Praise for *The Prepared Mind of a Leader*

"If you want to make a difference, read this book. Welter and Egmon show us more than a glimpse of the landscape beyond the boundaries of our habits, and a dynamic framework for navigating it. The eight skills are indispensable for anyone who aspires to be a leader."
  —Dale Burton, senior vice president, Devon Bank

"This is a practical guide for people in leadership positions or just interested in stepping out of their ordinary roles and boundaries. The authors give you insight into the mindset and associated skills of a successful, forward-thinking leader."
  —Rommin Adl, president and Chief Executive Officer, Strategic Management Group, Inc., A BTS Company

"Welter and Egmon do a great job of telling leaders how to prepare their minds for an uncertain future in clear, actionable steps. Anyone who wants to know how to 'see around the corner' needs to read this book."
  —Kaveh Safavi, chief medical officer, Solucient LLC

"The authors say that everyone, regardless of level in the organization, must have the skills of a *Prepared Mind of a Leader*—how true! Leadership is not just for people at the top."
  —Susan L. Henricks, president, RR Donnelley

THE PREPARED MIND OF A LEADER

Eight Skills Leaders Use to Innovate, Make Decisions, and Solve Problems

Bill Welter

Jean Egmon

JOSSEY-BASS
A Wiley Imprint
www.josseybass.com

Published by Jossey-Bass
A Wiley Imprint
989 Market Street, San Francisco, CA 94103-1741   www.josseybass.com

Jossey-Bass books and products are available through most bookstores. To contact Jossey-Bass directly
call our Customer Care Department within the U.S. at 800-956-7739, outside the U.S. at 317-572-3986,
or fax 317-572-4002.

Jossey-Bass also publishes its books in a variety of electronic formats. Some content that appears in
print may not be available in electronic books.

Library of Congress Cataloging-in-Publication Data
Welter, Bill.
  The prepared mind of a leader : eight skills leaders use to innovate, make decisions, and solve
problems / by Bill Welter, Jean Egmon.
     p. cm.
  Includes bibliographical references and index.
  ISBN-13: 978-0-7879-7680-4 (alk. paper)
  ISBN-10: 0-7879-7680-6 (alk. paper)
  1. Leadership. 2. Decision making. I. Egmon, Jean. II. Title.
  HD57.7.W4543 2006
  658.4'092—dc22

                                                              2005019337

Printed in the United States of America
FIRST EDITION
HB Printing   10 9 8 7 6 5 4 3 2 1

Contents

Bill dedicates this book to Marg.
Thanks for your patience and love.

Jean dedicates this book to G and Norma Egmon, who,
without even realizing it, taught me why and how to
cultivate and use a Prepared Mind in all areas of life.

CHANCE FAVORS THE PREPARED MIND

"Chance favors the prepared mind" was the statement Louis Pasteur, the nineteenth-century scientist, used to describe his remarkable ability to invent and innovate across a complex set of problems. When you look at Pasteur's accomplishments—from his studies of crystallization and fermentation that aided industries ranging from dairying to silk making, to his work with germs and microorganisms, which opened up whole new fields of scientific inquiry—you can see that he was truly ready for chance to "happen" to him.[1]

Pasteur's observation on the significance of a prepared mind was in the back of our minds as we looked at organizational successes and failures across a variety of industries, economic conditions, and business environments and observed the behaviors of the leaders of these organizations. We saw consistencies, and we wondered what the basis for these consistencies was and how they developed. What was going on beneath the surface of leader behaviors? What were leaders thinking or, in some cases, not thinking, as they made their decisions?

We believe "the prepared mind" is the hallmark of twenty-first-century leaders who are remarkable in their ability to sense, make sense (the development of an understanding of what they are sensing), decide, and act across a complex set of conditions. We also believe that the prepared mind is not a matter of chance. It is a matter of intentional preparation, and that is the purpose of this book: to help you build the skills of Prepared Mind leadership.

PREPARED MIND LEADERSHIP

In our working definition of Prepared Mind leadership, we see leadership as the practice of continuously envisioning opportunities for growth within complex, dynamic environments, built on core principles the organization is committed to sustaining and using as the basis for value delivered to all of its stakeholders.[2] Implied in our definition is that leaders, no matter where they are in the organization, are strategists in terms of making opportunities explicit and knowing why and when and how to move into and navigate the problems and opportunities they face.

You can be an individual contributor or a box on the organizational chart yet act as a leader in your organization—or fail to do so. Prepared Mind leadership is not limited by formal roles. In fact, the more we looked at acts of leadership, the more we realized the power, the responsibility, and the risk of "acting outside the narrow confines of your job description."[3] Furthermore, in this era of continuously shifting boundaries and relationships, and shorter job and strategy shelf lives, successful people learn to do just that, for their own good and for the good of their organizations. It's an organizational requirement that you perform your job, and perform it well. But leadership is a voluntary act.

Whether you hold a position of leadership in the traditional sense or decide that you are someone who will choose to step outside the strict confines of your job description, the intent of this book is to help you develop the skills of a Prepared Mind leader.

THE SKILLS OF A PREPARED MIND

Good leadership, like so many other things in life, is seen through a combination of skills. And like so many other things in life, you don't just "get better" at leadership; you improve your skills by regular practice. To use a sports metaphor, a good golfer has driving skills, putting skills, "rough" skills, bunker skills, and others. He or she is good only because of practice. And as we looked at organizational successes and failures in their innovation, decision making, and problem solving, we looked for mental skills that were being used or were absent.

We see eight fundamental skills delineating a Prepared Mind leader.

OBSERVING

The environment in which we live and operate is constantly changing. It's natural for us to look for confirming information about our view of the world, but it's often more important to look for disconfirming information. What have you been observing lately?

REASONING

People will want to know why you are proposing a course of action and will not follow your lead until they understand your explanation. What are your answers to the "Why?" question?

IMAGINING

The future is unknowable, but it can be visualized. Established industries, companies, policies, and practices are always challenged by new (imagined) ideas. What's running through your mind these days?

CHALLENGING

Any organization's business is built on assumptions. When is the last time you challenged your assumptions and tested their validity?

DECIDING

Face it, you get paid to make or influence decisions because action is essential to progress. Are you progressing or paralyzed?

LEARNING

Past knowledge got you to where you are today. It may or may not be effective in continuing to move you forward. What don't you know that you should?

ENABLING

You may be smart, but progress requires a concerted effort for any organization. Do the people around you have the knowledge and the means and, most important, the opportunity to progress?

REFLECTING

All decisions have trade-offs. We need to look at past decisions and understand the trade-offs we made and the consequences of those trade-offs. We also need to reflect forward (envision) and consider the trade-offs we are about to make. The problem is that we are time starved and never seem to have the time to just think. Have you spent any quiet thinking time lately?

THE MAP AND THE METHOD

How might you learn the skills of Prepared Mind leadership and then transfer this ability to work and other areas of your life as well? The map of how we approach the question is straightforward.

Part One sets the stage and explores several essential constructs for understanding what we mean by the Prepared Mind and how Prepared Mind leadership functions in a wide range of settings, from global behemoths to small-scale entrepreneurships.

Chapter One paints a broad-brush picture of the evolving future that requires us to be more prepared than ever before. In that context, we explore the particular meaning of Prepared Mind leadership and, with trigger questions peppered throughout, invite you to explore how these ideas apply to you and your organization's unique circumstances.

Chapter Two explains some of the fundamental constructs on which we built our model of Prepared Mind skills and our recommendations on how to develop them further and apply them in everyday life. The Sense-Response Cycle, the notion of opportunity space, the concept of mental maps and models, and the way we used what we call *anchoring concepts* to define and describe Prepared Mind leadership in action are the topics we explore here. We close this chapter with an overview of the eight skills of Prepared Mind leadership in the form of a quick self-evaluation.

The call to action in Part One is to take what you already know and recombine it with new knowledge in new ways. Part Two explores each of these critical abilities in depth: observing, reasoning, imagining, challenging, deciding, learning, enabling, and reflecting.

For each of the eight skills, we take a similar approach:

- Describe the skill and relate it to its anchoring concepts. We don't provide every key concept that underlies every skill, but we give you at least three key concepts for each skill. You can then choose to dig more deeply into how to develop and apply it.
- Provide several types of examples of the skill in action—sometimes hypothetical, sometimes from the business literature, sometimes from our own professional practice. We believe that by understanding the fundamentals of the skills, you will come to understand and use the power of Prepared Mind skills more effectively in everyday life, across a wide variety of situations.
- Offer a series of anchored exercises in every chapter that connects recommended skill-building activities and techniques to some of the concepts involved in deep understanding of the subject skill.
- Sprinkle trigger questions, additional skill-building tips and techniques, and thought-provoking scenarios and mini-cases that you can apply or translate to your own situation. For example, you could ask yourself, "What fundamentals of imagination was Howard Schultz using when he decided to buy Starbucks from the original owners?"
- Include a running example to spark your thinking about how the skills of a Prepared Mind might apply to the problem in your own situation. Titled "Everybody's Problem," we set up the scenario in Chapter Three and illustrate in some detail how the Prepared Mind might use that skill in thinking through and solving the problem of finding, acquiring, and retaining talent. The remaining chapters illustrate the application of the subject skill at three layers of a hypothetical organization and invite you to use the model from Chapter Three to explore the question for yourself and your organization in more depth.

The final chapter in the book ties it all together, illustrating the power of Prepared Mind leadership in meeting the challenges and opportunities of the future. It asks, "How will you prepare for your tomorrow?" and offers suggestions on how you can answer that question by using the Sense-Response Cycle and the eight skills of the Prepared Mind.

The subtext throughout Part Two is a constant invitation to practice. The exercises we provide in each chapter can serve as springboards for not only developing the Prepared Mind skills but also becoming more expert in understanding and using the skills ever more adeptly.

AN ONGOING INVITATION

As you consider the eight skills of the Prepared Mind, keep the question "Prepared for *what?*" in the back of your mind. You know your job and have certain depth in your area of expertise, but your expertise may or may not be helpful in navigating your future. Think about the work ahead of you as prepare to develop your Prepared Mind skills and apply them to your future.

You need the skill of observing because:

• Our world is larger than ever before. Many managers and executives have a general understanding of globalization, for example, but have not taken the time to look at how it will affect their job, their organization, their industry three, five, or ten years down the road. Or, to take another emerging issue, how many baby boom managers really understand the differences between themselves and the growing ranks of the "millennials," the generation born since the early 1980s?

• We cannot defend against new threats or take advantage of new opportunities if we don't see them in time. What's on the edge of your radar screen?

You need the skill of reasoning because:

• We need to (re)evaluate the assumptions we use to build our existing mental maps. Assumptions are wonderful mental short-cuts, but, like high blood pressure, they are silent killers when they are wrong.

• We need to understand other points of view to get the whole picture. Our view is only one view.

• We need to address unintended consequences before they surprise us.

You need the skill of imagining because:

• When we decide, we need alternatives to keep ourselves intellectually honest and sharp. If you decide based on the first possible solution to a problem, you are "satisficing." Satisficing may be a way to save time, but it often leads to mediocre solutions.

• Moving outside of my job description shifts me away from my comfort zone of known issues toward issues that are knowable and complex. I may have to build a new mental map, and that needs imagination.

You need the skill of challenging because:

• Expertise breeds conservatism, and conservatism can lead to stagnation. Remember that there is a fine line between being in the groove and being in a rut.

• Mental maps degrade slowly, and we need to be aware of this before it's too late.

You need the skill of deciding because:

• Leadership is experienced through the actions that are taken by the leader or by others.

• Time is not on our side. We cannot win by simply following the actions of the competition.

You need the skill of learning because:

• New and wonderful opportunities lie outside our current job description, and we need new knowledge and skills to take advantage of them.

• The larger environment in which we do business is generating new realities that have to be added to existing knowledge to create new knowledge.

You need the skill of enabling because:

- A leader needs talented and willing followers. All of us together are smarter than any one of us.
- Most organizations will fail if we try to go it alone.

You need the skill of reflecting because:

- We and our organizations learn more from understanding the reasons for failure than we do from studying someone else's best practices.
- Reflection primes the pump for early warning signs that we need to observe.

The competitive realities of the twenty-first century require as much "know why" as "know how," and although our goal is not to turn you into a cognitive scientist, we hope that you will want to peer beneath the skills of Prepared Mind leadership into related concepts and theories. We want you to have a tool kit that is deep and wide and will help you navigate a business environment that is more mentally, morally, and socially demanding than ever before. With a full set of Prepared Mind skills, you will have what you need to make the most of your future.

OUR FOUNDATION AND FRAMEWORKS

THE ONLY FOUNDATION WE HAVE

People and organizations have been prepared and unprepared throughout history, yet businesses continue to run, decisions and problems continue to be dealt with, and innovations continue to break through. So why is the need to have a Prepared Mind more critical than ever before?

To answer that question, we need to start with what we know. Contrary to the "clean sheet of paper" recommendations from the heyday of the reengineering movement, we humans *do not* start with a "clean sheet of paper" when we are constructing new knowledge and understanding in our minds. We build new knowledge and skills by appending new information to existing knowledge and skills and by recombining the old with the new in new ways.

We thus start with some of the important things we already know as business practitioners. These, combined with new information we gain from reading, listening, and experiencing business for ourselves with the application of the Prepared Mind skills, will set the stage for a new way of thinking. We have no choice but to build on today. It's the only foundation we have.

SIX GIVENS

We offer the following as what we know about the context for building a Prepared Mind. These are the givens, the context in which we operate:

- We know we operate in a system; we are not alone.
- We know that we are in the midst of multiple life cycle curves.

11

- We know that life cycle clock speed is accelerating.
- We know that progress requires us to actively sense and respond to the changes around us.
- We know that leadership is important during times of change.
- We know that every organization has a cascade of strategies, whether they know it or not.

As you think about these givens individually and then consider the connections among and between them, you will see a picture, a mosaic, of an evolving future that requires us to be more prepared than ever before.

There are more givens unique to you and your organization. What would you say they are? Are you listening to others in your organization who see connections you may not? Are you painting the picture and bringing others along the path of seeing the connections?

WE KNOW WE OPERATE IN A SYSTEM

When we investigate organizational successes and failures, the question of responsibility is often focused on the person in command. However, the system in which that leader is operating is just as powerful a determinant. Consider the realities of business life.

Collectively, companies are part of a system called "business." For much of the twentieth century, we followed the mechanistic thinking of the industrial revolution and considered ourselves to be part of a massive industrial machine (a "cog," with a specific role in a specific part of the machine, so to speak). By the end of the century, we changed the metaphor to that of ecology, which is more complex because the chains of cause and effect are co-evolving, they are much longer, and they are more interrelated. Your business is part of a business ecosystem. As with nature, if the ecosystem dies, all of the inhabitants die. Think of the airline industry as an ecosystem. Just how healthy is that entire ecology?

Like any other system, the system called business is a network of components, among them the human components or stakeholders: managers, executives, employees, competitors, suppliers, customers, and others who have relationships with one another. Both the components and relationships can change over time, and the strength of the relationships will wax and wane over time. In addition, any category of stakeholders can have multiple relationships. For example, competitors can buy from companies, sell to them, and also compete against them: same company—different relationships.

Changing any component or relationship can cause a string of other changes, which are not necessarily tightly linked in time or space. For example, when a competitor makes an improvement in quality control, a company's relationship with its own customers will change. What was good enough may no longer be so.

Now here is the tough part. In a complex system like business, we often do not know all the components. What people or organizations might affect or be affected by your decisions?

Furthermore, we often do not know the type or strength of the relationships between and among those people and organizations. Which relationships are becoming more or less relevant in your own ecology of business? For example, do your employees recognize themselves as having a contractual relationship or a loyalty relationship with the company? Will that loyalty relationship still hold after the latest round of layoffs?

The bottom line is that being prepared for the future is more complex than ever before. The leaders and companies that will succeed in this climate are those that appreciate the requirements of its many relationships, are able to change as they change, and can do so more quickly and more intelligently than their competition. Prepared Mind leaders are those who know how to work within the system while getting the system to realign or evolve in the direction they have imagined.

To get any system to change in a business ecology, we must first start with the people or stakeholders of the system: the decision makers behind other system components such as budgets, policies and governance, technological choices, and customer preferences. The Prepared Minds of successful leaders strive to understand what is on the minds (and in the hearts) of the stakeholders of their business ecology, and they design strategy and change from that understanding.

Prepared Mind Question

How do we make progress in a dynamic system with unknown components, unknown relationships, and unknown strength of relationships?

WE KNOW WE ARE IN THE MIDST
OF MULTIPLE LIFE CYCLE CURVES

Most of us are familiar with the standard product life cycle terminology of introduction and growth and maturity and decline (Figure 1.1). These are the stages that all products traverse from creation to elimination.

We also know that the same-shaped curve can be used to describe the life cycle of a business or an industry. And for those of us with enough years under our belt, we can see the same happening for most, if not all, management tools, techniques, and fads that have passed through our lives. Do you remember when Total Quality Management was hot (and then rapidly cooled off)? Do you remember the meteoric rise and fall of Quality Circles? How about the concept of employee empowerment? Is it mature, or on the decline, or already dead in your organization?

We live in the midst of simultaneous industry changes, company changes, product changes, technique changes, and fads—and all are at a different point in their own life cycle. There is so much evidence of the life cycle curve in our environment that we no longer take notice and consider it. We are like fish that don't see the water.

The hard part of all of this is that there is a big difference between knowing the cycle exists and knowing how to deal with it in

FIGURE 1.1. LIFE CYCLE CURVE

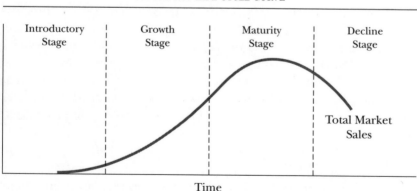

| Introductory Stage | Growth Stage | Maturity Stage | Decline Stage |

Total Market Sales

Time

a proactive manner. The curve is crystal clear when we look back on what has happened but almost impossible to anticipate as we look forward. We know the shape of the eventual curve that will play out, but we don't know how long the current phase will last and therefore when the curve will change direction. We also don't know how abrupt the change will be or to what degree the curve will change. And this is critically important when we think about the curve in the light of developing strategy.

Prepared Minds work within the current curve while thinking ahead of it. They also start seeing and helping others prepare for the new curve so the shift is truly evolutionary rather than a jolt to the system. Through skills such as imagining, learning, reflecting, teaching, and deciding, they determine when and how to ride the current curve and when and how to act beyond it.

Consider this. Would Motorola have lost the lead in cell phone technology if it had been prepared for the shift from analog to digital technology? We can look back and see that analog technology was in a decline long before Motorola did anything about it. It may have noticed the shift but clearly acted on it too late. What if Motorola leaders had noticed the curve in time to "jump the curve" to the digital life cycle? We can be sure that *someone* was jumping up and down and worried about the analog life cycle, but we have to ask why didn't they do anything in time to avoid the sudden maturing of the analog cycle.

The Prepared Mind senses changes in the direction of the life cycle curve before it's in full force and prepares the business for the new fundamentals while continuing to operate in the old fundamentals. Andy Grove, the cofounder and chairman of Intel, referred to these changes in direction of the life cycle curve as *strategic inflection points,* describing them as "a time in the life of business when its fundamentals are about to change."[1] This often means seeing the connection of something new in the greater environment, beyond our own industry. We have to learn to think through or imagine the possibilities of these out-of-industry changes on our own business's market, our organization's competencies, or other key factors in strategic decision making. For instance, have we truly thought through and begun to jump to the next curve that the flood of baby boom retirements will bring to bear on almost all industries and social systems?

Prepared Mind Question

We know we are in the midst of many life cycles. We know that shifts in their curves will herald new fundamentals for products, services, and businesses. But even in the fast-paced world of high technology, nothing happens overnight. There is always some sign of the changes about to hit, or even creep into, a company or an industry. Talk to some of the people who work with suppliers or customers. What new trends or technologies are they seeing? Are *you* paying any attention to them?

WE KNOW THAT CLOCK SPEED IS ACCELERATING

In the early 1990s, we were besieged with articles, speeches, and books addressing the topic of managing change. It was not a question of whether organizations could change, but whether they could change fast enough (or thoroughly enough) to get the benefits they needed. Most important, did leaders and workers change their mind-sets so they were more prepared and more agile to meet future changes, or did they simply survive one change after another?

Whether you embraced or fought the change movement, the reality is that thinking well and doing more, more quickly and more frequently than before, is an important variable in making progress. Move too fast, and your organization may expend resources as it moves down blind alleys: markets that will never materialize, problems that will self-resolve, and so on. Move too slowly, and problems may become too big to handle or opportunities may fall into the laps of competitors.[2] Look at Sears Roebuck and Company or Howard Johnson restaurants and ask yourself, "Is it what they did that got them in trouble—or is it what they didn't do?"

Prepared Minds know how to engage in thoughtful, real-time observation, analysis, and decision making in the midst of time-sensitive, resource-constrained, high-risk situations, and they know how to keep themselves and those around them focused on their core purpose and ultimate goals as they are making sense and deciding what to change and what to keep. They know how to walk the thin line between thinking and doing, between responding and reacting, between planning and experimenting. Also, they know how to engage others in continuous strategic iterations, understood as part of their normal course of doing business, and becoming smarter in the process. They don't hesitate to use tools such as scorecards and forecasts, but they don't just react or jump on the next new fad. They learn and change as they go.[3]

Prepared Mind Question

What do the people in your organization believe about your ability to "lead faster"? What values do you and they have in common?

WE KNOW THAT PROGRESS REQUIRES US TO ACTIVELY SENSE AND RESPOND TO THE CHANGES AROUND US

Survival and progress have always depended on the ability of the person or the organization to sense changes in the environment and then to respond in a timely and appropriate manner. Consider the early leader in electronic calculator industry, the Bomar Company (a manufacturer of LED displays), and its calculator, the Bomar Brain. Bomar had the lead and then lost it. What didn't the company adapt to?

Individually, we have all experienced the fight-or-flight syndrome. Something sudden happens, and we respond; in days gone by, this often was the difference between living and dying. Today, problems arise; we roll up our sleeves and attack the problem and feel tired, but satisfied, at the end of the day. We also know, but don't usually admit, that while we are often adept at handling "something big" that happens to us, we are lousy at dealing with small, slow changes. So we slowly let our relationships dissolve, or we slowly get out of shape.

And the same conditions happen in our business organizations. While some changes are fast (such as technological capacity), the impact on our day-to-day lives may feel slow or ambiguous unless we are, by nature, early adopters or unless we are prepared to see the change and its implications for our business. We go from being a hard-charging competitor to a company with bloated overhead expenses. We go from knowing our best customers to having a profile of a typical customer (which does not actually fit any particular customer). Margins slowly shrink, and we blame the dynamics of "the industry" instead of making the changes we should make in our organizations. One of the dangers of being strictly results driven is that we can spend so much energy "doing" and keeping up that we don't take the time to think ahead, until the inevitable is at our door and we feel compelled to react.[4]

It seems so simple, yet we manage to mess it up time and time again. What step or steps in the process were missed or delayed and caused Polaroid to miss the shift to digital photography? Our guess is that its leaders sensed it and made sense of it, but could not "pull the trigger" and decide to change the emphasis of the company. What food companies or restaurants missed the huge impact of the low-carb craze in 2004? Did Apple Computer possibly *cause* a shift in consumer electronics with its iPod music storage device? Time will tell.

Prepared Minds watch for anomalies—warning signs, surprises, new developments on the horizon—and ask if they fit their view of the world. If they do, then all is well. If they don't, then action must be taken. The danger in this simple scenario is the temptation to force-fit the anomalies into an existing view of the world and set of assumptions. To avoid this danger, they must continuously question the assumptions they and their organizations are making and ask for input from those closest to the action.

Prepared Mind Question

What can be done in your organization to help it slow down and take the time to make sense of new data and information? Is there a tie back to the organization's core purpose and ultimate goals and getting decision makers to think through the new situation in the light of those?

WE KNOW THAT LEADERSHIP IS IMPORTANT DURING TIMES OF CHANGE

The business scandals of the past few years have raised the need for better leadership of our businesses. Changes in global business conditions raise the need for global leaders. Changes in the technologies underlying our products and business operations raise the need for leaders who can transform our organizations. And yet, at the same time, we see the need to drive leadership lower in the organization to reduce response time, improve service, and deliver better value to customers.

What's the answer? The myriad of books and articles about the secrets of leadership make good points, but they have different perspectives to stress. Consider what some of the more objective minds have to say about the topic of leadership in business. Warren Bennis, a professor at the University of Southern California, focuses on the leadership of people in an organization and presents the need to foster conditions that support knowledge workers. From his point of view, this means providing purpose, developing an atmosphere of trust, fostering hope, and getting results.[5] Jim Kouzes and Barry Posner, the authors of the best-selling book *The Leadership Challenge,* now in its third edition, talk about the five practices of exemplary leaders: model the way, inspire a shared vision, challenge the process, enable others to act, and encourage the heart.[6] And Bill George, the former CEO of Medtronic, writes that he sees the qualities of a leader to include understanding the need for leadership, practicing solid values, leading with heart, establishing connected relationships, and demonstrating self-discipline.[7]

So we have three different points of view and all from people respected for their understanding of leadership. The words are different, but the meanings are clear. What do they have in common?

- Leadership is demonstrated in action, not just words. Therefore, acting on our organization's capabilities and capacity in the light of customer, employee, and shareholder needs is the acid test of good leadership.
- Leadership is found in the trust relationship with followers; it is not just a position in the power hierarchy. Therefore, the common ground for leadership and change is the point of alignment or convergence of our values, our employees' and customers' values, and the organization's values.
- Leaders know their purpose and the purpose of their organization. Therefore, we have to be prepared to answer the question, "Why are we doing this?"

So far, so good. But what about other realities of the twenty-first century?

One reality is that we have more knowledge workers than ever before, and they may or may not be part of an official hierarchy. They may, in the words of Charles Handy, be part of a shamrock organization, or a federal organization, or a "hive."[8] We may not have followers to lead as much as we have stakeholders to influence.

Another reality is that leadership deals with a wider sphere of influence as a result of globalization and the increased access to information and new technology. Leaders know more and are expected to know more, as are followers. In fact, those who twenty years ago may have been thought of as followers are charged with self-leadership and with acting on the information they have in the best interest of customers, the global organization, and the local culture and situation. Leadership is not confined to one job or to a predefined set of circumstances. It is situational and goes beyond the bounds of narrowly defined jobs. Like knowledge, leadership spreads with use.

All of these realities lead to our working definition of leadership. Leadership, as we think of it in the context of the Prepared Mind, takes Ronald Heifetz's notion of adaptive leadership and builds and expands on it.[9]

Heifetz's definition departs from many other theories of leadership in two respects. One is that he believes, as do we, that leadership is practice, not a particular position; it can be exercised from anywhere in the organization. Second, adaptive leadership requires deep learning and the challenging of mental maps to adapt to changed realities. This requires the person exercising adaptive leadership to think and act outside his or her usual or expected job description, and challenge others to do the same, in order to see or anticipate changes in the environment that require the adaptation of ways of thinking and ways of working.[10]

We build on the unique aspects of Heifetz's definition in the following ways. First, we believe that leadership practiced with a Prepared Mind not only adapts to changed environments but also is in the position to change environments by interacting with them in new ways. Adaptation is mutual. This notion of leadership moves from a traditional change management view of leadership to a view that more closely mirrors innovation and entrepreneurship.

The second way we build on Heifetz's definition is to acknowledge that to bring about effective opportunity and change, some core ideas in the current system need not change. In fact, they need to be reinforced and built on as foundational to success. In a study we did on turnaround companies that not only survived but became innovative, we found that the leadership authentically integrated and addressed the head, the heart, and the hands of business by building the new vision on something fundamental to the organization that did not have to change.[11] For one company, the idea of "empowered knowledge workers" released a whole new application of talent in a financial services organization and took them to a new level of motivation, performance, understanding the business of the business, and acting more innovatively in a changing market. For another company, it was the image of being scrappy that unleashed a desire to contribute to its competitiveness, cross-train, and even change product lines in order to a move from a commodities manufacturing business to a more knowledge-based science and engineering business. The bankers even held off dissolving the business not only because the new business model and numbers looked promising but also because the people of the company were so committed and willing to sacrifice to make it work.

The four aspects of leadership are (1) practicing outside the technical confines of one's job description, (2) challenging ways of thinking inside and outside the organization, (3) innovating to have an impact on the external environment as well as realizing the external environment's changing dynamics and potential impact on the internal environment of the organization, and (4) building the continuous process of change readiness on deeply held, sustainable principles. Therefore we define Prepared Mind leadership as *the practice of continuously envisioning and executing opportunities for growth within complex, dynamic environments, built on core principles the organization is committed to sustaining and using as the basis for value delivered to all of its stakeholders.* Prepared Mind leadership engages stakeholders in making changes in their ways of thinking and acting by leading them to develop their own ability to navigate the sense–make-sense–decide–act cycle, while maintaining their integrity by being grounded in principles shared with the organization.

This broader view seems to fit the realities of the world today quite well. Some of us are ordained leaders in our organizations. We have the appropriate title and the appropriate box on the company organization chart. Others of us are left with the unofficial title of "follower." However, reality of the need for speed and intelligence on the spot makes this distinction moot. We simply can't wait for the official chain of command to comprehend the changing world around us: we don't have the time, and the situation demands a response! Therefore, *everyone* has the responsibility (but often not the cultural permission) to work outside their job description to take advantage of opportunity that leads to strategic advantage. Leadership is seen in acting with foresight in the best interest of the organization's value chain, in line with personal and societal values. Prepared Minds enter the action anchored in purpose and unafraid to think and act differently than the status quo.

Prepared Mind Question

How has the responsibility for leadership changed in your organization? Are you seeing distributed leadership, or is the old semblance of hierarchy still in control?

WE KNOW THAT EVERY ORGANIZATION HAS A CASCADE OF STRATEGIES, WHETHER THEY KNOW IT OR NOT

Fundamentally, strategy is all about answering the question, "How will we accomplish a goal?" This could take place at the executive level of the corporation when the CEO asks, "How will we reinvigorate the revenue growth of this company?" and then goes on to answer the question by pursuing an acquisition of a complementary company. Moving down a notch, the president may ask herself, "How will I ensure the success of the acquisition?" and go on to answer her question by reorganizing the marketing and sales departments. Continuing the strategic cascade, the vice president of marketing has to answer the question of a combined marketing department, and the answer creates his strategy.

And so it goes: goals beget strategies, which become goals, which need a strategy, and on and on. This process could be planned and coordinated, where the intention at the top of the hierarchy links with execution at the bottom of the hierarchy; or it could happen in a disconnected fashion. In either case, the company has embarked on a series of strategies.

Models and patterns abound to describe the top-level strategy.[12] The problem for most managers and executives is that these models are only a starting point. They still have to figure out how to do the hard work of taking an elegant concept and fitting it to the realities of their industry and company. After that, they have to worry about the big issue of adoption. They have to take a company's goals and its general statement of strategy and make them real.

And so the work shifts from learning the basics of the strategy models to the day-to-day work of strategic thinking. It is hard work. It requires spending time pondering the multiple futures of the organization and determining what can be changed to reach or deal with those futures and, finally, considering the intended and unintended consequences of those changes. Just remember that strategic thinking at its core is simply good, critical thinking about the future of the organization.

This book is not strictly about strategic thinking, but thinking and acting strategically is a goal and result of Prepared Mind leadership, and this loose definition needs a bit of explanation.

First, when we think about strategy, we have to keep in mind the two key components of the future of the organization: goals and multiple futures. Strategy always is in response to understanding a goal. If you don't have one or if you won't share one, then the thinking process is nothing more than a shot in the dark. Also, every organization has multiple futures it has to consider.[13]

Second, when we engage in strategic thinking, we need to go beyond concepts and address those things we can actually change as we consider the adoption of the strategy. For example, quality is a concept. Improving quality may require changes to suppliers, machinery, employee training, and measurement systems.

Finally, strategic thinking must always consider the consequences of planned actions. This imperative is well expressed in one of the truisms from the discipline of systems thinking: every solution brings about a unique set of new problems. An example was the phenomenal success of GE's strategy in the 1990s. An unintended consequence was the raiding of GE for talent. GE was so good in its management team training and development that other companies saw it as a source of talent—and went after GE's best people.

Prepared Mind Question

Do the people at the bottom of the hierarchy have the same basic understanding of organizational goals as the executives do? Are corporate strategies meaningful to the workforce, or are they "just a bunch of words"?

CONNECTING THE DOTS

So why be concerned about developing and applying a Prepared Mind today? As a starting point, take the known aspects of business we've just related and consider some of the implications of those givens. As you do, think about the implications for your mental preparedness as well as that of your entire organization:

• Because globalization is a fact, the system called business is getting considerably more complex. Therefore, we need a mind that is open to new information and interpretation. Do you observe actively, or do you wait for something to hit you?

• Because the life cycle model underscores our world and because response time is shrinking, we need a mind that constantly looks ahead. How much time do you spend imagining the future conditions of competition?

• Because speed and balance are fundamental to success, we need a mind that is agile. Can you make decisions without all the facts? Are you willing to challenge today's paradigms?

• Because we need a process to prepare for navigating our future, we need a mind that is aware of its position in multiple organization, product, and concept life cycles and can observe the early warning signs of upcoming shifts. What warning signs do you use to see if your environment is changing? Can you explain the big picture to your peers and workers?

• Because leadership is critical in organizations, we need a mind that is willing to challenge and respond to challenges to take advantage of opportunities or intercept problems. When is the last time you considered the validity of the assumptions you're using in your job?

• Because strategy-in-action always trumps intention, we need a mind that deals with complexity. For every complex problem, there is a solution that is simple and easy to understand—and wrong. How prepared and willing are you to dive into the messiness of complex problems?

While we know that we need to understand and act on these things, knowing how is another story. The eight skills of the Prepared Mind provide the hows of taking what we already know about the business environment and creating new futures for strategic advantage and for the sustainability of the business system in which we act.

But first we look at the frameworks on which those skills are built.

CHAPTER TWO

FRAMEWORKS FOR INTENTIONAL PREPARATION

Louis Pasteur did not deny the role of chance, but he pointed to the work that comes before the luck. Preparation first; then the luck. Putting this into practice, we have to couple intention with our preparations. Intentional preparation means continuously looking for relationships and connections that if combined will result in new ideas, new solutions, new "luck."

To be prepared, you need to sense the early signals of the future and make sense of these signals, especially if they are in conflict with today's truths. You need to be better prepared for your future problems and opportunities and to possess the skills necessary to decide on a course of action and then execute that decision. As a leader, you also need to be able to help those who work with you—customers, employees, suppliers, and other stakeholders—and prepare their minds as well. Together you form a multifocal lens that creates a more competitive future by applying the eight skills of the prepared mind individually and collectively.

Intentional preparation for learning and practicing the eight skills begins with taking a look at the main tools we use to consider and integrate a vast array of thoughts and actions into a complete picture of Prepared Mind leadership.

The Sense-Response Cycle is the first of several frameworks we use to explain leadership behavior in terms of the eight Prepared Mind skills. Why skills? Skills show the mind in action, processing, making connections that motivate and enable external actions. Skills reflect the nexus of knowing and doing. Skills can be learned.

Skills can be broken down into concepts that are important to understand if we are to know when, why, and how to use the skills strategically and not just apply them haphazardly or simply because we have the ability.

The other frameworks for our thinking and recommendations are the ideas of opportunity space, mental maps, and anchoring concepts.

THE SENSE-RESPONSE CYCLE

Whether leaders are wrestling with problems, working on strategic innovations, or running their department, they are always faced with four major and recurring issues: (1) the need to *sense* the environment and changes in the environment, (2) the need to *make sense* of this input, (3) the need to *decide* on an appropriate course of action, and (4) the need to *act* on that decision. We term the process of dealing with those issues the *Sense-Response Cycle.*

We see the cycle at work in the actions of a dynamic CEO as she considers the acquisition of another company. And we see it when the executive vice president of a technology company authorizes a new R&D venture. But we also see all or part of it in action when:

- A factory worker stops the assembly line when she sees a quality problem.
- A salesperson calls a customer to inquire about the experience of procuring a new product.
- A marketing researcher spends lunch time with design engineers to make them aware of new industry trends.
- An investment banker notices a new application of an existing technology that has far-reaching implications for one of her customers and makes recommendations to the customer on ways he could use it in his business.

The activities of sensing, making sense, deciding, and acting are ongoing and cyclical (Figure 2.1). Once you have acted on something, you need to sense again and see the impact of your actions. Take a look at the basic steps of the Sense-Response Cycle

FIGURE 2.1. THE SENSE-RESPONSE CYCLE

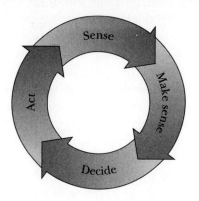

and consider the mental preparation and skills needed for each of the activities:

- We *sense* changes in our internal and external environments. Individual contributors and managers know the inputs to their job and (should) know when something is new or different. This activity is easy when we are working within the limits of our own job description; it gets much harder when we consider the larger context of our job or company. If we do not know enough of the larger context, we may not be in a position to sense anomalies.

- We *make sense* of these changes in the light of our purpose, circumstances, and goals. We know the rules of the game and compare the changes and the new things we have sensed to the expectations and assumptions that underlie our way of operating. There is a risk in viewing our purpose, circumstances, and goals too narrowly and thereby missing the implications for our deepest purposes and most ultimate goals. We have to think broadly and deeply while making sense of environmental information. Beyond the rules of the game, we need to make sense in the light of the purpose of the game.

- We *decide* on a course of action or inaction. If what we sense does indeed make sense, then we usually continue on the known and steady course. If what we sense does not in fact make sense to us, then we *should* decide on a course correction. Unfortunately, that is not always the case, and way too often we decide to wait and see. Remember that no decision is often a de facto decision.

• We *act* on the decision and get others to act. Ideally, this phase of activity should take place immediately after we decide on a course of action. Also, getting others to act usually happens more quickly and with more commitment on their part if they have been brought into the make-sense and decide phases. Making sense is often a social activity, ideally with Prepared Minds working together. Unfortunately, we often wait too long before we do what we already know we should do, and often we expect others to jump on board more quickly than their absorptive capacity allows.

• And then we repeat the cycle. In years gone by, this was done at a rather comfortable pace, and we had time to catch our breath before we embarked on the next round of disruptive activity. We could also get others to act on our decisions from a model of command and control. We know from looking at the pace of change in many industries that disruption has become a way of life. We also know that if we want those around us to be agile and prepared, we need to lead them less through command and control and more through letting them contribute. In fact, according to leadership researcher Ronald Heifetz, we are often better at working through this cycle if we make a point of listening to the voices of leadership from below—those who are on the front lines and often sense changes in the environment before we do.[1]

So where does this lead us as we think about the need for leadership in this century? First, it's more than just doing our job. Second, we have to sense and make sense of emerging problems and opportunities. Third, sense making has to lead to decision and action. Fourth, we need to be grounded in the mission and objectives of our organization; otherwise we won't know what to watch for, and our actions won't lead to progress for our organization.

These four descriptors are some of the hallmarks of Prepared Mind leadership in action. Each of the Prepared Mind skills supports a phase of the Sense-Response Cycle to one degree or another. Depending on the situation at hand, from problem solving to strategy to innovation, the emphasis on one skill or another may shift.

OPPORTUNITY SPACE

Some people do their job—no more, no less. They may be very good at their jobs, but that is what is expected of them, and we do not consider this the action of a leader. Other people do their job and then some—and if they go beyond their job description and move their organization forward, then they are acting as a leader. In both cases, it does not matter if you have people reporting to you. As we have stressed, an individual contributor can fit this description as well as the chief operating officer can. The more we considered the concept of opportunity space, the more we started to see some interesting characteristics.

The boundaries and shape of our opportunity space are constantly changing. Sometimes this seems to happen in an evolutionary manner, and other times there is a leap. Consider Honda Motors and Apple Computer. When Honda came to the United States, its perceived opportunity space was cruiser-weight motorcycles, until someone realized that the public was more interested in its little 90cc motorbikes. Now we think of Honda as "cars," but that's not what they saw in the 1960s. And then consider Apple Computer and how its opportunity space has expanded with the success of the iPod music player. Is Apple a computer company or a music company? Or both? Or has it defined another kind of company altogether?

Sometimes our opportunity space is stagnant and at other times quite turbulent. Think about the automobile industry and its dependence on the internal combustion engine. Although incremental improvements have been made all along, the opportunity space defined by the concept of "automobile" has been relatively stagnant since the demise of the Stanley Steamer in 1925. Now look at the opportunity space surrounding nanotechnology. It's almost limitless and the subject of books and science-fiction articles, but it's starting with the mundane application of making trousers more stain resistant.

Much of our opportunity space is unknown to us. We know our jobs and are comfortable with our existing network of clients, customers, competitors, and geography. And, in fact, these take up most of our time, so we don't even look to see what else might be out there. We can wait for it to be revealed to us, or we can navigate out to the edges of our known world and take a look. It's up to us.

Finally, and most important, our opportunity space is often self-defined. Learning to interpret the environment, even one that is filled with threats, unknowns, and ambiguities, and then imagining and building it into an opportunity and helping others see and build their opportunity space is part of the job of leadership. At the organizational level, we can read Theodore Levitt's classic *Harvard Business Review* article "Marketing Myopia" and see how the railroads nearly went out of business in the 1960s because they missed the rapid growth of the trucking industry; they defined their opportunity space as "railroads" and not "transportation."[2] The same thing happens with a talented engineer who decides to stay with the tried and true and finds herself with an obsolete skill set. The opportunity space is there, but we have to be willing to see it.

MENTAL MAPS

As you consider the challenge of navigating your personal and organizational opportunity space, consider the value that maps provide you in the physical world. Maps represent places we or others have been, multiple pathways between the places, and cues that point to destination spots and significant terrain changes along the way. Maps are representations of past journeys that we use as an anchoring reference to plan and navigate new journeys. The same is true for the maps in our minds.

Mentally, we have categories of information that we have picked up from prior experience or from learning from others' prior experiences and knowledge. We usually call these categories of information *concepts, ideas,* or *knowledge.* In our mind, we have roadways or connecting paths between our categories of information and keys that help us interpret the information. These connections are often thought of as mental models, theories, beliefs, and skills. In fact, when we get really accustomed to and proficient at going down a particular road, we say we have a skill. But, like Chicago (or almost any other city) in the summer, our mental roadways, especially our skills, are always under construction, and sometimes they have to be rebuilt, enlarged, or rerouted. To complete the map analogy, we have mental keys for interpreting information and for giving us shortcuts and pointers to special terrain and anomalies among our information. These mental map symbols and keys include things like language, rituals, even biases and emotions.

Mental maps, just like other maps, become useful when we are going somewhere or doing something that requires direction. But no matter what kind of map you use, you want and need maps that are both coherent and current. Mental maps are coherent when they are orderly and logical. When we pick up a road map, we expect it to have scale and a consistent level of detail and abstraction. That is why maps provided by chambers of commerce, which often show a blowup of local businesses but not street addresses, are not very helpful once you are out of the shopping area. And maps of all sorts are valuable for navigating only if they are current. A map of the United States from the 1950s would not show today's interstate highway system and would not help the traveler motoring from New York to Los Angeles.

Think of the details from your mental map that you use for your organization. Are those details current? Was the mental map of the U.S. automobile industry current in the 1970s when the Big Three all but ignored the Japanese manufacturers? Move forward to 2005, and ask if the current automotive leaders have Korean manufacturers on their maps. Should they? Time will tell.

Or take this down to the personal level and ask yourself about your mental map of employee relations. By now, the average middle manager is aware of employee demographics and how they relate to issues of salary, benefits, communication, and motivation. But does your map include the wants, needs, and points of view of the latest wave of employees—the millennials, who are just now entering the job market? If it doesn't, your mental map is about to become obsolete. Think about it. In sheer numbers, this generation is about the size of the baby boom generation, but they are significantly different. They grew up with computers, the Internet, and instant communication. They also saw their parents and older siblings suffer job losses as businesses chased after the holy grail of "lean and mean." Their wants and needs may be significantly different from your wants and needs.

Think of mental maps as different combinations of categories of information, connections within and between those categories, and keys that help us recognize new information and how to interpret it.[3] To keep our mental maps coherent and current, we can always ask ourselves three questions:

- What information do I need to sense, make sense, decide, and act on the current situation or in a new opportunity space?
- What connections can I be making between categories of old and new information that I have not made before that would help me sense, make sense, and maybe decide and act in new ways?
- What other keys for interpreting the information could I apply to see this situation in new ways?

Don't try to rewrite a mental map as big as the world; give yourself some constraints, like one or two answers for each of these questions, as a start. Also, as a leader, you will want to engage others in these questions to see whether their mental maps are coherent and current for seeing and navigating the opportunities that lie ahead.

We will give you exercises like these throughout the book so you can practice seeing and navigating opportunity spaces by applying the Prepared Mind skills. We will also help you learn and understand the anchoring concepts and connections under the skills so you can learn to apply them effectively across situations and domains.

As you take this journey through the Prepared Mind, we recommend you carry in your back pocket a variety of your own cases to use when applying the reading and doing the exercises. You will also need a commitment to asking yourself questions and letting us ask you questions along the way. There is nothing like a good question to force you to consider, "Where do I want to go from here?" and "How did I get there before?" and "How will I get there now?"

ANCHORING CONCEPTS

As you may remember, about 10 percent of an iceberg can be seen above the waterline; the rest lies out of sight.[4] And so it is with the Prepared Mind. Just as with a physical iceberg, where most of the important stuff is beyond what you can see, the same is true of the Prepared Mind. You have to go deep to get the whole picture.

One implication is that anyone wishing to have a prepared mind must be able to think in the abstract. The skills are observable; the reason that the skills are powerful is barely discernable. All of us have seen and experienced the behaviors associated with the Prepared Mind for much of our lives. But we may not be aware of the skills and the cognitive and behavioral theories underlying those behaviors.

You would never claim to be an expert financial businessperson if you didn't understand basic concepts such as transactions, accruals, and discounted cash flow and the impact they can have on your business decisions, skills, and practice. Likewise, you would hesitate to call yourself an expert business leader and thinker if you didn't understand basic concepts underlying the Prepared Mind skills and the impact they can have on your business decisions, skills, and practice.

This simple metaphor of an iceberg is meant to get you ready for exploring the Prepared Mind, from the submerged concepts that anchor the eight skills, all the way up to specific behaviors or acts you see above the waterline of business. Also, you can start on the surface, with an observation of an action, and then take a deeper dive down through the Prepared Mind skills to their anchoring concepts. Understanding these concepts, as well as learning these skills, helps you understand and explain action, build more ways of framing issues and solving problems, and perform with greater mental agility. Traversing the iceberg up and down makes you smarter and more equipped as a business leader to navigate all kinds of business problems.

Above the waterline are all the things that you observe with your five senses. Your observations begin the Sense-Response Cycle. What do you make of Walgreens popping up on corners across America? Quarterly trade deficit figures? Quarterly earnings reports? The words and tone of a political campaign speech? Seventy-five messages in your e-mail in-box? Requests that you attend three conflicting or overlapping meetings? And the list goes on. The things at the tip of the iceberg are the blessings and the curse of leading in the knowledge era. We have a lot of data and information in our line of sight at all times. Some of it we ask for; some of it we don't. But the net result is that there is a lot to sense.

To sort, filter, and attach value, we have to immediately go to the next level to use knowledge and skills that are invisible but allow us to make sense and eventually shape the things we see and do. We use Prepared Mind skills such as learning, reflecting, and imagining to ask ourselves questions about what we see and experience. For instance, we may ask ourselves, "What happened in our organization the last time a competitor cut its prices? How did we respond? Why? Who won that battle? What did it do to our brand?" Or we might allow what we see to spur our imaginations into different questions that start a chain of strategic thinking and reasoning. For instance, if we see that labor prices are much cheaper abroad than in the United States, we might ask, "What would it look like if we moved our manufacturing and support offshore? What costs would we save that we could fold back into innovation or investor earnings? What sorts of hiring practices would we have to learn to enable us to move jobs? If we cut jobs here, how will that affect our relationship with our community?" In other words, we start to think about what we see and make sense of it in ways that may lead us to new decisions and actions. However, be careful if you stop there.

Many errors are made because people do not go deep enough. Too many decisions get made after this initial level of analysis and planning. We do not dare to withstand pressures to move quickly, or we don't know which deeper questions to ask, or we fail to think things through by considering underlying fundamentals. For instance, many mergers and acquisitions fail because the decision makers did not think about cultural compatibility (or incompatibility) when two companies merge and attempt to produce results in new ways. The make-sense cycle stops when one company learns what equipment the other uses and what its operating procedures are. Often we hear the postmortem, "It looked good on paper." In the Sense-Response Cycle, this is moving to decide too soon, when there was more making sense to do. Research tells us that experts spend more time in this upfront stage of making sense, planning, and thinking things through before deciding and acting. They achieve their desired results in less time than others who decide fast and then have to backtrack, repairing but still not reflecting. Chris Argyris starts to get at this with his notion of double-loop learning, and Peter Senge touches on it with his notion of systems thinking, but doing the work of going below the waterline of the iceberg is more than using mental processes. It involves knowing the relevant concepts, theories, and content that underlie whatever it is we are thinking through.[5]

When we dive below the waterline, we are trying to understand the fundamentals underlying the business decisions we are thinking through—the Prepared Mind skills we are using. Theoretical fundamentals, such as supply and demand and motivation theories, are examples of underlying forces that influence business intentions, decisions, and results. For instance, supply and demand are important to every decision we make about pricing and labor. Extrinsic and intrinsic motivators have a bearing on the results of any initiative we have to retain our best employees. At a more macro level, when we read articles about the unemployment rate or interest rate, if we are smart, we read well below the headlines to see if the economic fundamentals are in good shape or if the statistic is indicating a shift in economic health.

When we dare to dive to this depth, we ask ourselves, "What are the key anchoring concepts and theories underlying the issue? What do those concepts mean, and what do they imply when you engineer them into a decision?" When you hit on the anchoring concepts, you may even start to change the way you see the issue, which will open new doors for your analysis, decisions, and actions.

We often watch really smart people think through issues. They ask a lot of questions, and then magic happens, or so it seems. We attribute their ability to brilliance and creativity. In reality, the key is often that they are thinking at the level of fundamentals and anchoring concepts and theories, and they make sense at that level.

At the top level of the Prepared Mind iceberg are the behaviors we see that result from using the eight skills. If we hear someone say, "Walk me through your thinking about investment options," we can bet that he or she is using the skill of enabling to help make someone else's skill of reasoning more explicit. However, if we really want to help others learn how to reason more effectively, we go to the deepest level and ask questions or demonstrate the use of anchoring concepts for the skill of reasoning.

When we follow up with someone who has just walked us through his or her thinking about investments with a question like,

"Tell me how you are *defining* margins, or share with me your *assumptions* about hedging," we are drawing on the fundamentals of theory building and hypothesis testing. And although those terms are not common business-speak, we use them all the time. And if you are using the enabling skill and the person seems eager to learn from you, you have a teachable moment when you can name what you just did so the person now knows what theory building looks like in practice and has a new concept to use going forward. If, as a means of enabling, you say, "I saw where you were going with your thinking, but I did not understand the link between your second and third point," you are not only gently using the skill of challenging but also bringing into the light the fundamentals of logic or linear thinking.

BRINGING IT ALL BACK HOME

Let's look at these frameworks from your personal point of view. You have a job, and for the most part, you know the scope and responsibility of it. Furthermore, the longer you do your job, the more familiar it becomes. You expended a lot of energy in the sense and make-sense phases of your job when you first engaged it, but as time went by, you internalized what has to be done and you can just focus on the decide and act phases of the Sense-Response Cycle. You become fast and efficient. Think of this as the "job box" that we enter mentally and physically when we go to work. We sense that little else is new, and so there is no need to make sense and, consequently, no new decision to make. We may be very efficient at what we do today, but we are not preparing ourselves or our organization for the future.

What happens when you combine the Sense-Response Cycle with our definition of Prepared Mind leadership? You get the picture shown in Figure 2.2.

You can operate the cycle within the boundaries of your existing job description, or you can take a chance and operate just outside the lines. Why should you work outside the boundaries of your job? Well, to be blunt, you can look at this defensively and face the fact that your job *is* going to change and you may as well have some voice in the change.

Think back a few pages to the concept (and reality) of the life cycles. As you move along the life cycle curves of your products,

Figure 2.2. Expanding the Sense-Response Cycle
Beyond Job Description Boundaries

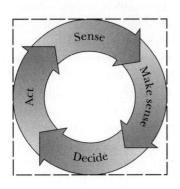
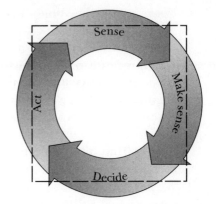

services, company, and industry, you always have to prepare for the unknown beyond every strategic inflection point, the point where the fundamentals may certainly change. And if you know your job description will change *after* the inflection point, you may as well prepare *before* the inflection point.

Think of it this way. As you approach an inflection point, you have two choices: do your job, or expand your job to meet the future. If you decide to just do your job, you continue to operate in a status quo mode and wait for someone else to make sense of the situation and change your job description (or, heaven forbid, eliminate it). But if you decide to expand your job, you have to operate in all four phases of the Sense-Response Cycle, slightly outside the limits or confines of your job description. We don't know what our future will be, but we do know that we can prepare ourselves.

We see leadership in the actions of individuals who break out of the confines of their job description to take advantage of opportunities in their environment. The difference between this and "defending your job," as described above, is a question of motivation and consideration of your needs, as well as the needs of your organization.

This description of leadership—the willingness and ability to work beyond formal job descriptions for the betterment of the organization—supports and aligns with five powerful questions that drive organizational progress:

1. *Where are we?* The role of leadership is to assess your position in the larger context of the systems within which you operate. Not knowing your starting point is to begin without knowing your strengths or weaknesses.
2. *Where do we want to go?* Part of a leader's role is to help an organization focus on a destination. Not knowing your destination is akin to wandering in the desert.
3. *How do we get from where we are to where we want to be?* What decisions will we have to take to get from here to there? Action without a plan is a sure-fire way to waste resources.
4. *What assumptions are we making about our situation?* Do you know what you should and, more important, should *not* take for granted?
5. *How is our opportunity space changing?* Tomorrow is not yesterday; new problems will arise, and new opportunities will present themselves. Will you see the differences in time?

The first three questions are the obvious ones underlying the creation of a strategy, whether it's for a corporation, a department, or your own career. The fourth question, the uncovering of assumptions, is critical to having a good foundation for the first three questions. And the fifth question highlights the need for understanding and developing a Prepared Mind.

Prepared Mind Question

What are your answers to these five questions for your role in your organization?

We all have a pace we prefer within the Sense-Response Cycle; however, changes in our opportunity space, whether caused by competitors or customers or new technology, require us to run the cycle at ever higher frequency or face the danger of becoming irrelevant. Even if we are not responding to changes in our environment or taking advantage of opportunities, our familiarity with our job allows us to speed up the cycle, with all the attendant risks inherent in working faster and faster. Speed can be dangerous;

change for the sake of change puts us in danger of losing our balance. We need a balancing mechanism, a supporting framework, a foundation on which to build our leadership values and skills.

The Prepared Mind leaders we know are grounded in the ability and willingness to examine their mental maps, expand on them, and, when necessary, discard the outdated and build new ones. They then use these updated maps to operate their own Sense-Response Cycle at the speed needed to take advantage of opportunities that lie outside the boundaries of their job description. The skills needed to make this concept a reality are addressed in Part Two.

But first, try a quick self-evaluation as a preview of the eight skills of Prepared Mind leadership and an opportunity to take what you already know and combine it with some of these new frameworks in new ways.

HOW PREPARED ARE YOU?

Preparedness is found in the exercise of specific, learnable skills, and the eight Prepared Mind leadership skills are the most important. You may be good at some and not so good at others, but you need them all, and this book will help you get better, no matter how good you already are. How good are you at these skills?

- Observing: Can you describe an embryonic trend affecting your industry? Do you know your newest customer needs? What "strange data" have you noticed recently? None? Do you really think there are no surprises on the way?
- Imagining: What "new story" could you write for you company? Can you envision the domination of your industry by a competitor? By your company? What bold moves did they take? What conditions are in place for this to happen?
- Reasoning: How does your company make its money? Could you explain the impact of losing a good customer? How much money does a "bad" customer cost you? Do you know? Do you care? Or is that "accounting's job"?
- Challenging: Is there any way to convince your boss that the company strategy needs to be changed? What do you stand for? What are your values? Do you truly believe the words of your company's mission statement?

- Deciding: How often does the buck stop with you? Are you capable of dealing with risky situations, or is everything moved to committee for a decision? Do you move fast enough to avoid evolving problems or to take advantage of new opportunities?
- Learning: In the words of Steven Covey's *Seven Habits,* what do you do to "sharpen the saw"?[6] Are terms such as *Six Sigma, customer relationship management, knowledge management, and middleware* meaningful to you, or are they just buzzwords as far as you're concerned?
- Enabling: Do the people around you learn from your words and actions? Is what they are learning from you making them more valuable to the organization? How do you help them become leaders?
- Reflecting: What did you learn from your last mistake, and how has it changed your behavior? What did your company learn from the last product or service launch, and what should change for the next launch?

These are the eight skills of the Prepared Mind. In Part Two, you can explore them in more detail and discover how to develop and apply them in your own situation.

THE SKILLS OF PREPARED MIND LEADERSHIP

$\boxed{\text{CHAPTER THREE}}$

OBSERVING
Seeing Beyond the Obvious

A valuable race horse, Silver Blaze, is stolen from its stable. Inspector Gregory of Scotland Yard asks Sherlock Holmes if any particular aspect of the crime calls for additional study. Holmes replies, "Yes," and points to "the curious incident of the dog in the nighttime." Inspector Gregory replies, "The dog did nothing in the nighttime." "That," says Holmes, "was the curious incident."[1]

Arthur Conan Doyle's enduring Sherlock Holmes has fascinated us with his powers of observation for over a century. His ability to find and make sense of the smallest clues was consistently the pivot point to solving the mystery at hand. The stories of the detective are not shoot-'em-up adventures; rather, they are stories of the power of observation. In the language of the Prepared Mind, Holmes's opportunity space was the world of crime, and his mental map was the mind of the criminal.

Shift to the 1980s. John Naisbitt's *Megatrends* soared to the top of the best-seller list and stayed there for sixty weeks. Naisbitt was doing something that any of us *could* have done: report on what he was seeing and the patterns that were evolving. His secret? He had the curiosity and took the time to look for emerging trends. Shift again. Faith Popcorn carried that ability to detect grand movements into the 1990s with her regular "Popcorn Reports" of trends and observations. Shift once more, and today we see Clay Christensen and his Strategy and Innovation team at Harvard Business School sending out biweekly commentary on stories they have seen in recent business publications that relate to changes in the business environment and the potential for innovation. Their opportunity space? Society at large. Their mental map? The evolution of new trends and discontinuities in established ones.[2]

Whether it's Sherlock or John or Faith or Clay, we find the ability to observe both interesting and somewhat mysterious. How is it that they see what we don't? Why are they so far ahead of the rest of us? The simple truth is that they see things because they look for things. It sounds trite and easy, but if it's so easy, then why do so many companies get surprised by events happening around them?

LOOKING AND SEEING

Why didn't GM pay attention to Toyota decades ago, and why are all of us not paying attention to Hyundai in the opening decade of the twenty-first century? What are you missing because you are not actively observing? The directive "look for things" is relatively simple, but putting it into practice is quite difficult. Observing is not a passive endeavor. It is a very active process and closely aligned with the concepts of paradigms explained by Thomas Kuhn in the early 1960s and that of mindfulness put forth by Ellen Langer in the 1990s.

Thomas Kuhn, then a professor emeritus of philosophy at MIT, wrote the landmark book *The Structure of Scientific Revolutions* as a historical overview and explanation of a practice that he referred to as paradigms. "The study of paradigms," he wrote,

> is what mainly prepared the student for membership in the particular scientific community for which he will later practice. Because he there joins men who learned the bases of their field from the same concrete models, his subsequent practice will seldom evoke overt disagreement over fundamentals. Men whose research is based on shared paradigms are committed to the same rules and standards for scientific practice.[3]

In other words, because scientists in a given field have the same models, they understand the world in the same way.

Kuhn wrote about the history of science, but the observation holds true for the practice of management and leadership. The problem for the scientist and leader alike is that the expression, "I'll believe it when I see it," is supplanted with the unspoken phrase, "Because I believe it, I see it." All too often, we see what we believe and deny what we see because we don't believe.

Later Kuhn discusses the impact of a changed paradigm—and this is the important part for us as we try to improve our ability to observe: "When paradigms change, the world itself changes with them. Led by a new paradigm, scientists adopt new instruments and *look in new places*. Even more important, during revolutions scientists *see new and different things* when looking with familiar instruments in places they have looked before [emphasis added]."[4]

The Prepared Mind leadership issue here is that paradigms are wonderful shortcuts as we think about the world, but they are deadly if they are not attuned with reality. When that happens we see, but we don't observe.

Similarly, Ellen Langer, a social psychologist and Harvard professor, has written extensively on the topic of mindfulness and, more important, mindful behavior. In her research, she has identified three characteristics of applying a mindful approach to our day-to-day activities: (1) the ongoing creation of new categories, that is, new shades of gray; (2) openness to new information that may not fit in existing categories; and (3) an awareness of multiple points of view, that is, the realization that our point of view is not the only one.[5]

Langer's second characteristic, being open to new information, strikes at the essence of the skill of observing and, going back to Kuhn's observations, the difficulty of truly observing the world as it is. All of us are bombarded with increasing waves of data and sensory inputs, and whether we realize it or not, we have become increasingly resistant. It's not so much a case of having to pay attention to the news of the world as it is a case of knowing when to change our filters so that the important stuff comes in.

The business world has been obsessed with change and managing change for at least the past thirty years, and we have long overcome the temptation to hunker down and wait for it to blow over. We see the big changes hitting our business and try to figure out how to bring our organization in line with them. We engage big-name consultants and their methodologies, and sometimes things get aligned. And yet for the most part, we ignore the day-to-day small changes that are all around us. Why? We just don't see them. The problem is that these small changes build up, and all too often, they sneak up on us.

OBSERVING BY THE PREPARED MIND

> We do not see things as they are; we see them as we are.
> —Anaïs Nin

Observing, as we think about it in terms of the Prepared Mind, is the skill of taking in new data from the environment and integrating them with what we already know in order to select, categorize, and represent the data as something meaningful in our minds. That "something meaningful" activates further making sense of the situation and begins to shape the boundaries of the opportunity space. The challenge here is somewhat akin to the admonition to think outside the box. However, in this case, the challenge is to be willing to change the size or even the shape of the box.

Consider the importance of the timing of our observations in the Sense-Response Cycle. Data are hitting us constantly, and we often wrestle with the issue of when to convert the data to information that we can try to make sense of. If we sense that the data point to a competitive change after it is well under way, we are almost surely in reaction mode and are faced with a good news–bad news scenario.

The good news about being in reaction mode is that the course of action is clear, often painfully clear, to us at the time. But since we have to react, we mostly follow the competitor's moves. For example, the competition may have released a new product. As we make sense of the impact of this new product release, we realize that we have to match the product's features and benefits. And so we launch a focused (and sometimes frenzied) reverse-engineering effort to copy the product and get it to the market as soon as possible. The bad news is that our competition got there first, so our options were constrained. They set the rules of the game, and we had no choice but to match them. Competitor intelligence was focused on what they (and others) did, and our reaction was to copy their actions.

Wouldn't it be better to focus on what the competition is capable of and sense it *sooner* by observing leading indicators? Your sales force knows when a competitor's product or service hits the street. What about your R&D people? Do they observe what's in the papers and speeches of your competitor's R&D people? If they do, do you listen to them when they tell you about the "exciting things" that the competitor is doing?

And so we have two scenarios. One is the scenario of reacting to a competitive move after it has been completed. The alternate scenario is one of observing the clues laid out before us. How might this alternate scenario play out? In this scenario, we watch patent filings, talk with suppliers and headhunters we both use, make sales calls on their most progressive customers, listen to their speakers at industry events, and generally observe the competitive ecosystem in which we both live. This ability to observe gives us an earlier sense of where they are going and gives us time to make sense of their potential actions. Maybe we come to the same conclusion about the need for upgraded products; maybe we come to a different conclusion. The point is that we have the opportunity to act instead of react: more options are open to us because we have more time. The skill of observing is key to shifting more of our most precious resource, time, toward the work of sensing and making sense of the world and its changes.

So here's the situation we all face: we can wait and see the obvious, or we can improve our personal and organizational ability to observe and therefore sense the clues that in hindsight will seem so very obvious.

THE PARADOX OF OBSERVING: WE OFTEN SEE, BUT WE DON'T ALWAYS OBSERVE

When it comes to the skill of observing, we might expect to dwell on behaviors, scenarios, instances of concrete things we see, hear, taste, touch, or smell. Observation seems like the ultimate skill for the opening activity of the Sense-Response Cycle: that of sensing. However, if the skill of observing were just about data in our environment, how would we explain the fact that we don't make observations about everything our senses take in? How would we explain the phenomenon that two companies can be in the same environment and make different observations?

Observation, in the way we think of it in the leader's Prepared Mind, is not just about taking in raw data from the environment. Observing with a Prepared Mind includes looking for meaning. The quest for the meaning behind data affects how we interpret what we observe and what we observe in the first place.

There are obvious things like statistics and ratios or stories from our consultants that are meant to help us understand our position in the current business environment. We may hear speeches being given to a board of directors or feel the handshake of people coming into a meeting. We may see long lines or short lines. We may savor familiar flavors or experience strange tastes in dishes that are foreign to us. The list goes on.

But problems with the skill of observing are usually not associated with lack of data from the environment. We generally have plenty of data, even too much data. Problems more often come from not knowing what to pay attention to in the midst of all that data. Also, we often spend energy on "urgent" things that are less meaningful in the big picture of our business and family lives yet fail to observe subtle signs that point to the need to activate the Sense-Response Cycle for making decisions and taking action that will have real import.

Problems also arise when we attribute the wrong meaning to data. For instance, we may come up with a theory of why a business strategy did or did not work, but actually we fail to look at deeper possible causes addressed by Chris Argyris's notion of double-loop learning.[6] The first loop addresses the fit between our mental maps and incoming data. The second loop addresses the question, "Do we have the correct mental map?"

Failure to act can begin with the failure to observe. This often happens because we want coherence with what we already know; we may observe something new in the environment but then make it fit what we already know. We focus only on those features that seem familiar or frame what we see as a familiar scenario. Consequently we fail to see the underlying structural differences and implications. Think about the cell phones you have owned over the past ten years. Now ask yourself, "When did Motorola notice the shift from analog to digital? When did Nokia notice the shift from technology to cool design?" The answer, in both cases, is "Too late."

Three Anchoring Concepts

To improve our ability to observe, we can learn techniques that make us better observers. For instance, we could develop a skill-building plan that looks something like this:

1. Notice one new thing going on in my company every day and record what it means to me in a journal.
2. Visit geographically dispersed offices and observe the differences in work style, what people have on their desks, and other things that show differences in culture.
3. Read more articles and books about my industry, and write a summary as to where I think the future of the industry is going, based on my observations of things discussed in the article.

However, learning techniques is not enough for the Prepared Mind. If you wish to be flexible and strategic in your thinking and application of the Prepared Mind skills, you need to understand the roots of the skills and the concepts that anchor them and provide the foundation for skill building and overcoming the risks and challenges of using each skill.

The three anchoring concepts of observing are (1) attention, (2) perception, and (3) pattern recognition.

Attention

The Attention Economy has become more than a book title; it has become a worldview for many business executives in and out of industries that have traditionally been paid to get people's attention: advertising, marketing, and television, for example.[7]

The operating assumption underlying the attention economy worldview is that customers have many options and many things vying for their attention, and more and more customers have the power to turn off traditional attention getters such as the sixty-second television commercial. Therefore, in order to reach customers and get them to begin to know and believe what we want them to know and believe about us, we need to design products, services, businesses, and advertisements in such a way that they link to customer values and vehicles already in use, are emotionally and cognitively compelling, and yet seem unobtrusive. This is not just about selling soap or cars. This view applies to recruiting and managing talent, gaining attention and commitment for causes and charities, even getting our children to learn in school. Whether we agree with this worldview or not, it draws our attention to a classic concept from the world of cognitive psychology: attention.

In 1890, William James wrote, "Everyone knows what attention is. It is the taking possession of the mind, in clear and vivid form, of one out of what seem several simultaneously possible objects or trains of thought. Focalization, concentration, of consciousness are of its essence. It implies withdrawal from some things in order to deal effectively with others."[8] What James offered as a definition more than a century ago still holds true today.

To put it in a nutshell, attention is the mental process we use to select what we will further process mentally. Our sensory organs can take in many pieces of data, but only those pieces that we attend to will become an observation worth making sense of in our minds.

Like so many of the other skills and foundational concepts of the Prepared Mind, attention is at least in part determined by what is already on our minds. Have you ever had the experience of buying a new car and then suddenly noticing many cars on the street that look like the car you just bought? It is not that a rash of people suddenly high-tailed it to the local car dealer to buy a car just like yours. Rather, we start to see our car everywhere because we tend to attend to things that remind us of things that are fresh in our minds, or have strong emotion attached to them, or address a problem, need, or question we are wrestling with in our working memory. Often, too, our attention is drawn to things that are very dissimilar to knowledge, skills, and images already in our mental store of prior knowledge. Have you ever had to tell your child, "Don't stare, honey," when someone passes by who does not look like people the child is used to seeing in her world?

Attention is a requirement for the skill of observing. It is the filter through which we choose what to sense and make sense of. If we want to improve our skill of observing, we will need to become more aware of our habits of attention and make more conscious decisions of what to pay attention to and ask others to bring to our attention.

"Have You Ever Wondered" Tip

Here is a little consolation for multitaskers who ask, "Can we attend to more than one task at a time?"

The best conditions for performing two tasks together are when the two tasks are dissimilar from each other, when they are relatively easy tasks, and when they are well-practiced tasks. The worst conditions are when the tasks are highly similar, difficult, and have been practiced very little. The practical application here is to work on dissimilar, familiar tasks at the same time, like brushing your teeth and brainstorming ideas for your presentation.

Source: Michael W. Eysenck and Mark T. Keane, *Cognitive Psychology: A Student's Handbook* (Mahwah, N.J.: Erlbaum, 1990).

PERCEPTION

If attention is like catching the eye of the girl or boy across the room at the high school dance, then perception is the dance that ensues and turns the night into an experience. Perception takes the next step in processing the data from our environment and turning them into something meaningful. It too is required to activate the skill of observing. One technical definition of *perception* is that it "is the means by which information acquired from the environment via the sense organs is transformed into experiences of objects, events, sounds, tastes, etc."[9] In other words, perception is the process for turning information into experience. Perception takes attention to the next level and turns our observations into experiences that make us think and feel, even if perceiving seems automatic or unconscious to us some of the time.

When we are in the act of perceiving, our minds are dancing. Who are the partners in the dance? One partner is the information from the environment (the number, the tone of voice, the news story, the face). The other partner is our mental map: a select group of concepts, networked relationships between concepts, hypotheses, expectations, and knowledge that we have acquired from previous experiences and have stored in our memory. Perception, like the skill of learning, involves constructing meaning by combining new information with old knowledge. Perception is not as deep a process as learning, but it is a necessary foundation for many of the eight skills of the Prepared Mind.

When we offered Anaïs Nin's observation earlier, "We do not see things as they are, we see things as we are," we were in part referring to the role of prior knowledge (including beliefs, preferences, biases, and recognized attributes) in seeing and perceiving. In some respects, our minds are prepared to take in new things based on what is already there. One reason that the skill of observing is so vital to building the Prepared Mind is that we must constantly be adding to and reshaping our mental maps if we are to develop our leadership capability beyond what it is today. We have to make a conscious effort to broaden and deepen our ways of attending, perceiving, and seeing patterns in our observations that translate to richer networks of concepts and ideas in our minds.

PATTERN RECOGNITION

The third anchoring concept for the skill of observing is pattern recognition. Pattern recognition adds a layer of complexity to attention and perceiving because it detects and discriminates recurring combinations of things in the environment and begins to direct our making sense toward relevant patterns rather than having us just see and react to singular experiences. Many psychologists believe that we can recognize patterns because we can associate similarities in recurrent events to networks of ideas in our minds. In a way, our minds are like tapestries with patterns that allow us to fit new threads into them.

For instance, if we see a company continuing to lay off people in waves, we may start to think that it needs to reduce cost and that the business may be in trouble. Why would we notice the layoffs as a pattern and associate them with such a hypothesis? Because prior knowledge from personal experience, reading the newspaper, listening to the news, and watching other companies take similar actions has formed a pattern in our mind that layoffs are associated with cost reduction and cost reduction is associated with business risk. It is not just the similarity of features that helps us see the pattern. It is the relation between features that have given us a structure in which to place an observation. So we have the concept of layoff related to the concept of cost reduction related to the concept of unemployment. If we see enough of these relationships, we usually start to predict a larger pattern we might call "troubled economy."

If we are given enough context, we can learn to look for patterns. For instance, if we are reminded that fall is coming because school is starting all around Chicago, the concept of "fall in the Midwest" cues all kinds of patterns in our mind. We prepare ourselves to see the first leaves change color, and then we begin to look for more color change and even predict the next pattern of leaves falling off trees.

Patterns are a very efficient way for us to organize observations and not be overwhelmed by a multitude of singular events. The danger is that we may prematurely assign an event to a pattern and miss variations that could take our thinking and responses in new directions. If something occurs that we think should fit into a pattern but it does not, it usually activates the Sense-Response Cycle to an even greater degree. For instance, last year we had a cold summer in Chicago. Instead of the usual pattern of leaves changing color in September and October, we saw leaves changing color in August. That got people's attention. In business meetings and social gatherings, people talked about the leaves changing early, trying to make sense together and even predict what the winter would be like.

The skill of observing depends on our ability to see patterns. It also depends on our ability to see when things do not fit our existing patterns. It is the latter that often signals a threat or opportunity in our world.

CONNECTING TO THE CONCEPTS: ANCHORED EXERCISES TO IMPROVE YOUR SKILL OF OBSERVING

SCAN FOR TRENDS

In John Naisbitt's *Megatrends,* the trends themselves were interesting, but the enduring value of the book was the method Naisbitt and his associates used to identify the trends. Their method was based on our three anchoring concepts for the skill of observing:

attention, perception, and pattern recognition. Naisbitt and his associates scanned a number of newspapers and magazines from different geographical areas searching for articles about different industries. Over time, they saw the trends and the opportunity space for major areas for innovation that were bubbling up, and they categorized them into products, services, demands, and other business and social issues they expected to emerge over the next ten years.

Their method is something each of us can do individually or as a group of leaders. An abbreviated version is to do a thematic analysis once or twice a year, even if it is just reading the annual "new technology trends" or "hottest innovation" issues from magazines such as *Fortune, Business Week,* and MIT's *Technology Review.* Observing growing demands in business and developing capabilities in technology combine to set us on the path of recognizing opportunities and issues.

CONNECT THE DOTS

The Prepared Mind leaders we know are especially good at connecting the dots. For instance, one CEO in health care tracks innovations, legislation, and emerging opportunities in arenas such as telecommunication, education, and government. From there, he connects the dots to issues that will be just around the corner for health care, such as privacy concerns around potential television systems for patient monitoring. He then prepares his organization to think through the implications not only for the design of hospitals but also unintended consequences on factors such as staffing and finance.

You can improve your observing skills by simply paying attention across domains and keeping company with leaders from different industries to hear what they are facing and how they are thinking about it. Perceiving connections across industries helps us see things we might otherwise miss and helps us deepen our recognition of the systems or interconnected view of this world that is based on webs of knowledge. Think tanks, university forums, renaissance weekends, even cocktail parties are all great places to observe across domains.

The Cycle of Observing

If we are going to be prepared for our future, we need to keep ourselves open and honest by better observing the changes around us. Some changes are obvious, others very subtle. The obvious changes attract everyone's attention, but only the best Prepared Minds note the subtle ones. Consider the questions illustrated in the Sense-Response Cycle as a way to leverage attention, perception, and recognition. Use Figure 3.1 as a starting point.

Figure 3.1. The Sense-Response Cycle of Observing

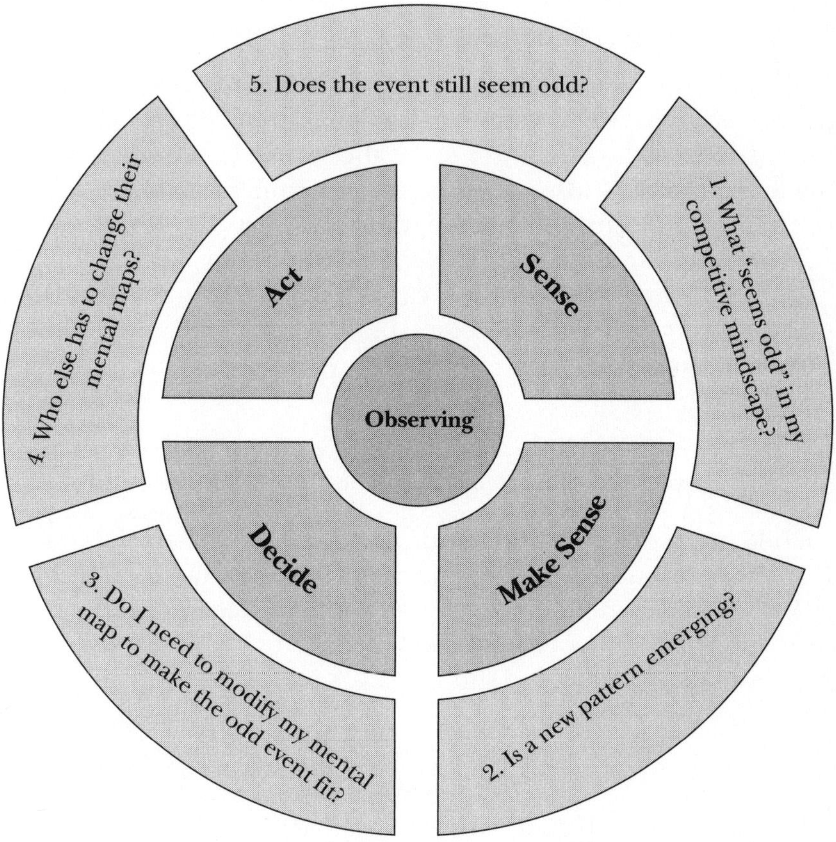

- 5. Does the event still seem odd?
- 4. Who else has to change their mental maps?
- 1. What "seems odd" in my competitive mindscape?
- Act
- Sense
- Observing
- Decide
- Make Sense
- 3. Do I need to modify my mental map to make the odd event fit?
- 2. Is a new pattern emerging?

1. WHAT "SEEMS ODD" IN MY COMPETITIVE MINDSCAPE?

In 1955, St. Joseph Lead was number 299 on the Fortune 500 list. What a great business! Lead was used in paint, in gasoline, in solder, and for plumbing, to name just some of its uses. What "odd" events did St. Joseph Lead miss? That is, what was happening before their very eyes that did not fit their mental maps? What might its executives have done if they had seen them early on? Sometimes an odd event is just that: odd. Sometimes odd events are "the canary in the coal mine." What odd events have you ignored in the past few years?

2. IS A NEW PATTERN EMERGING?

One of the ways we can make sense of odd events is to see if a new pattern is emerging. What were the signals that led Toyota to take the risk with its hybrid automobile, the Prius? There was no existing market for hybrids. There was no government mandate. Surely there were not enough hard data to support the design, engineering, and development of such an automobile. Yet as of 2005, Toyota has more orders than capacity for manufacturing this model. Honda is close on its heels, but the rest of the auto industry is playing catch-up.

3. DO I NEED TO MODIFY MY MENTAL MAP TO MAKE THE ODD EVENT FIT?

An odd event does not add to our knowledge if we deny it because it does not fit our existing mental map. To quote Sherlock Holmes in "A Scandal in Bohemia": "It is a capital mistake to theorize before one has data. Insensibly one begins to twist facts to suit theories, instead of theories to suit facts."

4. WHO ELSE HAS TO CHANGE THEIR MENTAL MAPS?

One of the big failings of large organizational change projects is that once the leadership "gets it," they assume that everyone gets it. Not true. We need to spend considerably more energy both understanding and, when needed, modifying the mental maps of all those who are involved with the change.

5. DOES THE EVENT STILL SEEM ODD?

If we have done a good job of leading our organization and taking advantage of the problem or opportunity we faced, then the whole organization can look back at the event and admonish themselves for not seeing it sooner. However, if the event still seems odd, then we will still have parts of the organization in denial.

BENEFITS, RISKS, AND CHALLENGES OF OBSERVING

Developing and using any of the eight Prepared Mind skills carries benefits, risks, and challenges. Here is our starting list for the skill of observing, but the most important list is the one that is specific to you. So don't just assume that we have given you a comprehensive view. Add to, subtract from, and modify our list to fit your reality.

BENEFITS OF IMPROVING YOUR SKILL OF OBSERVATION

Improving a skill takes time and energy. Before expending either, we need to be assured that the benefits are worth the effort. Consider the following points.

Strategic Focus

Skilled observation focuses your attention so you can be more deliberate and strategic about what you are thinking through. Since most of us are time-starved, we need to occasionally lift our head, look around, and see what has changed. Our opportunity space is dynamic; just because we understood it during the recent strategic planning session doesn't mean it stayed that way.

Self-Revelation

Working on your observation skills points out your habits of categorizing and labeling that may be efficient but could be limiting to your business thinking. Look for unusual events in your opportunity space. If they don't fit your existing mental map, you may need to modify the maps.

Enriched Point of View

Practicing observation encourages diversity of thinking among your team in what they notice and how they think. The same event may have different meaning depending on the person's point of view. The composite picture is always richer than yours alone.

New Perspectives

Systematic observation allows you to take a step back from doing and make a conscious effort to see new things that may affect what you are doing or the way you are doing it. Ask yourself, "What's the big picture around here?" and see if your efforts are still aligned.

RISKS OF OBSERVING

An overemphasis on a newly developed skill can result in experiencing certain downside risks. Consider the following points.

Indecisiveness

The skill of observing is important for the sense and make-sense activities of the Sense-Response Cycle. However, if we just keep collecting data, we almost always find information that supports both sides of an argument. This can lead to indecisiveness, paralysis, and fear of acting. Committing ourselves to put the skill of deciding into action, with the help of skills like reasoning, can help us move through the cycle and not be caught in a cycle of all inputs and no outputs.

Sideline Players

Have you ever had someone on your team at work or even in your neighborhood who is always filled with ideas, observations, and opinions, but when it comes time to step up and do something with them, this person says, "No, that's not me," or, "That's not my job." Given that the Prepared Mind definition of leadership includes working outside the boundaries of one's job, being observant on the sidelines is hardly leadership. The skills of deciding, challenging, and enabling can help someone step up and do something with what he or she observes.

There is an old principle used in the community of theater directors that if you want someone to offer observations and contribute ideas to the creative process, you, as the leader, have to enable the others by asking them for their observations three times. The first time, they will do it thinking it will never be acted on. If you do use the ideas in a decision or action and you ask them a second time, they will contribute their observations with the hypothesis that the first time was a fluke and their ideas will not be used again. If you find a way to use them and ask them a third time, they will offer their observations with healthy yet hopeful skepticism. If you use what they give you, they will then continue to make observations and contribute them to the group.

Breeding Skepticism and Cynicism Beyond Healthiness or Helpfulness

One of us works in a university environment where people are paid to analyze, criticize, and uncover the dark side of things. There is nothing like working with a twenty-one-year-old student who has become such an excellent observer and critic of society that he makes Eeyore, the sad donkey from the Winnie-the-Pooh books, look like an optimist.

The Prepared Mind skills of challenging, learning, imagining, and enabling are key to moving beyond cynicism, no matter what the environment is. Challenging and learning can work hand in hand in getting the skeptic or cynic to remember a time in his or her life when the pattern observed led to positive outcomes. Sharing counterexperiences and asking them to imagine outcomes beyond their immediate observable world are all important in enabling people not to get lost in their own morass of observations.

Taking Your Own Observation as Truth

Even masters at attending, perceiving, and recognizing patterns are not always right. This is why making sense of observations with others who have different perspectives is critical before jumping to a conclusion. We are likely to be better off if we approach the skill of observing from a learning stance rather than a decision stance. The skills of challenging, imagining, and reflecting are particularly helpful in helping us take in the data we see, hear, touch, feel, or smell, and turn them over to understand them as early pointers to a variety of possible explanations and implications.

CHALLENGES TO OBSERVING

It's pretty clear that the ability to observe is critical to seeing the future before it crashes against our doors. However, we read regularly about the failure of business leaders to observe the changes hitting them and their organizations. They "missed the market" or "failed to respond" or were "surprised" by competitive moves. The bottom line is that they and their organization failed to observe.

What gets in the way of our ability to attend to, perceive, and recognize patterns from the information in our environment? Some of the obvious ones are:

- Information overload
- Limited cognitive load capacity
- Routines
- Underusing the skills of Learning and Reflection
- Fixation on today

Information Overload

We are exposed to so much information and stimulus at once that we do not know what to pay attention to, let alone process and discriminate for patterns. Prepared Minds become strategic about their information intake. For instance, they learn to go into new situations with specific questions or goals in mind that will focus their observations. They may also distribute observation responsibilities among their colleagues, who then later can compare notes. Skills like imagining and reasoning can help us chunk information into scenarios or into logic flows that give us a framework for managing great amounts of information. Learning strategies such as the use of matrices and concept maps can serve as visual aids to help us organize our information and see relationships among concepts.

Limited Cognitive Load Capacity

The reason that we cannot perform two similar, difficult, unpracticed tasks at once is that our working memories have a limited capacity; we cannot load them with too much complex, simultaneous thinking. The skills of learning and reflecting are very helpful in providing tools to help carry the load.

For instance, Prepared Minds take notes so they do not have to rely solely on their memories to hold and process new information. Another trick is to take a break from the information intake action, let yourself categorize what you have seen so far, and begin to form patterns and themes so when you step back into the fray, you can reduce load by placing new information in the categories you just formed. Prepared Minds do this all the time by stopping the conversation and summarizing what they have heard so far. They may also devise mnemonic schemes like the ones we used as kids to remember the notes on the music scale (Every Good Boy Does Fine). Also, sometimes Prepared Minds physically remove themselves from situations just long enough to process what they have just heard.

Routines

Some aspects of the Prepared Mind require extra conscious effort to fight against our natural patterns such as being creatures of habit. We see what we expect to see.[10] Routines are efficient, but if, for instance, we always drive to work on the same route, or always visit the same place on vacation, or always read the same kinds of books, we will fail to observe whole chunks of the world that may be very relevant to us and our business.

We may also not have the rich, complex, internal mental maps that are formed from having the variety of experiences required to identify, process, store, and make sense out of what we observe, especially that which is unfamiliar. If we lack context, we will be limited in what we observe and consequently limit our opportunity space.

Prepared Minds expose themselves to new and varied people, places, and things regularly. Some of the brightest, most successful, and most interesting Prepared Minds we have known naturally and explicitly associate what they observe with history they have read, cultures they have visited, artwork they have viewed, philosophical and theological ideas they have contemplated, and nature they have witnessed.

The skills of challenging and imagining can be helpful in not becoming victims of routine. We can challenge ourselves to walk a different path or look at an issue with a new lens, and we can invite others with different experiences to challenge us. We knew a vice president of human resources who asked the vice president of finance to challenge him by framing a people issue in terms of dollars and investment. It gave the HR vice president new things to observe when making business decisions about staffing. Imagining forces us to picture scenarios that are not part of our routines. When we plant just one new "what if?" image in our minds, we immediately begin to see new things or see things in new ways.

Underusing the Skills of Learning and Reflection

Haven't the times when you needed to learn something led you to being more open to observing a new class of things that might help you in your learning? Working the other way, when we take in a lot of information, it will fall to the cutting room floor unless we commit ourselves to being more reflective and using what we observe as fodder for our reflection. Reflecting allows us the time and motivation to make meaning out of all the information we have; it allows us to make sense out of what sometimes seems like nonsense. Unfortunately, it often takes a strong, almost overwhelming, often perceived as negative event, like a death in the family or a job loss, to cause us to reflect on what we observe and observe things we may have missed when going through the motions of the routines of life. However, if we set aside time to journal, meditate, pray, draw, or whatever else it is that helps us reflect, we open our minds to deeper and broader observations.

Fixation on Today

We are so focused on the problems of today that we neglect to lift our head and look for tomorrow. In 1994 when Gary Hamel and C. K. Prahalad published *Competing for the Future,* one of their startling observations was the small amount of time senior executives spent thinking about the future of the companies.[11] Considering the recurring themes of downsizing, rightsizing, leanness, and cost reduction over the past fifteen years, we doubt that today's executives are spending any more time considering the future and looking for clues of what might be emerging. So while we can easily think of challenges that prevent us from being good observers, we also need to be aware of the signs and risks of overusing the skill of observation and how, taken to the extreme, it can actually hinder our minds and our ability to sense, make sense, decide, and act.

APPLIED OBSERVATION: THE TALENT PROBLEM

We will use the talent problem as an ongoing example of the use of the eight Prepared Mind skills. This example is developed here and will be shown in sidebars in the following seven chapters.

The problem of acquiring, developing, and retaining the right talent is familiar to every organization that expects to survive and grow. What kinds of questions and what activities might a Prepared Mind leader consider in thinking about this issue from the observing point of view?

An executive might inquire into the benchmark practices for talent acquisition, development, and retention. However, she should also be aware of seeing only the obvious, superficial activities.

A middle manager might look into evolving trends that the organization is not prepared to handle. An example might be seeing an early retirement trend. A coworker might also see others who are falling behind in the application of a new technology but are not being properly developed. An analysis of SAP (a comprehensive enterprisewide software package) failures might discover too many ill-prepared workers.

And an individual contributor might communicate emerging problems seen in the field or on the shop floor.

Now let's go deeper. One of the most effective ways to practice the skill of observing is to ask questions leading from its three anchoring concepts of attention, perception, and pattern recognition. In our example here, you would first break open the talent retention issue to select some key aspects to look at in more depth. For instance, what are your criteria for talent? Would others have different opinions? How would your competitors define talent? Now take the concept of retention and ask similar questions. Then use the anchoring concepts to form questions to dig even deeper. With this process you will build a list or map of ideas to use as food for thinking through the issue with extra effort given to the skill of observing—for example:

Definitions

- Talent: Graduate degree, good performance scores from clients; good leadership scores from team; specializes in more than one area
- Retention: Stay with the firm seven plus years; hold two or more positions

Anchored Questions

- Attention: Focus, selection for further processing

  What employees should I focus on? Given my unpacking of the term *talent*, what are my criteria for selecting a group to analyze?
  Why is talent retention important to the firm and to me? Why should I invest time in giving it more thought?

- Perception: Transform information into experience and meaning

  What does the loss of talent mean to me and to the firm? What kind of experience do people have that works in a high-turnover environment versus what I imagine it could be like if more talented people stuck around longer?
  What do all these data about turnover spikes two years after graduate school mean? What does it say that most people defined as talented have held only one position in the firm?

- Pattern recognition: Detecting, discriminating, recurring combinations of interconnected information

  What patterns are emerging if all of the colleagues I have known who have left did so after they had worked three years with the firm and then completed their master's degree? What do the firmwide data show in this regard?
  Is there some link between turnover and time in the firm, graduate degree, and lack of promotion?

Notice that these questions simultaneously begin to make sense out of what has already been observed and suggest new areas to observe.

What have you observed about the talent problem at your organization?

BUILDING YOUR SKILLS

Here are a few more techniques to use to build the skill of observing.

LEARN THE WARNING SIGNS

The American Cancer Society has educated legions of women to be better, proactive observers of their own bodies and some of the warning signs of breast cancer. Because they know what to look for and understand the danger of a missed observation, they remain vigilant.

Some warning signs for a business at risk have been well known for quite some time, and yet we still ignore them. Consider the following examples. If they apply to your business, are you observing them?

- Low inventory turns
- High personnel turnover
- Ongoing discounts
- Reduced cash flow
- Repetitive customer complaints
- Increasing Accounts Receivable days

LOOK THROUGH DIFFERENT EYES

Bill goes to a party with his wife and after the party she asks him how a friend is feeling. Bill says, "Gee, I don't know. We talked about sports and business. I guess he's feeling fine." His wife responds, "Well, his skin color seemed wrong, and his respirations seemed a bit fast. Something's wrong." Bill was trained as an engineer; his wife, a nurse. Their observations of the same person were different because they were looking through different eyes.

What if you observed your industry through the eyes of a newspaper reporter? Would you see the human story behind your decisions? Would you see the story behind the story that, truth be told, is more interesting than just the facts behind your current dilemma?

What if you observed your business through the eyes of an ecologist? Would you see the forces at play that are slowly destroying the entire competitive ecosystem? Is the weakest player in your ecosystem thriving or slowly dying? Which of the competitive interrelationships is changing, and is that good or bad for you in the long term?

What if you observed your stakeholders through the eyes of a great chef? What "presentation" is ideal? What combinations would give your business a unique flavor?

There are many more eyes that we can use to improve our ability to observe. However, none is more important than looking at your company, industry, or ecosystem through the eyes of a child. We smile at the ability of a child to see things that we take for granted and ask wonderfully simple, yet often unanswerable, questions. The child in you once looked at the sky and asked why it was blue. And often the adults around you could only answer, "Because."

When was the last time you looked at your business and asked obvious, but unanswerable questions? Who are your most and least profitable customers? What do your fastest-growing customers want next?

MORE QUESTIONS TO CONSIDER

- **Intentional obsolescence.** The harvested ice industry (which prospered for two hundred years) mastered the core capabilities of cutting, transporting, and storing ice. Mechanical ice making made these capabilities irrelevant.

  Make a list of the capabilities on which your industry relies. What can you make obsolete? What if your competition made any of them obsolete? What will the Internet make obsolete?

- **Tipping points.** When does one rock rolling down a hill cause an avalanche? When does ice melt? When will buying your favorite product "tip" from retail stores to the Internet?

  When will your business design become obsolete? *Can't happen*, you think? Don't fool yourself. List some borderline trends, things that just *might* affect you. Come back to the list in a few months to see if they have increased in size or momentum.

- **Go for the old.** In-line roller skates were invented in the early nineteenth century but did not become practical until modern materials could be used.

  Look at your business or profession. What's old that could benefit from new methods or technology? No ideas? Go to the library and find an old Sears catalogue. Any ideas now? List a few ideas and keep asking people, "What would you think if I . . . ?"

GO FORTH AND OBSERVE

Make a commitment to leave this chapter prepared to apply the skill of observing, even if it is with just one strategy in mind. The strategy could be to improve your attention, which could mean opening your lens or narrowing your focus, depending on where you feel you need to develop your attention ability. The strategy could also be around becoming aware of your own perceptions or what meaning you are attaching to information. The strategy could give you practice in seeing patterns, perhaps among things that on the surface seem different but underneath are all part of the same issue.

The skill of observing sets the horizon and the boundaries of your opportunity space. The Prepared Mind is a keen observer and a great opportunist.

I try to hear things through the ears of others, and see things through their eyes.
—Leonard Riggio, CEO, Barnes & Noble

The Prepared Mind deliberately seeks new perspectives by asking questions and listening to others who see the customers or visiting the assembly line to ask, "What is working and what is not working for you about this product?"[12]

CHAPTER FOUR

REASONING
Moving from the Known
to the Undetermined

Reasoning is the stuff of detectives, teachers, and scientists. We marvel at Sherlock Holmes and his ability to immerse himself in thinking about the clues over many pipes of tobacco. And having sweated through college logic courses, we have been exposed to more logic traps than we can remember—or even care to remember. We read about the early years of the search for understanding DNA and are amazed at how the scientists figured it out. Surely they must all be quite gifted!

Reasoning is also the stuff of the business practitioner. It is found in understanding the "way we do business." It is, or at least it should be, the very foundation of our strategy. Sometimes it is well done; other times it is not so well done.

Toyota's strategy of just-in-time (JIT) manufacturing did not come out of thin air. Managers and executives had to reason their way through the reality of the automotive industry in the 1970s and "connect the dots" to come up with a new way of competing. We now accept JIT as a common approach to manufacturing strategy, yet it was anything but that when Toyota started it. The danger we now face is that many executives accept JIT as *the* inventory and operations approach—and they ignore the reality of global outsourcing, dock strikes, and the response time of a far-flung operation. It still makes sense, but not all the time.

We can look at the U.S. airlines and marvel at their price competition—and ask ourselves how they got trapped into a strategy that is slowly destroying the industry. Reasoning over the short term shows the potential for filling seats by cutting prices, but over the long term (especially in an industry that has too much capacity and is undifferentiated), this only destroys total industry value.

A SHORT COURSE IN THE SKILL OF REASONING

Reasoning is one of those concepts that is often lumped in with other activities of the mind, such as thinking, judging, analyzing, concluding, deciding, arguing, and making sense. All of these concepts are important and related to reasoning. However, we know that part of deep learning involves conceptual understanding. It follows, then, that if our goal is to learn what reasoning is and how it works so we can be more adept in practicing it as a skill, then it is important to know specifically what reasoning is and where it fits in the scheme of the Prepared Mind.

Note how the previous two sentences reflect the pattern of reasoning: the statement of premises, or what we believe to be facts about the world; the application of a rule-based process, often stated in the form of if-then statements; and conclusions that can be tested against other conclusions for validity. You can see those elements when we break the sentences apart:

Premise 1: "Learning involves conceptual understanding."

Premise 2: ". . . [we want] to learn what reasoning is and how it works so we can become more adept in practicing it as a skill."

Rule: "It follows, then, that . . ."

Conclusion: ". . . it is important to know specifically what reasoning is."

At its core, reasoning is a rule-based process for deciding what to believe. The fact that it is rule based implies that there is a rational movement from one idea to another by seeing connections of logic between the ideas and by drawing conclusions from given premises. Reasoning is the rational chain of thought we go through when using what we believe to be known truths or premises to build toward and arrive at previously undetected truths. Reasoning is the skill behind sound argumentation (argumentation in a rhetorical sense, that is, and not necessarily implying conflict).

Reasoning can be deductive: drawing specific, valid conclusions from premises that are known to be true. Deductive reasoning is sometimes known as "reasoning down." One way to remember this is to picture an upside-down pyramid that illustrates going from the general to the particular. For instance, if it is a general rule that prices rise when demand outstrips supply, we can reason that if demand is currently greater than supply, prices will rise.

Reasoning can also be inductive: "reasoning up" or drawing more general and likely (but not 100 percent guaranteed) conclusions from a series of specific premises or observations or what we believe to be facts. Think of a pyramid that illustrates going from particulars at the top to general conclusions at the bottom. Inductive reasoning is how hypotheses and theories are constructed in science. We use the skill of observing to gather enough instances or data points that lead us to infer certain patterns, generalities, or conclusions that can be tested over time by collecting more data and information.

Here is a simple economic example to illustrate inductive reasoning. Let's say that data show the price of gasoline at the pump is rising. Let's say that data also show that the Organization of Petroleum Exporting Countries (OPEC) holds the majority percentage of the world's oil supply. We also know one of the basic rules of economics: when demand outstrips supply, prices generally rise. Then we might come to the reasoned conclusion that OPEC is constraining oil supply. Note that we may be right, but we may be in error, in part because we may not have all the premises and facts we need to flesh out the chain of logic. We can, however, take this conclusion and test it against other data.

Right away, we can see how important reasoning is in the Sense-Response Cycle. In order to believe something, make a decision, and act, we must rely on reasoning, even when we do not have all of the facts or all of the premises. Decision making and leadership under uncertainty require the skill of reasoning, along with other skills of the Prepared Mind. Reasoning provides a mechanism or set of rules or procedures for coming to conclusions in an orderly way that can be supported (or refuted) by evidence to support our propositions.

Reasoning is an ongoing process; it does not take place just once and forever. Our opportunity space is constantly evolving, and if we don't make sense of the impact of that evolution, we will end up making all of our decisions based on what was once true—but may no longer be so. Can you get better at reasoning, or are you stuck with the mental horsepower you've been using for most of your career? The answer is, "Of course, you can get better," but it often takes some retooling because most of us have been conditioned over the years to find the "right" answer and give that answer back to our teachers or our bosses. Unfortunately for many of us, our education did not prepare us to reason. It was focused on the memorization of facts, not the development of mental processes.

Anchoring Concepts of Reasoning

Underlying the skill of reasoning are three core concepts and processes that are often used loosely or taken for granted when people talk about thinking in general, and reasoning in particular: mental models, information processing, and rationality. If we want to improve our reasoning skill, we need to improve our understanding and use of these three concepts and their allied processes.

Mental Models

Made popular by Peter Senge and *The Fifth Discipline* in the early 1990s, the term *mental model* has become synonymous to many as what we think and believe and how we think and believe.[1] Actually, a mental model is much more specific than that and acts like the physical models we build (as in engineering and architecture) to show how we think the parts of a particular object fit together to make it work. If we have a model of a car, we represent what parts we think need to be present to make the car work and meet the design specifications (or standards) we have proposed. We then test our models against various ways to design a car and see which is the more valid design. In some respects, a model represents our theory of a particular thing. The model may or may not withstand the tests of pressure, user preference, and road tests, but we bet our predictions about the car based on the way we model it. Change a factor or change a relationship between factors, and you change the model.

Mentally, we do the same thing when we are trying to reason through a problem and come to a conclusion on which to act; that is, we build models in our minds about the way specific things

Know the Common Mistakes

We know from everyday experience that this conceptually simple process of reasoning is fraught with difficulties—for example:

- *Reasoning to achieve the wrong goal.* This is akin to an ill child's plea, "Make the pain go away." We can make the pain go away, but if we don't address the underlying illness, we have to be ready for another symptom to arise. In the business world, this would translate into a decision to counter the competitor's last move without actually addressing evolving customer needs.
- *Not looking past the first opportunity.* This is a way to satisfice, but it's also a symptom of lazy thinking or succumbing to the pressures of not enough time. An example is the approach many companies took to address the concern about falling profits. Cost cutting and head count reduction are "obvious," but unless the company is thriving on the revenue line of the income statement, cost cutting is not enough.
- *Coming to a conclusion based on weak or missing evidence.* This is often the result of starting with a conclusion and finding as little evidence as possible to support the forgone con-

should work and what factors will be critical to their working that way. If we are good at reasoning, we test our model before we commit to it. For instance, we may ask someone to use the skill of challenging to present other models of the way our object works, or we may engage in an argument to test our theory.

This model usually determines the way we behave. So if we are about to go into a negotiation, for instance, and have a mental model that negotiation consists of winners and losers, splitting a known and limited pool of resources, we will reason and come to the conclusion that the winner will end up with more of the given pool and the loser will end up with less.

Furthermore, if we have a mental model that winning is good and losing is bad, we will do everything in our power to end up clusion. The stereotypical version of this story is that of an executive who wants to try something simply because he likes it and no evidence is necessary. An example is the creation of Samsung Motors in the late 1990s.[1] Kun-Hee Lee, the chairman of Samsung Industries, loved cars, and the company proceeded to give him an auto company, although all evidence would have shown this to be a poor idea. The industry had too much capacity, and Samsung had nothing unique to give it any competitive advantage.

- *Building an argument based on bad assumptions.* This often is the result of convergence of changing industry needs, time pressure, and an unwillingness to challenge existing mental models. In this case, we often find companies that fall back on past truths and practices. Consider Sears Roebuck's reluctance to leave the department store concept in spite of overwhelming evidence that it was outdated.

---

1. This story is described in Sidney Finkelstein, *Why Smart Executives Fail* (New York: Portfolio, 2003).

with more money of the limited pool than the other person. We will reason to a definite conclusion and goal, based on a very narrow and limited set of things we know in order to make our reasoning fit our mental model of "negotiate to win and make someone else lose." Unless we test this model against other methods of negotiation, we will likely go through life with a win-lose premise about negotiation.

If win-win is our mental model for negotiation instead, we will reason that our first goal is to find out what everyone wants, whether it is evident in the pool of resources or not. Then we will reason that if we can find a way so that everyone gets something they want, everyone will walk away from the negotiation happy and a winner. But if our win-win model is tested and we end up feeling we got the short end of the stick, we may change our mental model for the particular act of negotiation.

Notice that *mental models* are different from *mental maps*. Mental models consider only a relatively small amount of the content we have in our minds and a small number of connections between that content, all in service to a specific issue. If, for instance, we considered more of what we know and value and hold in our mental maps about dealing with people with needs, which is true of people who are in negotiation (for example, the golden rule, listening skills, how to combine to enlarge the current resource pool), we might change our mental model or move to an entirely different set of models (for example, how to merge versus how to compete).

Still, when our mental models are active, they are shaping our reasoning paths down specific channels. The conclusions we draw may make sense according to the mental models we are using. However, the conclusions may be faulty, incomplete, or unacceptable to others if we are not more aware and agile with our mental models, drawing from our bigger mental map.

When it is said that someone is able to see the big picture, that is, reason by considering premises and conclusions from many different and relevant angles, it usually means that the person was able to try on many different mental models and realize the conclusions that they led to, tapping into a bigger mental map for different ways to gain perspective and reason through the situation with greater flexibility. In other words, people who reason well and are less prone to error are those who process information more completely in the premises and possible conclusions.[2]

INFORMATION PROCESSING

When the fields of cognitive science and artificial intelligence burst onto the scene in the 1950s, they did so in part in reaction against behavioral sciences that said in essence that the only things worth knowing and studying scientifically were things that could be observed, for instance, human behaviors. The cognitive scientists believed there was value in coming to understand things not observable through human behavior but sometimes implied by that behavior, that is, the human mind and the processes of thinking. Also, for practical reasons, if they could mirror and enhance the human power of computing and program machines to do some of that work, then the world could be more productive, with machines doing more of the computational and transactional work and humans doing more of the higher-level thinking and conceptual and creative work.

That bit of history is important for understanding the power of the metaphor that began the cognitive and knowledge era revolution: that the human mind is like a computer.[3] In order to get where we are today with information technology, we had to understand the human mind as an information processor and then build models of that process into our machines. While some today bristle at the metaphor and think it is dehumanizing, a lot of value comes from considering the information processing capability of the human mind. For one thing, it helps us understand in greater detail the rule-based process for reasoning chains or "programs" we use to consider, combine, compute, and come to conclusions.

The information processing model of human thinking and reasoning basically follows the pattern illustrated in Figure 4.1. We take in data from the environment through observation and perception. For instance, we hear a customer complaint. We search our memories and mental maps trying to retrieve similar information or slots in which to place the new information. We have rules in our memories that direct where we put this new information. If this information is about a customer issue, we act on it by passing it to marketing. If it involves a technology issue, we pass it along to information technology. If it is feedback from one of our biggest customers, maybe our rule is to gather more information and act on it ourselves. We retrieve that prior knowledge and either fit the new information into it as a near-perfect match, or we transform the information to fit our prior knowledge. This is why, for instance, we sometimes miss new opportunities or threats in our environment. For efficiency's sake, we often make new information look like things we already know how to handle.

We may then transmit the new information into our memories, or we may work on transforming the information or our minds more rigorously, especially if the skills of learning and challenging are being applied. If we are poised to learn, we transform our prior knowledge and adjust our mental maps to contain the new information. For instance, when Sam Walton founded Wal-Mart, he

FIGURE 4.1. INFORMATION PROCESSING MODEL

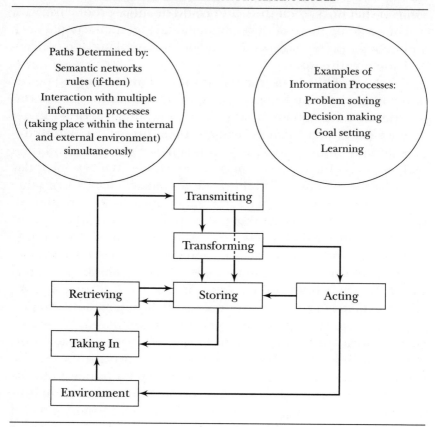

adjusted his mental map to include the option of major discount stores in small towns as a market. We often take this newly constructed or adapted information and act on it to meet our goals (for example, we decide and or act), and then we look for feedback information from the environment to tell us if our information processing and use of it furthered our goals. We then store the new knowledge or conclusions we draw in our long-term memory for use as prior knowledge in the future.

You can see how systematic, orderly, rule based, and reasonable this process is. In the process of reasoning, we are framing information in the form of premises, applying rules already in place in our memories. The new knowledge structures we create by going through the information processing model become the conclusions we act on and hope to get positive feedback about from the environment or our own consciences. We generally do not enter into reasoning or activate our information processing system unless we have a goal to achieve, a problem to solve, a decision to make. Assuming we have the motivation to think through something rationally, humans have an information processing capability that still outperforms machines. It follows, then, that if we want to improve our skill of reasoning, one way is to work on expanding or enhancing the various components and links of the information processing model.

RATIONALITY

We are living in an era filled with uncertainty and acknowledged complexity. We are overwhelmed with data, yet we seldom feel we have enough information to guarantee particular outcomes to our decisions. We are also emphasizing things like emotional intelligence, social networks, and relationships. In this context, the concept of rationality sounds old and stodgy. The eighteenth century, known as the Age of Reason, highlighted the rational man (rarely the rational woman). We are in the twenty-first century. Are we promoting a throwback to the good old days of linear, rational thinking and control? Not completely. If we were, we would not be emphasizing Prepared Mind skills such as imagining and challenging. Still, we cannot throw the baby out with the bathwater. Reasoning, and the philosophy and practices of rationality that underlie it, are still important knowledge to understand and use.

Rationality helps us arrive at beliefs and truths by helping us organize and interpret our observations and experiences of the world and draw conclusions from them that move us beyond the confines of our immediate experience. Rationality gives us tested, proven, or, at least, verifiable principles that we can use to guide our future observations, decisions, and actions. Typically rationality assumes we are thinking through information within the boundaries of rules and constraints. We are thinking "inside the box" on purpose.

Consider how necessary this is and how much progress we have made by employing rationality. For instance, scientific disciplines are defined by a few key concepts, rules, and methods that focus the scientific method (itself a tool for rational thought and reasoning) on a specific body of knowledge. Without rationality, we would not know what to believe or why to believe it, and we would not know where the bounds of one discipline or profession began and others ended. We would have not laws—physical, social, legal, or otherwise. We would have no method for consensus around problem solving and decision making. We would be in chaos.

If we rely only on rationality to its extreme and allow no room for emotion, imagination, faith, intuition, and other less evidence-based influencers of thought and action, we would not be creative, innovative, or even human. We would be like Spock from *Star Trek* to the extreme. However, without a healthy respect and use of rationality, we would be utterly confused and disordered. We would likely not have structures to create, innovate, or keep us alive and human.

Rationality is an old disposition that is timeless in its application. It, along with mental models and information processing, makes us efficient and often more disciplined in our thinking. The core concepts that underlie the skill of reasoning are powerful ones to understand and employ when converging and focusing our thinking toward a decision and action.

CONNECTING TO THE CONCEPTS: ANCHORED EXERCISES TO IMPROVE YOUR SKILL OF REASONING

ASSUMPTION TESTING

Many of the so-called communication problems in organizations stem from our failure to question the assumptions that lead to assertions or decisions. What assumptions have you and others made? Do all of you have the same set of assumptions. If so, have they been recently tested for validity? This is another way of asking if those involved in the discussion are reasoning from the same premises and have the same mental models.

TALK ALOUD

There are various formal methods of learning and mentoring that call for talk-aloud techniques. For example, when experts model to novices how to do a task, the novices catch on more readily if the expert talks out loud about what he is doing and why he is doing it each step of the way. In other words, he walks them through their information processing system and likely reveals his mental models and assumptions about a particular facet of how the world works.

Even informally explaining your reasoning behind an opinion or decision is a good way to check your validity and your own rational thought processes, information processing, and mental models. Especially if you are open to questioning by those who are hearing you reveal your reasoning, you can check your own clarity and either explain in new ways or reconsider aspects of your reasoning system.

DIG

Dig into the reasons that support the conclusion. Test for rationality. Are the reasons true? Do they in fact support the conclusion to which you've come? Be very careful here. If you start with a conclusion (certainly not unheard of), you need to evaluate it, not defend it.

COCKTAIL NAPKIN EXERCISE

Through years of consulting, we have discovered that some of the most compelling business models and ideas have been invented on cocktail napkins. At cocktail parties or on airplanes, often a cocktail napkin is the only medium readily available on which to visually represent concepts and connections between them, usually with a causal reasoning assumption built within them. Whether we realize it or not, when we illustrate a version of how we think the world works on a cocktail napkin, we are building a model and illustrating our own mental model about a particular aspect of the world.

The challenge of this exercise is to make your reasoning clear with a simple picture that others can look at and understand easily by applying their own information processing system and coming to a conclusion that it is rational and sound. In a way, sharing an illustrated cocktail napkin is like facing the same challenges teachers face when trying to connect with the thought processes of their students. If you can illustrate it on a cocktail napkin, you have reasoned with clarity and conciseness.

Here is the generic form of the exercise:

1. Pose the business issue you are trying to understand.
2. Generate a list of factors you think contribute to the issue.
3. Chunk your list into categories.
4. Label the categories with the intention of making these categories the factors in your model.
5. Map out the factors and links between them on the cocktail napkin so anyone can see how you think the factors relate to each other and what these relationships cause.
6. Explain your reasoning out loud.

ELEMENTARY, MY DEAR WATSON

In the past year in academia and in business, we have heard people refer to Sherlock Holmes in presentations and articles about five times more often than just ten years ago. What does that suggest? One idea is that as the world of information is getting busier and more complex, we are looking for a role model who looks under the data that are there (and the data that aren't there) and can use superb skills of information processing and rationality to come to conclusions.

A fun, fast, and increasingly popular way to increase your own skill of reasoning is to read Sherlock Holmes with two goals in mind:

- Try to think with keen rationality through the clues as the story progresses and see if you come to the same conclusions as Sherlock. In most of his stories, he actually lets Watson know when he has figured out the mystery. That is a clue that all the needed information has been revealed and processed to draw a conclusion.
- Listen or read carefully when Holmes explains his reasoning to Watson, Scotland Yard, and others. Go back and review the clues and his chain of reasoning and how he connected the dots. What mental models was he activating? How did he select information to process versus what to let go?

As reading good literature implicitly improves your vocabulary, reading good reasoning will help you practice and increase your own skill.

GAMES AND PUZZLES

Treat yourself to books of puzzles and games that test and exercise thinking skills. You can pick up these books in most bookstores, usually on the shelf right next to the crossword puzzles. You can also work your way through various levels of difficulty. What will likely prove humbling at first can turn into a highly productive way to develop your Prepared Mind on business trips and time on airplanes. You can also learn which information processing methods or steps you tend to rely on and which ones you need to improve. In a broad sense, there are games that challenge everything from logic, to spatial reasoning, to analytical ability, to creative thought. People with Prepared Minds have found motivating ways to puzzle about things in every domain of their lives. Some are just more explicit about it than others.

THE CYCLE OF REASONING

The Prepared Mind skills are developed for a reason, and one reason is to improve your ability to work the Sense-Response Cycle. Consider how the five questions illustrated in Figure 4.2 show how the skill of reasoning applies to any and all phases in the cycle. We are taking a deep dive into these questions inasmuch as reasoning is essential to innovation, decision making, and problem solving, especially in these times of change.

1. ARE MY MENTAL MAPS CORRECT?

This question takes us to the interface between sensing and making sense. Our objective is to use what we are sensing to come to a conclusion and ultimately make a decision.

How do you and your organization make sense of the world? How many of these phrases do you hear in your company's halls and offices?

"Let's run the numbers on this before we make a decision."

"What did the focus group say?"

"Let me look at your project plan."

"This doesn't make sense. How can we connect the dots?"

"We need help; better call the consultants."

FIGURE 4.2. THE SENSE-RESPONSE CYCLE OF REASONING

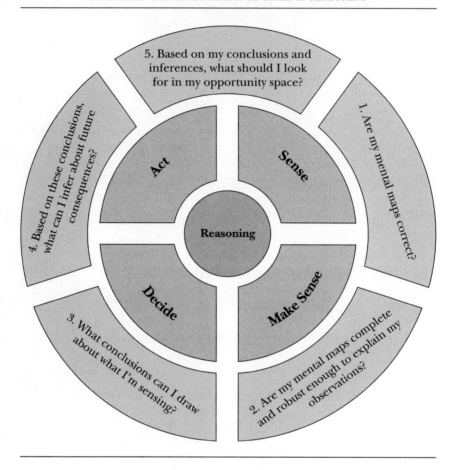

5. Based on my conclusions and inferences, what should I look for in my opportunity space?

1. Are my mental maps correct?

4. Based on these conclusions, what can I infer about future consequences?

Act

Sense

Reasoning

Decide

Make Sense

3. What conclusions can I draw about what I'm sensing?

2. Are my mental maps complete and robust enough to explain my observations?

All of these statements (and there are scores more) reveal mental maps in action.

When we run the numbers, we seek a numerical understanding of how things should be, and we want to use this understanding to confirm a current situation. Every time we run a projected return on investment calculation to evaluate a new product or a new project, we are using an existing and accepted approach to make sense of our world. We have expectations of cause and effect and add new data to see what the result should look like.

When we use a focus group to evaluate a potential new offering, we have an expectation that outside forces, like real consumers, can tell us something about the offering. We have guesses, and we want to confirm those guesses. Our existing mental maps are not robust enough, so we get other points of view to make them more predictive.

When we ask to review a colleague's project plan, we are asking to review her model of causes and effect. We have an objective, and the plan should show us the steps needed to achieve milestones that will eventually result in the accomplishment of the objective. The mental map of the project may be a one-time effort, or it may be built on previous projects and we are modifying it to fit current circumstances.

The question of connecting the dots is a bit of a good news–bad news routine. The good news is that we have sensed something happening in our environment that is so new or different that it just doesn't make sense to us. If we continue along this good-news path, we will either create a new mental map of our opportunity space or modify an existing map. The bad news is that sometimes we deny what we are sensing and keep using the old mental map for making a decision.

Sometimes we call the consultants because we need more people to accomplish a task that we could do ourselves if we only had enough capacity. For example, it may be a big systems project like the Y2K projects of a few years ago. Information technology directors all over the world knew what had to be done; they just did not have enough people to do it. However, there are times when we call the consultants because we need someone to help us make sense of what's going on in our world. Real strategic consulting is just that: working together to build a competitive model that works for you rather than coming in with a canned solution.

When you make sense of something, your mental activity falls along a continuum from reasoning about events to comparing events. Think about how often you experience something and say to yourself, "Oh, that's just like what happened when we . . ." Or you use an analogy or metaphor to compare a new event to something familiar. This is making sense by comparison. It is generally fast and relatively easy. But when we are new to a situation, like a new job, we have little to compare it to so we figure it out for ourselves. This is making sense by reasoning, and it is usually slower and harder than the use of comparison.

However, making sense is rarely an either-or situation. Because the development of new knowledge is the addition of information to old knowledge, we often take a blended approach to making sense of changes in our opportunity space. We sense something, call on an existing mental model, and then, if needed, modify the model to explain reality.

How do you know if your mental models are correct? The answer is found in the basics of the scientific method. Treat your mental models as hypotheses, and make sure you look for information that proves them to be wrong, which is contrary to our natural inclinations. Most of us like to be right, and we look for confirmation all the time. However, if we look only for confirming information, we are likely to fool ourselves. We need to be open to disconfirming information and its ability to keep us on the right track.

All mental models are built on assumptions. Are your assumptions still valid? Remember that assumptions don't go bad all at once; they start to go bad slowly. Should you be concerned that yours are beginning to "spoil"? Yes. It's worth the look.

2. Are My Mental Maps Complete and Robust Enough?

Before we address this question, we need to take another look at the concept of opportunity space and what might trigger the need for more robust mental models. Our opportunity space is a mental construct that includes problems, opportunities, new information, and new relationships. It is dynamic and expands or contracts depending on our view of the world; it is not defined by someone else. Rather, we set the bounds. And therein lie the problems and opportunities associated with the issue of robustness. To make this more concrete, consider the opportunity spaces of Starbucks' Howard Schultz and his counterpart at Folgers Coffee.

What's in Starbucks' opportunity space? It's easy to see geographical expansion, competition, bean suppliers, changing demographics, and all of the same things that are in the Folgers space. However, Schultz sees music in his opportunity space as well, and in mid-2004, he made a move into letting customers download (legally) their favorite music and burn customized CDs to take with them. Will it succeed? Time will tell. But it's clear that Schultz senses a bigger opportunity space than that of just the coffee business. And that brings us back to the issue of complete and robust mental maps and the findings of the German psychologist Dietrich Dörner.

Dörner conducted a series of studies in the late 1980s that resulted in the book *The Logic of Failure.*[4] The results of his studies can be summarized as follows:

- *Real-world situations are complex (lots of interrelated parts), but we try to simplify.* We see this happen every time a leader grabs onto a current fad and does not take the time to see if the "solution" is actually needed. Think back over your work experience and evaluate the thinking that went into the decisions to adopt "lights-out" automation, TQM, reengineering, Six Sigma, manufacturing resource planning software, enterprise resource planning software such as SAP, customer relationship management (CRM) processes, and others. Complex problems do not react well to simple solutions, and simple solutions are often the result of incomplete mental maps.

- *Real-world systems (like business) have many hidden variables.* To use Dörner's term, they are "intransparent." The implication here is that we don't dig deep enough to make our mental map complete enough to reflect reality. One of the best tools we have is still the "five whys" of TQM. Why? Because it forces you to go deeper and deeper into the issue and the proposed solution.

- *Real-world situations have an internal dynamic of their own.* Consequently, there is a lot of "noise" as a result of the system's operating at its own pace. As we develop and modify our mental maps, we have to consider the noise factors and the impact that they have our thinking. Consider this: a major role of people in a leadership position is to position their organization for the future. Yet the great majority of management time is spent on the problems of today—much of which is simply "noise" that should be handled by someone with less responsibility.

Ask yourself, "Do my existing mental maps adequately explain the events I'm seeing in my opportunity space?" Making sense should focus on retroactive or proactive explanation: we need to know what has happened and why, and we need to know what will happen and why. Unfortunately, when we can't explain events to our own satisfaction, we tend to revert to superstition or fantasy. We blame "luck" or "the fates"—which is comforting for the uneducated but not very helpful.

"Have You Ever Wondered?" Tip

How can you make your mental maps more complete and robust? As a start, you might want to avoid considering your maps as complete; they need to remain a work-in-progress inasmuch as our opportunity space is constantly changing and evolving. Also, you might want to consider the "noise" in your opportunity space and make sure your mental maps are aligned with the real issues and not the noise. For example, we constantly come across companies that are working on their "morale problems." However, poor morale is a symptom (an effect), not the real problem. As important as good morale is to a company, poor morale is simply noise. What's the real problem that has to be addressed?

Finally, you may want to sit down with organizational outsiders and explain your issues to them. Will they see what you're seeing? If not, then your mental model may need to be modified.

---

3. WHAT CONCLUSIONS CAN I DRAW ABOUT WHAT I'M SENSING?

The Sense-Response Cycle is meant to be just that—a cycle—and it should be completed and repeated at a frequency that keeps you ahead of the pace of change in your opportunity space. Therefore, the purpose of the make-sense phase of the cycle is to come to an appropriate conclusion about the things we have sensed that can then be used as the basis for deciding an appropriate course of action. And the conclusion or conclusions must have acceptable, relevant, and strong reasons.

Acceptable reasons are those that show a real cause-and-effect relationship and do so consistently. For example, if you have experienced a rise in sales due to an increase in advertising expenditures, then you might conclude that spending money on advertising will result in increased sales. But it pays to remember that past reasons may not fit the reality of today's opportunity space. Perhaps your increase in advertising coincided with a competitor's decision to cut back on advertising. As an example, consider the relationship between mass advertising on network television and an increase in product sales. For the longest time, it was a case of spend more (on advertising) to get more (sales). What changed? The audience changed. You can spend more than ever before on network television advertising, but the audience is smaller, so the sales boost is inevitably smaller.

And just because the boss decrees something does not make it acceptable from a reasoning point of view. Other unacceptable reasons are those that cross the line from ethical to unethical, legal to illegal, and moral to immoral. Manipulating revenue or profit projections may cause an increase in stock price, but they are unacceptable. Unfortunately, if you have detected an executive fiat in your opportunity space, there is little you can do about it other than to try and recast it into something that makes sense from another perspective.

Ask yourself, "What's new in my opportunity space? Am I seeing events that are not aligned with my existing mental maps? If so, is it because my mental maps are wrong, or is it that events have caused my maps to need to expand?" The danger here is that we will deny what we are seeing and fall back on mental maps that no longer support our reality.

4. BASED ON THESE CONCLUSIONS, WHAT CAN I INFER ABOUT FUTURE CONSEQUENCES?

Leaders have to make sense of their opportunity space in order to decide on a course of action. In addition, we have to remain mindful that actions we take today will have future consequences, both good and bad. Consider the widespread implementation of stock incentive plans in the 1990s and the use of the insecticide DDT during World War II as two examples.

Incentive plans have been a part of business life for quite a while. The competitive boom in the 1990s led to more incentive plans, and more generous plans, than we had seen in the past. The motive was to get business executives to work for the long-term benefit of the company and its stockholders. Existing incentive plans usually focus on short-term measurements like annual profits. Many business thinkers were concerned that executives were taking courses of action that benefited them in the short term but left the company weaker for the longer run. The solution was to make more of them owners, or owners of a bigger piece of the corporate pie; by having a bigger stake in the company through stock ownership, it was thought that they would be more inclined to take a long-term view. And that was a valid approach for most of the executives involved in such plans. However, we now know that some executives soon realized that since they could sell the shares that they acquired, they could reap a nice short-term profit by taking quick or even illegal actions to raise the stock price. We should have seen this coming because we learned a very valuable lesson from killing mosquitoes: the lesson of unintended consequences.

One of the major killers of American and Japanese soldiers in the South Pacific during World War II was malaria, a terrible disease carried by mosquitoes. The war against these insects was won by the American development of DDT. It was so effective that DDT was used as a general insecticide on U.S. farms in the 1950s and 1960s. The immediate consequence was good: increased crop yields. However, the long-term consequence was not felt until the late 1960s when Rachel Carson wrote her eye-opening book, *Silent Spring,* and we collectively realized the devastation that the chemical was having on the environment.[5] DDT was finally banned in the United States in 1972. We may not have discontinued the use of DDT during the war if we had known about its side effects, but as we now know, its widespread use should have had more forethought.

We cannot see the future. However, that should not keep us from considering, as the management sage Peter Drucker puts it, the "futurity of present decisions."[6] Coming to an understanding of the future impacts of our decisions takes time, concentrated thought, and a cross-functional approach to thinking. We need to map out the strings of causes and potential effects of our major decisions and make sure we look for unintended consequences as well as the desired consequences. Not all of the if-then statements can be considered absolute, so we have to think about probabilities and branches. And because we will soon reach beyond our area of expertise, we need to bring other experts into the discussion.

5. BASED ON MY CONCLUSIONS AND INFERENCES, WHAT SHOULD I LOOK FOR IN MY OPPORTUNITY SPACE?

Although the Sense-Response Cycle is shown as a one-way cycle, the truth of the matter is that we often have to loop back and run the cycle through iterations. Most of us are faced with the potential for data overload. There is simply more going on in the world than we can attend to. However, one of the primary reasons for trying to make sense of our opportunity space is to determine those things that we need to sense in the first place.

For example, if we spend the time to make sense of poor morale in our company, we will come to an understanding of the policies and practices that cause morale to drop. We can then monitor the work environment for those policies and practices. Are there warning signs in the environment? By using my mental maps, can I predict future events that will take place because of my actions or the actions of others? Have I considered how I will take advantage of these changes? Am I making "future sense"?

BENEFITS, RISKS AND CHALLENGES OF REASONING

Here is our starting list of the benefits, risks, and challenges associated with developing and using the skill of reasoning. Add to, subtract from, and modify them to fit your reality.

BENEFITS OF IMPROVING YOUR SKILL OF REASONING

Improving a skill takes time and energy, and before expending either, we need to be assured that the benefits are worth the effort. Consider the following points.

Greater Clarity

We can connect the dots for those followers who need to know *why* we are embarking on a particular course of action. Sometimes we would like it if the people around us would simply do what we want them to do. However, we owe it to them and to ourselves to be able to explain the rationale for planned actions and programs. Furthermore, we have the opportunity to improve our reasoning by having it challenged by the very people who have to act on our decisions.

Defensible Positions

We can defend our actions. Leaders are in the position of affecting those around them by their decisions. Our decisions may be popular, or may not be popular, but we should always be in a position to explain why we did what we did.

Improved Decision Making

Reasoning slows us down—in a good way. As we were preparing the manuscript of this book, we interviewed many business managers and executives and explained the Sense-Response Cycle to them. One of the common reactions we received was having people point to the diagram of the cycle and explain that all too often, they saw people jump from the activity of sense to the activity of decide (or even act) without taking the time to make sense of what they were seeing. Developing the habit of reasoning is a way to insert a pause, however slight, in the Sense-Response Cycle, where it is needed most.

RISKS OF REASONING

An overemphasis on a newly developed skill can result in experiencing downside risks. Consider the following points.

Leaving Others Behind

We may be seen as being too far ahead of the pack. People who are adept at reasoning are often out in front of the rest of the organization. The ability to develop scenarios or to conceive of long cause-and-effect chains may leave you unsupported by the rest of the organization. The skill of enabling is needed to help others see our thinking and develop their own skill of reasoning.

Coming to Wrong Conclusions

Using obsolete mental maps can lead to wrong conclusions. In the 1980s, the concept of JIT made no sense at all to those people who saw lots of inventory as necessary to factory production. In the 1990s, Dell's concept of selling computers over the Web made little sense to companies with a retail mental map. After all, you couldn't even touch the computer you were buying! The skills of learning and challenging keep us constantly fresh and updating our mental maps.

Analysis Paralysis

We can often get most of the answer to whatever situation we are faced with in a relatively short period of time. However, for the risk averse, there may be a need to have the absolute, 100 percent complete answer before they move. In today's competitive environment, time is *not* on their side. Knowing the skill of deciding must be acted on and setting limits to our time for analysis can help move us past reasoning to deciding and action. We must be able to accept risks and include them in our reasoning process, knowing that reasoning does not mean certainty.

Working Backward

By "working backward" we mean starting with a conclusion and then defending that conclusion rather than evaluating it with objective reasoning. This is generally the case when an executive comes out with a dictate ("We will be a Six Sigma company by the end of the year!") and then the people around him or her are asked to "evaluate" the idea. Too many projects have come in over budget and late because the "evaluation" was certainly not objective. Executives need to have those around them employ the skill of challenging. Reasoning and deciding always need to begin with a clear definition of the problem, not an assumption of the solution.

CHALLENGES TO REASONING

We know that we should improve our skills; however we are all faced with barriers and obstacles. Consider the following points.

Finding Sufficient Time to Use the Skill

Organizations have spent the past fifteen years becoming leaner, and more and more managers and executives complain of being time starved. The activity of making sense and the reasoning that goes along takes time. Unfortunately too few of us take the time to think though our problems and opportunities. We just want to get to the next item on our to-do list. Committing oneself and one's organization to learning and reflecting will necessarily slow it down enough to reason.

Perspective

Objectivity may be tough for experienced leaders. The longer you have been in a company or a position, the finer the line is between being "in the groove" and being "in a rut." This goes back to the admonition we gave you in Chapter Three. The cry of "I'll believe it when I see it" gets replaced with, "Because I believe it, I see it." How else could you explain Motorola's delay in making sense of digital technology in the mid-1990s? How else could you explain the dot-com bubble at the turn of this century? Once again, the skills of learning and reflecting keep the Prepared Mind open to change.

Admitting You Need Help

Many of us came up through the ranks of our organization. Unfortunately, in today's business environment, so much is new (globalization, technology, business models) that many of us have to turn to our youngest workers for help, and we are hesitant to do so. We have not included the skill of humility in the Prepared Mind, but perhaps we should. A stance toward learning and enabling, though, necessarily opens one to learning from others and enabling others by letting them teach us.

The Reductive Fallacy

Of all of the mental traps we have to face, none is more dangerous to strategic thought than the reductive fallacy, which occurs when we reduce complexity to simplicity in causal explanations. We try to keep our information processing fast and easy when actually it is messy and interconnected. We witness this every time an executive tries to find the silver bullet for the problem she is facing. It is seductive to think that we can quickly improve things by implementing Six Sigma, or installing CRM, or automating the people out of the production process. But when we look to a simple solution to deal with the complexity of business, then we are living the reductive fallacy.

Applied Reasoning: The Talent Problem

What kinds of questions and what activities might Prepared Mind leaders consider as they think about the problem of acquiring, developing, and retaining the right talent from the reasoning point of view?

- An executive might consider if she is in danger of committing a common mistake by reasoning to achieve the wrong goal. For example, in the short term, she might ignore company bench strength to achieve profit goals. However, a longer-term view might show that to be the wrong choice. Where will she get the next generation of leaders?
- A middle manager might find ways to make his team more talented as a whole by developing a mental model of what a high-performance team might look like in his organization. What does real synergy look in your organization? Consider the picture of an operating aircraft carrier during times of conflict. The team knows what to do and can certainly out-perform the individual skills of each of the members.
- An individual contributor might consider the impact of teaching his boss the basics of the tools and technologies that have developed since the boss was in school. The boss has the bigger picture and the bigger responsibility. Think of how good you could both be if the boss was smarter about your capabilities.

BUILDING YOUR SKILLS

Here are a few more ideas for building your skill of reasoning.

IS EVERYBODY LIKE YOU?

Find a thinking partner who is *not* like you—someone with a different background and different set of skills. List some of your ideas or problems, and get your partner to ask questions about them. Some will seem "dumb"; others will absolutely astound you.

ARE YOU THINKING BIG ENOUGH?

Thomas Edison's vision was for a lighting *system*. The light bulb was only one step along the way. Take your work or home situation, and think bigger. What does it look like? Describe the full context in which your situation lies.

PICK ON SOMEONE ELSE

Having a hard time being objective about yourself? List all the things that are wrong with *another* industry, company, or person. Now look inward: How many of them apply to your industry, your company, or yourself? How might someone else's solution benefit you or your company?

GO FORTH AND REASON

We know from research and experience that the most powerful way to change our thinking and abilities in any domain is to engage in an exercise that taps into our emotion, cognition, and behavior and is something we can use in our daily life. Try one of the exercises from this chapter at work over the next few days to begin improving your skill of reasoning.

Reason and truth will prevail at last.
            —Samuel Adams

The Prepared Mind is a rational mind, taking care to distinguish between opinions (claims) and reasoned arguments. Reasoning means probing (rather than accepting) a claim to expose the logic and facts at work. Constructing well-reasoned arguments requires focus on three things: the conclusion or result, the reasons that support the conclusion, and the evidence that suggests each reason is true.[7]

IMAGINING
Envisioning the Future
Before It Arrives

Imagination is the beginning of creation. You imagine
what you desire, you will what you imagine and at last
you create what you will.
GEORGE BERNARD SHAW, 1950

Shaw considered imagination to be the beginning of creation. All of us need to create our own future, based on the particular problems and opportunities in our opportunity space. Yet most of us do not consider ourselves to be imaginative. We were when we were young, but many of us lost this capacity over the years. Unless you went to art school or drama school, your education probably did not encourage imagining.

Just as we have a personal dilemma, we have an organizational dilemma. We need the skill of imagining if we are to find the twenty-first-century holy grail of growth through innovation, but we have past and present forces driving it into submission. The quantitative view (read bias) of many business practices eliminates imagining a solution. We have to "run the numbers" before we can try something new.

BE PREPARED TO IMAGINE

Of the eight skills of the Prepared Mind, the ability to imagine is the maverick. We may agree that it's needed for the arts, but many of us live in the fact-based, objective world of business. We have a love affair with data. Yet in the face of the unknown, a little imagination is a most valuable asset. Consider the power of this skill if you could:

- Imagine another business model. Now that we have moved beyond the dot-com and dot-bomb, we have to conceive of new uses of the Internet.
- Imagine your competitors' next moves, and launch a preemptive move. Or would you rather wait and let them set the rules of the game?
- Imagine wild success, and build toward it. If your management time is spent on safe, incremental moves, you may need a good dose of imagination.
- Imagine dismal failure, and defend against it. The 9/11 Commission report about the attacks on the World Trade Center and the Pentagon put much of the blame on our collective lack of imagination. This tragedy should also be a lesson.
- Imagine what the next generation of workers will expect of you and your organization. Are these young people wrong? No, but they are different, and many of us can't imagine working with them. We had better start.

Imagining is the starting point of all of these. Some of your dreams will come true; others will not. But life is so much more exciting if you can dream, and this may be the most fundamental difference between leaders and the rest of us. Leaders have a dream.

Leaders imagine the future, both the future of opportunities and the future of threats. Imagining fuels our ability to picture a new reality and start planning for it before there is even concrete evidence to validate it. New business models and practices start in someone's mind before they ever enter the competitive landscape. If all we do is benchmark (copy) the competition, we will have to live in a world of competitive parity and compete on price. Need a familiar example? Look at the major U.S. airlines at the end of the twentieth century.

In a world where decision making is increasingly time sensitive, creating a mental scenario that follows the chain of events from where we are to where we want to be is a powerful device. We can mentally rehearse a decision, visualize its impact in advance, and save precious time by avoiding pitfalls that can be anticipated. We can imagine.

DEFINING IMAGINING

Imagining is the skill of picturing something mentally that may or may not have been represented physically before in our experience. In order to see with the mind's eye, in order to dream, in order to envision what the future can look like before it arrives, we need the skill of imagining. This skill is what helps us see the opportunity in opportunity space. Imagining is the prerequisite skill for creativity and innovation that take what we imagine and turn it into an object or experience that others can observe.

Chance favors the Prepared Mind, and we have to be prepared to imagine the opportunity space beyond our current job description and organizational scope of work. Without this skill, we have to wait for sensed events to unfold before we can make sense of them, and we will be doomed to spend our organizational life reacting to the ideas and actions of others.

AN INSIDE-OUT VIEW OF IMAGINING

The key to true Prepared Mind leadership is found at the heart of Michael Porter's succinct view of strategy: after you have reached the competitive state of the art, you have to "do different things or do things differently" to capture and maintain competitive advantage.[1] Living up to that standard requires an ability to envision the new, the novel, and the yet-to-be-imagined.

Imagining is the most difficult skill to see evidence of because, by definition, it is mental, not behavioral. However, when we heard Ronald Reagan asking us to picture "a city on a hill," we know that his rhetoric was drawing on our internal ability to paint pictures in our minds and attach meaning to them.[2] We were being asked to activate our imaginations to prepare us to see and do things differently. John Lennon's song "Imagine" gives us plenty of ways to picture a different world from the way things were in the late 1960s and early 1970s, when the song sprang from his imagination. Imagination uses the things we observe as its fodder, but the new composition of things we see springs from the inside out. Our minds prepare us to see new pictures of reality.

At times, our skill of observing picks up on external representations of things, like music, poetry, movie scripts, and children's play acting, and we attribute those external expressions to the internal ability and process of imagining. In fact, Howard Gardner attributed patterns of this ability to the existence of "multiple intelligences."[3] For example, when we say someone has musical intelligence, especially in the ability to write and arrange music, we are naming a particular pattern or application of imagining. Someone who can sit down at a blank computer screen or a blank sheet of paper and write a story is using the skill of imagining to express the use of linguistic intelligence.

Perhaps one reason that the skill of imagining is often cited as the least used of the Prepared Mind skills in business is that the focus on business for so long has been on what we can see and represent with numbers. Somewhere we have forgotten that at their core, numbers and math are symbolic artifacts of our imaginations that seek to represent abstract ideas in more commonly understood forms. Still, the patterns of great businesspeople, especially those thought of as leaders, change agents, and entrepreneurs, have all pointed to the skill of imagining and the importance of beginning with distinct ideas and concepts that take the shape of business models, new products and services, new ways of working, new markets. To go where we have never gone before in business, to be innovative, requires imagination.

So in our definition of Prepared Mind leadership, the skill of imagining is not a "nice-to-have" but a "must have." There is particular power in realizing that leadership is not just about adapting to changed realities in the environment but creating new realities by innovative impact on the external and internal environments. It isn't enough to wait for change to be on us: we have to anticipate it, imagine it, create it, and meet it. Much like the hockey legend Wayne Gretzky, who would "skate to where the puck would be," Prepared Mind leaders are able to imagine where things like new technologies, government regulations, and competitive moves will hit, and they get there early, at least mentally, so they can leverage scenarios of the future and control the game. Conceiving of new realities is the first step in actually creating them and gaining first-mover advantage. In many ways, the skill of imagining distinguishes leading from managing.

Predictive modeling, forecasting, competitive intelligence, and other tools of business strategy that sound very rational and focused on reasoning and decision making all depend on the skill of imagining, because they require us to envision patterns and implications. As much as we like to be rational in how we think about business, the skill of imagining requires us to be a little irrational at times—but smart too. Imagination provides the compelling vision of what will be valuable to current and future customers, even when all the data are not in.

If reasoning can be conceived as logically thinking through a series of if-then statements, the skill of imagining provides the "ifs." It frees us to nominate and consider new assumptions, new mental models, and tap into our store of mental map material to imagine new combinations of things that others have not yet created.

ANCHORING CONCEPTS OF IMAGINING

In order to understand and develop the skill of imagining in ourselves, we have to engineer our methods from three of the unique human abilities that the skill of imagination rests on:

- Forethought
- Imagery
- Analogical thinking

FORETHOUGHT

The everyday expression for forethought is "thinking ahead." We think in future time and try to predict the consequences of our actions. It helps us decide which path to take and the impact our decisions and actions will have on us and the people and world around us. In the Sense-Response Cycle, forethought allows us to "see" what the outcomes of decide and act might look like when we are still back at making sense. To envision the future, we have to imagine different scenarios of what the future will look like, and then we usually choose the most desirable path—desirable based on what we value.

Most of us have heard the old saying, "Hindsight is 20–20." When we are looking ahead and not behind, we do well to base our forethought on insight. Insight comes from combining prior knowledge with imagined outcomes, and comparing them to values and principles that are stable and socially and morally acceptable. This capability helps us imagine and helps us enact the aspect of Prepared Mind leadership that calls on us to build the continuous process of change readiness and innovation on deeply held, sustainable principles. Especially during times of uncertainty, when we do not have all the information we need to make a decision and predict its outcome with relative certainty, we have to imagine new ways to make the underlying principles to our business show up in the world in such a way that they engage others, particularly customers. We have to activate our capacity for forethought to engage in some serious mental play and imagine different scenarios in our mind, allowing for risk and uncertainty, while staying true to core values and principles. This is a daily charge of Prepared Mind leaders.

Some tricks for sparking our capacity for forethought include asking ourselves, and those around us, questions about what could happen and using logic to play out the different paths. Also, we can picture an ideal situation, or at least one that is better than the current situation, and plan toward that. The concepts of self-fulfilling prophecy and the Pygmalion effect reflect this idea of imagining. You see in yourself, or in others, what you want or expect to see. Doing so helps your image become actualized by how you act in congruence with that image. On an individual level, for example, if you see yourself as a high achiever, you will likely do things that reinforce the image of high achiever; not surprisingly, you will become widely known as a high achiever based on the empirical evidence of your performance. The same holds true for work groups and whole organizations.

The capacity for forethought can also yield negative images and keep a person from going down a certain path. In a research study one of us conducted with turnaround companies, we learned that a CEO led the business back to profitability and continuing innovation not by imagining the company with more of the same customers it used to have when business was good (the image even the board had in their minds as the way to turn it around). Instead, he used other Prepared Mind skills such as observing, learning, and reflecting to see that the environment was changing: the product that had been 70 percent of the business and its bread and butter would soon become a commodity and more cheaply made abroad. He saw a small percentage of the company's capacity dedicated to a different high-tech capability, and he imagined the products they could make with that technology and the customers they could serve. He used forethought to see a new company, and so the new company is what emerged from bankruptcy—not new in terms of structure or people, but in terms of the products it made and the customers it attracted.

This skill of setting up mental options to help us decide on which one to act requires representing these scenarios in our minds. These images seem real, or at least realizable, and they provide us motivation and technique for following through. Athletes use imagery all the time when they are visualizing a particular golf stroke or tennis serve. Like Gretzky, they "skate to where the puck would be." Prepared Minds know that imagery is a must in business performance too.

IMAGERY

The power of what and how we represent things in our minds and retrieve those images of things to sense, make sense, decide, and act has been discussed as far back as Aristotle. To share just one ancient trick that has very modern applications, consider the imagery technique that ancient orators used to connect the main points of their speech to certain objects in the room, within a certain order. For example, Cicero associated his point about strength with a pillar in the room, courage with a picture of a lion on the wall, truth with a burning torch hanging from a pillar. These visual cues sparked retrieval of the concepts stored in their memories and allowed them to give their great speeches by memory by just scanning the objects in the room.

The CEO we discussed in the section on forethought also had a real talent for using imagery. He used the image of a junkyard dog (taken from the Jim Croce song, "Bad, Bad Leroy Brown") to symbolize his tenacity and that of the workforce. That image became so powerful that one of the employees brought in a huge, scrappy-looking stuffed dog that became the symbol of turnaround and victory for the company. It also became the title of a new rewards program for innovative ideas. To win "The Junkyard Dog

Award" became a source of pride, admiration, and healthy competitiveness among the workers.

There is debate, as is the case with almost all foundational concepts, as to the nature of imagery and representations in our mind. For instance, do we store features or structures of an object or idea in our minds, or do we store computations or connections between features and structures? The answer is probably "both." Recall that our mental maps include categories of data and information and connections between those categories and the elements within them. Often this content and these connections are stored and represented in images.

For our purposes, the Prepared Mind consciously remembers images and recombines them to build new images for the future. Vision, in one sense, is the recombination of previously stored images that give us a view of the future. Images, which have both emotion and logic embedded in them, combine into a coherent story that shows us our goals, maps out our path, and ignites our energy to do something new and nonhabitual. Imagery allows us to create new realities through recombination.

But how do we go about this task of recombining what could be billions of images into new coherent forms? As is the case with so many skills of thinking and doing, we use our past to bridge to the future. Analogies, in particular, are efficient and powerful ways to use the familiar to bridge to the unfamiliar and set off on a new pathway to add to our mental map.

ANALOGICAL THINKING

Analogies are partial similarities between different situations that allow us to make further inferences. Analogies and metaphors are bridging strategies. They take the old and bridge to the new by connecting links based on what is similar between them. Analogies help us cross the chasm from our past and current state to our future, at least in our minds. And once we can represent "the other side" in our minds, we are more likely to take the steps to reach it.

The ability and habit of thinking analogically, that is, looking for similar structures and patterns between situations that on the surface may appear different, is one of the most efficient and creative things Prepared Mind thinkers can do. Analogical thinking allows us to import a complex system of interrelated knowledge from one domain to another. Analogical thinking always requires us to look below the surface for underlying common structures, methods, and concepts at work.

Notice that the definition and power of analogies come from connecting different domains and different situations. This does not just mean connecting accounting and finance, law and human resources, experience in the oil energy with experience in the financial services industry, and so on. It can mean those things and the changing professional knowledge landscape that is making it more and more imperative to become a deep generalist (that is, combining deep, specialized expertise with a wide range of exposures and applications).

However, we can also use our pasts and our passions as fodder for our analogical thinking. In fact, we do it all the time. Think how many sports metaphors are used in the business world. Often leaders whom we label charismatic and compelling are really good at using examples from nonbusiness areas of their lives (for example, history, family, volunteer experiences, movies, even quotes from great literature) to introduce new ideas and pathways to the future. One of us heard a general manager tell his top leaders that he thought everything they would ever run into in business could be seen in the game of hockey. After a chuckle all around, he went on to give examples that bridged what they knew about successful hockey teams with what they were facing as a company undergoing tumultuous change.

Maybe one reason they say leadership is both art and science is that the art of imagining, based on forethought, imagery, and analogical thinking, paints the picture of a future when all the evidence is not yet available.

CONNECTING TO THE CONCEPTS: ANCHORED EXERCISES TO IMPROVE THE SKILL OF IMAGINING

VICARIOUS LEADER

There is a long-lived story that for years after Walt Disney died, employees in the company, including those in charge of what Walt called "imagineering," when confronted with a dilemma or stuck in a creative rut, would ask themselves, "What would Walt do?" Perhaps the answer was not as important as always calling on the vision of the company to inspire breakthrough thinking.

To learn vicariously from others, we have to rely on the anchoring concepts of forethought, internal representation, and the ability to think analogically. Even if we are relying on the image of someone from the past, we have to have the forethought to project them ahead to the current situation. Perhaps we even picture them advising us and giving us examples from their own experience to support the advice. This painting of the picture in our minds requires internal representation. Imagining their examples means that we are thinking analogically, looking for similarities between our favorite leaders and ourselves, their situations and ours.

Pretend in your own mind or out loud with a trusted friend that you are your favorite, most admired leader. This could be a leader who is living or deceased. The leader could be from business, government, religion, history, or family. Now give that leader a specific issue to solve or a specific trend to analyze and tell you the implications in general and for the world you wish to affect.

In other words, give the leader a problem and imagine what he or she would say. Interview this person (or interview yourself as you role-play that leader). What would you ask? How would you frame the situation? What do you imagine this leader saying in terms of underlying principles? Opportunity space? Effects across the system socially, economically, personally? What advice would that leader give? What examples would this person give from his or her own life to illustrate the advice?

WALKING IN THE SHOES OF AN ANGEL INVESTOR

Pretend that an angel investor has chosen you to lead a company based on your reputation for great leadership and entrepreneurial spirit. What business idea would get you really jazzed? If you were to give your angel investor a plan for the first sixty days of the business, what would you do? What would you offer as a business product and business model, and why?

This is a great way to improve your imagination and also turn it into something you might actually pursue by building on the concept of forethought. Entrepreneurs are great at using forethought to have a vision and internally represent it in their minds before externally representing it in the form of a pitch, a story, or a business model to others. Entrepreneurs, though, are like all of us: they do not come up with ideas totally from the blue. They think analogically and look for ways to connect what they already know to what they sense the market needs.

METAPHOR MAKING OR POETRY IN EVERYDAY ACTION

We know that imagination and innovation are built somewhat on new information merging with ideas we already carry around in our minds. We think analogically or metaphorically to look for similarities of things that might at first appear different. This ability to make metaphors not only increases your skills of translation and communication but can also be an aid to increasing your imagination by building on things you experience in your everyday world.

Assign yourself a day a week as your metaphor-making day. Try it for a week. Promise yourself to make a metaphor out of five things you see or experience that day. It can be as simple as looking at an object, seeing a word, or having an interaction and then asking yourself, "What does this remind me of? What is this like?"

If you need some ideas to get started, begin by paying attention to metaphors others use. From that, you can sense others' analogical thinking, which gives you insights into their mental maps and biases. Think about the companies you have been in where the language is in large part framed in war metaphors—"We're going to battle," "Heads are going to roll," "Cover your back end"—compared to cultures where the metaphors are around sports: "Step up to the plate," "Go the extra mile," "We have a strong bench."

If you want to change minds and change cultures, begin by planting new metaphors that help people think of different analogues and internally represent their ideas with a different focus.

Keep a notebook of your creative ideas and links. Eventually you might start to play with metaphors to business and from that come up with some innovative and outstanding products and services.

RIDING THE TRENDS

Every year, the major business magazines publish their "best of" and "trends" lists. As a skill-building exercise, collect these lists from *Business Week, Fortune, Business 2.0,* or even nonbusiness magazines such as *Newsweek* and *People*. Use forethought to take five items from across the lists and imagine how they could (1) inspire a product or service for your business, (2) point to a market need and a value proposition waiting to happen, and (3) have ripple effects and an impact on your current business.

Again, you will get practice in imagining, and you will also get real ideas that you can and should attend to as implications for your business.

PRODUCT AND SERVICE SYNTHESIS

Remember the TV show *MacGyver*? Whenever MacGyver was in a jam, he would take objects around him and build a solution, from wind sails to communication devices to fuel carriers, MacGyver always imagined and built solutions from the things around him. If you watch a group of six-year-old children, they do the same thing: washing machine boxes become castles, throw rugs become moats full of crocodiles, and wrapping paper tubes become weapons to fend off those crocodiles. MacGyver and kids are great at analogical thinking.

In that same spirit, choose three of your favorite products or objects in your everyday environment, and imagine combining them to become some unique product or service with a value proposition that no one can beat. Start looking for similarities of functions, shapes, colors, or some other criteria. For motivation, take an actual practical problem you are trying to solve and combine objects to solve it. If you have a difficult time becoming playful enough, surround yourself with a couple of six year olds as your design team. You may be amazed at what you discover together.

Kids make great use out of their ability to think analogically and internally represent worlds that adults seem to have forgotten. If nothing else, interacting with them gives us permission to free up our imagination.

SCENARIOS

A classic business strategy technique that calls on the skill of imagining is scenario planning. Scenario planning especially builds on the anchoring concept of forethought and the ability to internally represent multiple possibilities or pictures of the future. People will employ this method in different ways. For purposes of improving your skill of imagining, the method is not as important as the essence of taking trajectories or segments of your business and imagining different scenarios (global and local) that could play out five, ten, or fifteen years down the road. They could be as big as OPEC's doubling the price of oil or as specific as your top salespeople quitting. Imagine the consequences and what you could do, and then prepare or act in advance so your best scenarios are more likely to happen and your worst scenarios are not. However, do not jump to solutions. Spend some time on imagining what could happen and using other Prepared Mind skills such as reasoning to think through the impacts on your business.

THE CYCLE OF IMAGINING

We can see and react to those things we observe in the here and now but can only imagine the future. Consider the questions posed in Figure 5.1 as a starting point.

1. WHAT COULD THIS EVENT, PROBLEM, OR ISSUE MEAN IN THE LONG RUN?

We sense things in our environment and sometimes simply ignore them. However, there are times when the event is a clue, indicating something greater to come. Say you lose a long-time, loyal customer to an upstart competitor. Is it a one-time event, or could it be a clue that this new competitor is about to change the competitive landscape? Use your ability for forethought, and create some good news–bad news scenarios.

2. WHAT ALTERNATIVE CONCLUSIONS ARE POSSIBLE?

Staying with the example, we could conclude that the competitor was simply lucky or that the old customer is simply no longer loyal. Could an alternative conclusion be that the competitor is better? Could it be that the industry is slowly changing and we have not responded to the changes? Sometimes we reach conclusions that are less painful rather than face the facts that are evolving (however slowly) in front of our eyes. What if you shifted

FIGURE 5.1. THE SENSE-RESPONSE CYCLE OF IMAGINING

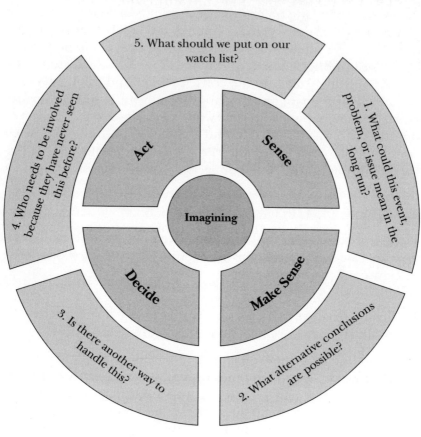

your customer metaphor from "long-standing relationships" to "every day is a new day"?

3. IS THERE ANOTHER WAY TO HANDLE THIS?

We all have tried-and-true routines to dealing with the many decisions that have to be made in our organizations. However, every now and then, we need to invent new, game-changing solutions. How many ways can you play your competitive game? Can you imagine breaking competitive rules? Can you imagine creating a new game?

4. Who Needs to Be Involved Because They Have Never Seen This Before?

While our "reasoning brain" might see the need for knowledge-able experts, our "imaginative brain" might want to try smart strangers! There are two good reasons that we occasionally need a new pair of eyes looking at the implementation of strategic decisions. First, we have to prevent falling into a rut and doing things as we've always done them. Second, we need to groom our future leaders by giving them new problems and opportunities to tackle.

5. What Should We Put on Our Watch List?

We need to constantly update and upgrade our watch list if we are going to continue to sense and make sense of all of the changes surrounding us. Yesterday's competitors are not necessarily to-morrow's competitors. Yesterday's opportunities are history. What about tomorrow? Or do we think that there is a formula that we can apply? All of the fallen icons of the past had a formula, but they neglected to keep looking for the clues that would lead them to discard or modify their formula. The Sense-Response Cycle is running faster than ever before. What's the next new thing you should be trying to sense?

Benefits, Risks, and Challenges of Imagining

All of the Prepared Mind skills have benefits, risks, and challenges associated with their development and use. Here is our starting list for the skill of imagining; add to, subtract from, and modify to fit your reality.

Benefits of Improving Your Skill of Imagining

Improving a skill takes time and energy, and before expending either, we need to be assured that the benefits are worth the effort. Consider the following points.

Enriched Vision
We are able to visualize a potential future and make plans to achieve it or avoid it. Business executives often run a "visioning"

session to take an elusive goal and make it more tangible in the minds of their followers. Unless our business is merely an extension of today, this exercise in visioning has to be built on what we can imagine.

Contingency Plans

We are able to build contingency plans for the projects and programs that are essential to our progress. The exercise of determining what could go wrong is an exercise of the imagination. We can mentally be the competitor, or the machine, or the business environment and sense how they might react. There are times when we need to think the unthinkable in order to protect our workers and assets.

Innovation

Whether we are innovating a product, a service, a business model, or a new way of working and executing our strategy, we need the skill of imagining to imagine a better state and what new possibilities will look like in action. We have to imagine strategy, and we have to imagine the execution to get there.

Improve the Other Prepared Mind Skills

When we exercise our skill of imagining, we see the world differently. That new view of reality or a possible new reality unleashes new options for the other skills of the Prepared Mind. For example, we start to observe things we did not notice before because our imagination has primed our mental map to get ready to look for new landmarks. The rest of the skills also get new life breathed into them when we animate our minds with imagination.

RISKS OF IMAGINING

An overemphasis on a newly developed skill can result in experiencing downside risks. Consider the following points.

Credibility on the Line

If we spend too much time in our imaginary world and not enough time dealing with current issues, we might be seen (and treated) as a dreamer. If this happens too often, we might lose credibility with the very people we are trying to influence.

Threaten the Status Quo

We may be seen as someone who challenges the status quo and therefore someone who is "dangerous." People with dreams are rarely dreaming of stasis; they dream of change, and as we know too well, change is often perceived as dangerous to the people in charge.

CHALLENGES TO IMAGINING

What gets in the way of our ability to exercise forethought, use imagery, and draw on analogies? As part of the preparation for this book, we interviewed dozens of business executives, and as part of the interview process, we asked them to name the most *under*developed skills of the eight skills we have identified. The skill of imagining was regularly mentioned as being underdeveloped in most business organizations.

Why do so few businesspeople consider themselves to be good at imagining? Here are six challenges that you have to overcome:

- A limited view
- Focus on facts
- Limited analogues
- No time
- Seriousness without humor
- Ingrained habits

A Limited View

If you are like most other people in business, you have a limited view of what creativity is and who is creative. Most of us think that creativity is a mysterious gift. Somehow magic happens in the mind, and a masterpiece appears. Anything short of that is not creative. In fact, creativity is complex. However, the imagination aspect of it is based on human capabilities and experiences each of us already has had and just need to practice reassembling in new ways.

Consider the impact that the system of formal education has had on us. We entered the system at an age when a big cardboard box could be magically transformed into a boat, or a cave, or a fort, or a spaceship, or anything else. In other words, we entered the system at the height of our powers of childhood imagination. And for the next twelve or sixteen or more years of formal education, we became socialized to color inside the lines and to speak up only when we had *the* right answer. We searched for perfect knowledge and as an unintended consequence lost the ability to imagine. Think of the long-term consequences on the ability to create strategy when the underlying talents are being stunted at the earliest opportunity. We suspect that future leaders will be even less able to imagine a strategy that is based on coloring outside the lines.

As Prepared Mind leaders, we can call out others' creativity when we see it and find a way to use it. One CEO we studied found a way for two of his staff to use their creative talent in videotaping and home movie making to capture the company meeting and replay highlights in the cafeteria. Was it the most polished presentation the company could have used? No. But the point was that the employees got the opportunity to expend more of themselves for the business and their colleagues noticed and became more fully engaged as well.

Focus on Facts

We act as though only the facts are real. We have collectively spent the past half-century on a quantification binge. We don't want opinions; we want facts. We don't value anything unless we can run the numbers and prove our point of view. Time spent imagining a future state of our business has been supplanted by time spent building spreadsheets. Numbers have replaced dreams.

Limited Analogues

We lack rich, vivid, varied experiences from reading, travel, conversations, and other everyday enriching pursuits that we do not take the time for or fail to reflect on, so our storehouse of analogues is not very robust in our memories. Prepared Minds know how to quickly pull in knowledge from their mental maps to take them and others to new destinations.

In addition to reading, travel, and other pursuits, imagination is enhanced or repressed by physical and psychological factors in the workplace. Colors help, art helps, and music and quiet both help. Look at the work space of some of your most creative people; you are very likely to see toys and junk lying around. The stuff is there for a reason: to stimulate the senses and feed the imagination. Similarly, we can be sure that we can kill all overt acts of imagination by only accepting "proof" (that is, numerical analysis) that something is worth pursuing. Or we can make sure our R&D people give us a string of boring (but "safe") product line extensions by coming down hard on all failures. We may need the psychological sense of safety that comes with this, but we may also be stifling the creative energies of those around us.

No Time

"Time starvation" could be nominated as a killer to all the skills. However, how we spend our time is a decision. We have to make up our minds to observe, imagine, learn, and so forth, and we find ways to do these things in the midst of everyday life, whether we are standing on deck with a four year old or standing in a boardroom with a chairman. The key here is not to assume you can put off "this imagining stuff" until you have the time; you never will under those circumstances. So take a tip from a small business owner we worked for years ago. He scheduled "library time" every week and went to the public library to think about his business. Sometimes he worked on an emerging problem. Sometimes he paged through magazines to get ideas for new products. The point is that he faced up to his time constraint and fit thinking time into his busy schedule.

Along with not taking time, we have a cultured need to look busy. Think about your own job for a few minutes. Do you have the time to sit back, put your feet up on the desk, close your eyes, and imagine a better way? And even if you have the time, would you want to be caught daydreaming by your boss? After all, you would not look busy, and what would she think! No, we've taken the most basic skill and relegated it to company-sponsored (and scheduled) brainstorming sessions and retreats when we have to tackle a big issue.

When we think of the skill of challenging, we usually think of challenging our own or others' ideas or logic. We can also challenge ourselves and our calendars to work on the skill of imagining by setting aside time for a reading retreat, attending a talk, or even just having lunch with an interesting person with whom to brainstorm. We have also found it useful to leverage mindless tasks like taking a shower or brushing our teeth. Keep a pad of paper and a pen nearby, and write down ideas that you imagine when you don't think you are thinking but you really are.

Seriousness Without Humor

What makes something funny is that it calls our attention to something ironic, some connection that we did not think of before that makes us think about the situation in new ways. Humor gives us perspective. Being a business leader is very serious business, and we tend to believe that we might offend someone with humor, so we are careful to stick to reasoning and linear thinking. However, think of leaders you have admired. Wasn't there something very human about them that used humor in a kind and sometimes instructional way? No matter what you thought of Ronald Reagan's politics, it is commonly accepted that he was a strong leader with a great sense of humor who could say clever, imaginative things on his feet.

Humor is also a great tool for enabling others to speak their minds, share their perspectives, and see things, particularly ironic things, in a new light. An executive who circulated highlighted articles to his senior staff that emphasized the company's new direction also sent around *New Yorker* cartoons and other pieces of humor that helped the staff keep perspective and feel open.

Ingrained Habits

Stephen Covey says that one of the seven habits of highly effective people is to begin with the end in mind.[4] Most businesspeople are good at this; we are, after all, goal oriented. Most of us have learned to analyze, forecast in linear ways, and reason. We know what results we want, and we know a few basic ways to get there. And we use them over and over again, even when they don't work. Maybe the end is appropriate, and maybe even the general strategy is fitting.

However, the way we frame, execute, and enroll others in strategy is what Prepared Mind leadership is about. It requires that we think and act beyond traditional acceptable paths to business, particularly in this age of complexity. For example, we often act as if the responsibility for innovation belongs in the marketing department or in R&D. But imagination is not simply the purview of these departments. It should be encouraged and fostered throughout the company, and businesses should constantly imagine new ways to use all the assets at their disposal. This may result in completely new products and technologies, but our thinking should not be limited to products and technologies. Imagination was no less part of the picture when Toyota created JIT manufacturing and changed the entire automotive industry in the process.

Think back to the CEO who came up with the image of the junk-yard dog. The company turned this symbol into an award for any-one in the company who came up with a creative idea that could save the company money or make it money. People no longer waited for a particular department to be creative. They learned that the skill of imagining could be put to work anywhere in the business.

Applied Imagining: The Talent Problem

What kinds of questions and activities might Prepared Mind lead-ers consider as they think about the talent problem from the imag-ining point of view?

- An executive might imagine operating the organization with a world-class team of people. What skills would they have? How would they interact? What if your competitive metaphor shifted from grabbing a bigger piece of the pie to simply en-larging the entire pie? Or, better yet, baking a brand new pie? Now who would you need on your team?
- How do we make the best situation out of what we have? A middle manager might want a different team, but she has what she has (especially in the lean organizations of today). How could she take this average group and turn them into a high-performance team? What discussions should they have? How could they be stretched? What if they cross-trained?
- An individual contributor might imagine the perfect boss-subordinate relationship and its impact on the entire team. What does he have to do to make the existing relationship improve? Although we are always ready for "them" to change and get better, we have control only over our own actions and reactions? What does a perfect working relationship look like? And how can you make it happen?

What imaginative solution could you use to solve the talent prob-lem at your organization?

BUILDING YOUR SKILLS

There are any number of good books that have large lists of specific tools and exercises you can use to improve your ability to imagine. *A Whack on the Side of the Head* and *Thinkertoys* are two of the enduring best in this category.[5] The tools we are outlining here are broader in nature.

CREATIVITY DAY BY DAY

Draw on the human capacity for forethought and imagery one day at a time, and then ramp up to more of a future state. Before you leave work at the end of each day, look at your calendar for the next day's meetings. Pick one, and make explicit to yourself the business and interpersonal goals of the meeting—yours and those participating.

Let's say you want those in the meeting to like one another and act as one team; specifically, you want the meeting to be a forum for deciding what to do with limited resources. Imagine what actions would be occurring in the meeting if your goals were being met. What questions would you be asking? What image could you use to convey a sense of unity that they would appreciate? Picture yourself telling a story using that image. Before you know it, you have rehearsed the meeting, much of which you can use the next day. And if one of the things you envision is asking people to brainstorm or come up with unusual ways to share resources, you are asking them to use their imaginations as well.

SWITCH YOUR FOCUS

Draw on your own analogies from other experiences in different facets in your life when your ideas, hunches, instincts, or dreams materialized into something beneficial for you and for those you worked or lived or played with you. Ask yourself what is similar between those experiences and the current situation, and acknowledge your own instincts this time, just as you did before. Remember that you always have the skills of challenging and reasoning to test them in real time.

CONSIDER THE ROAD LESS TRAVELED

Once again, the use of imagery and forethought can help us come up with new products and new ways of working, no matter where we are in the organization. In fact, there is a growing business for providing companies with creatively designed spaces for doing strategic planning. We have seen everything from rooms painted orange, to Play-Doh on meeting tables, to basketball hoops on the lawn. The idea is to free up people from their usual physical constraints and images that keep them thinking in terms of status quo. These playful images are meant to spur new ideas and thinking ahead, sometimes in outlandish ways, in order to come up with workable new ideas. A more tangible example is the use of design in all aspects of business. Designers can bring in sketches of everything from new workplace arrangements to new products to new images of teams working together. Sometimes if we can see what others have imagined for us, we can think ahead to what these ideas might look like in our real worlds.

MORE QUESTIONS TO CONSIDER

Here are three more ways to trigger your use of your imagination. Each is tied to a short anecdote.

- **Swatch this.** Swatch, the Swiss watch company, marketed the watch as a fashion accessory, not a timepiece. By crossing from timepieces into fashion, Swatch grew explosively.

  In what category have you placed yourself, your product, or your company? What else could you be? Imagine three other categories in which you might fit.

- **Oh, Henry.** Henry Ford did not invent the automobile. He did not invent the assembly line. But what a combination!

  Have some fun. List a dozen combinations that would create something new (and maybe useful) for your business. Be goofy at first if you want; we are normally too serious and need self-permission to do nonserious stuff like imagining new things.

- **Too old?** Ray Kroc was a fifty-two-year-old milkshake machine salesman when he came upon a hamburger stand in California. He bought the franchise rights from the McDonald brothers, and the rest of the story is well known.

  Name a dozen things that you are too old to start. Are you really too old?

GO FORTH AND IMAGINE

Read the story of Jean and her four-year-old friend, and see if you can apply the lesson to your organizational life. We bet you can.

Jean and the Fireflies

Picture yourself in the situation of talking with a four-year-old little boy about his imaginary friends. Standing on an outside deck on a warm summer evening, just as the lightning bugs were coming out, this little guy started to paint the picture of two of his best friends, Buce and Humpty Dumpty. There was an elaborate imagination at work that entailed telling me that they lived in their own apartment, drove a sports car together, and would stop by to pick my little friend up and take him to play and eat blueberries.

Being pretty good at the skill of enabling, I asked him all sorts of questions that allowed him to run with imagination. However, I was caught off guard when he asked me to tell him about my imaginary friend. Being forty years since I have had an imaginary friend, I squirmed. Yet I knew he expected me to play along.

I looked out and saw the lightning bugs and recalled that they are also known as "fireflies." Almost simultaneously, my internal hard drive was searching wildly for analogous connections. If the four year old could borrow from Mother Goose and make Humpty Dumpty one of his best friends, I reasoned that I could search my memory for stories and characters that made me laugh. Remember the unexpected twist at the end of the movie *Usual Suspects*? The Kevin Spacey character, Verbal Kint, was brilliant at combining the skills of observing and imagining. In my own little scenario, I landed on "Rufus T. Firefly," whom I characterized as the leader of the imaginary country of Freedonia, played by Groucho Marx in the movie *Duck Soup*.

So I shared stories of my imaginary friend, Rufus T. Firefly, a name that just lit up my little friend. I imagined aspects of Groucho Marx and myself combining (a scary thought) as a friend to this four year old and started making up stories that had Rufus and me going on rides in the sports car with Buce, Humpty, and my little friend. Based on my values and pictures of the future, I shared that Rufus was writing a book on leadership, based on his time as leader of Freedonia. My Rufus also loved to play golf and share jokes, both of which delighted my little friend.

That exchange reminded me how fun it was to imagine. It also reminded me we often need aspects of four-year-old intelligence in business and our adult lives. Four year olds are very in touch with their human capabilities of forethought, internal representation, and thinking analogically in ways that show what they value now and picture in their future: friends, memorable book and movie characters, sports cars, play, blueberries.

There are times when we need to let our imagination fly ahead of us. What can you imagine is in your future?

CHAPTER SIX

CHALLENGING
Pushing for Higher and Deeper Thinking

> *The ultimate measure of a man is not where he stands*
> *in moments of comfort, but where he stands at times of*
> *challenge and controversy.*
> MARTIN LUTHER KING JR.

The skill of challenging centers on questioning the obvious answers and the path of least resistance in favor of what is the right thing, given the circumstances, and who you are fundamentally as a person or as an organization. We often think of challenging as pitting one point of view or one set of skills against another, and in the end, we end up with winners and losers. The common understanding behind the concept of challenge is built around a zero-sum game: one team wins, the other loses; one company increases sales, the others decrease sales; one person is right, the other is wrong. And on it goes. However, as we think of challenging as a skill of the Prepared Mind, the goal is for everyone to win—not through consensus or compromise necessarily but by pushing for higher and deeper thinking through opportunities, strategies, and tactics.

The common behaviors, scenarios, and outputs we see that we attribute to challenging tend to be things like counterpoints, debates, and arguments to poke holes in claims, questions that ask the speaker to show if and how her idea works in a different context. When we think of challenging, we tend to think of discourse rather than dialogue. We think of it in black and white, stark binary terms of good versus bad, right versus wrong, my way versus your way. It all seems very democratic, and it rests on the assumption that this tension of opposites will produce a stronger, more innovative conclusion. This view of the dialectical challenge works much of the time. However, it is not the only form of challenge.

We challenge you to also think of challenging as an invitation to consider something new and not necessarily something opposite. Also, consider how we can challenge our own thinking, with or without the help of someone taking another side. Some of the things we see when we open up the skill of challenging include multiple options or streams of thought, a spoken statement about the organization's mission and values, questioning to help people think through motives and consequences in advance of taking action, and a sharing of what is better, stronger, wiser in the person (or organization) who is being challenged and a call to rise to that higher level. Remember that the object is not win-lose but thought and synthesis toward the best possible decision and action.

CHALLENGING BY THE PREPARED MIND

The skill of challenging is sometimes an obvious, overt act, as in the conflict created over a competitor's latest move. Sometimes it's subtle and in the background, as in confirming your and your organization's beliefs. Sometimes it's motivational, as in setting goals that stretch people beyond their comfort zone. It can be found in your response to slow industry change as well as your response to a crisis. For the Prepared Mind leader, challenging means to offer different ways of seeing or different views altogether of what is real and actionable. In other words, the challenge may be around how one is thinking or what one is thinking. We need to challenge ourselves whenever we build, modify, and abandon our mental models in order to build new ones.

There are four specific aspects of challenging that may need explanation and exploration. As you consider the skill of challenging, we want you to consider it as:

- A calling into question
- A test of one's abilities

- An act or statement of defiance
- A call to engage in competition

A CALLING INTO QUESTION

Consider the challenge you pose when you ask the ultimate business question: What business are we in? Answering this question gives rise to a wide range of possibilities for any business. At one extreme of the answer continuum is the "stick to your knitting" and "core competency" response of the 1980s and 1990s: doing what you're best at and focusing on your core competency. At the other extreme are the conglomerates of the 1970s and the feeling that "we can manage anything": we can be anything we say we are. Focusing on your core competency is important—as long as it fits the evolving needs of your customers and clients.

Consider the reality that Kodak has faced recently: its core competency has been and is *film,* but its customers only want *pictures.* Kodak has taken too long to challenge the basic question of its business definition: What business is it in? The answer to this basic challenge is not simple or academic; in fact, it will trigger closing of factories, reallocation of R&D monies, potential stockholder revolt, and a move into the converging worlds of film-based and electronic cameras, cell phones, and personal digital assistants. It's clear from the outside that not answering the challenge will lead to a painful decline in revenues and profits. But the answer is not always obvious or easy for those inside the organization.

Similarly, expanding the scope of your business is a good way to grow—as long as you don't get into situations where your ignorance of the context makes you dangerous. Consider the conglomerates of the 1970s. At one time, ITT was in the businesses of renting cars (Avis), running hotels (Sheraton), making bread (Wonder Bread), and fertilizing lawns (Scotts fertilizer). ITT exists today, but as a much smaller and more focused company. The siren call of synergy was challenged, but not until the company almost self-destructed.

A TEST OF ONE'S ABILITIES

Consider the question posed by looking at your business from the outside, from the point of view of customers and competitors: Are you moving fast enough? Do your customers perceive your company as meeting their evolving needs in a timely manner? Do your competitors respect you for industry leadership, or do they take advantage of your lagging position? When you consider the question of "Fast enough?" in the light of the Sense–Response Cycle, we see that there are two fundamentally different aspects to this.

First, can we avoid the dangers of "active inertia" and change fast enough to satisfy our customers' needs?[1] Active inertia is the condition of doing what you've always done (and doing it well) but missing the curve in the road. It's not what you do that gets you in trouble; it's when you keep doing what you've always done. As an example, you have only to look at your cell phone. Motorola was king of the cell phone business, but it did not move fast enough to take advantage of the shift from analog to digital technology. And then for a few years, it seemed as if Nokia could do no wrong— until it was slow in responding to customers' desires for cell phones with digital camera capabilities.

The second aspect of "fast enough" overlaps with the first question of defining your business. A useful lens here is Joseph Schumpeter's notion of "creative destruction," denoting a "process of industrial mutation that incessantly revolutionizes the economic structure from within, incessantly destroying the old one, incessantly creating a new one."[2] In other words, industries are constantly morphing into something new. And that is the challenge to an agile leader: if you change your organization more slowly than the industry changes, you are in danger of becoming irrelevant.

AN ACT OR STATEMENT OF DEFIANCE

It is easy to think of challenging one's competitors and others outside the company. But we want you to consider the situation of using the skill of challenging as a support to the ultimate question confronting senior executives: What do we have to do to balance our actions in support of customers, employees, and stockholders? You cannot keep everyone satisfied and still maintain the long-term health of your company. Take a moment and think of the challenges (and what you have to challenge) as you try to keep your three main constituencies in a balanced state:

- Customers want good products and services, when and where they want them, and at a reasonable price. To serve their needs, you may need to consider keeping inventories low, changing your offering regularly, outsourcing as needed, and focusing on competitive pricing—for a start.

- Employees want challenging, steady work and good pay and benefits. To serve their needs, you may need to consider keeping the factory open during slack time, maintaining work in-house, and building inventory.
- Stockholders want growing revenue, steadily growing profits, and long-term stock appreciation. To serve their needs, you may need to cut costs, milk your "cash cows," and price as high as allowable.

The need to balance the needs of all three constituencies has been discussed in articles and workshops that focus on providing long-term value, so we are not going to address the issue of why trade-offs are needed to keep all three in balance. (Balance is needed only if you want to survive in the long term. If all you care about is the short term, then focus on the shareholders and milk this cash cow for all it's worth.) However, a few words on what has to be challenged and how you might go about doing so are in order.

Business executives and managers spend a considerable amount of time discussing the issue of value for customers and clients. Andy Grove of Intel challenged the consumer's perception of the value of Intel's microprocessors though the "Intel Inside" branding campaign. We are willing to pay for those things that we value—and Intel had to challenge the point of view of consumers regarding the value they were receiving from Intel. Unless Intel had brought the notion of the processor to our attention, would any of us really care about what was making our PCs run? And by changing the end consumer's expectations, Intel was able to leverage its reputation with its direct consumers, the PC manufacturers.

Jack Stack and his management team at Springfield Remanufacturing Corp. (now called SRC) had to challenge the role of "the worker" in both their minds and the minds of their employees. Springfield Remanufacturing Corp. was formed through a management buyout of an International Harvester division.[3] The management team thought they could bring the failing division to prosperity, but they found out they needed more: they needed everyone to understand the business and how it made its money.

With their back to the proverbial wall, Stack and his team had to challenge the notion of the relationship between management and the workforce. Stack and his team are best known for their innovative open-book approach to business. In this approach, taken almost out of desperation, Stack provided the opportunity and, most important, the challenge to his workers to understand the financial condition of the company in order to make more relevant business-based decisions. The biggest challenge, however, may have been to Stack and his fellow executives. Letting the workers see the books and participate in the decision process is quite a challenge to those who have formerly been the only ones in the know.

Finally, we need to challenge the stockholders of any company to consider the long-term viability of the company and balance immediate rewards against long-term gains. In 2004, for example, we watched Kodak continue to struggle to reinvent itself and at the same time convince some of its larger shareholders of the need to spend precious free cash from continuing operations on risky digital formats. The experiments and ventures may or may not work, but simply listening to the shareholders who are focused on short-term gains (dividends) would surely have hastened the company's decline into a film-only niche player.

The situations we have described can be summarized as the three major challenges of any organization, the ones that form the core responsibility of senior executives: identity, speed, and trade-offs. And although these are the responsibility of the executive team, Prepared Mind leaders throughout the organization are not off the hook. They see relevant events in their opportunity space relating to these major challenges, and it is their responsibility to challenge the senior executives to address the event.

A CALL TO ENGAGE IN COMPETITION

This aspect of challenging sits at the heart of strategy. Landline-based telephone companies have been challenged to rethink their business with the onrush of cellular technology. Cell phone makers have been challenged to think about their product identity. Is it a phone, a camera, a PDA, or even an entertainment channel? Technology is moving faster and faster, and the quest of being different and, simultaneously, relevant is a daunting challenge. However, having different and better products is not the only way to engage in competition.

Consider for a moment the findings of Michael Treacy and Fred Wiersema's best-selling *Discipline of Market Leaders*.[4] In studying the actions of market leaders, they looked at a modified version of Michael Porter's earlier "formula" (he did not present it as a formula, but it soon was used as such) to either be the low-cost producer or differentiate yourself in order to win. Their findings focused on operational excellence (needed to become a low-cost producer), product leadership, and customer "intimacy" (both forms of differentiation). Their conclusion was that winners excelled in one of these three disciplines and were at least as good as the competition in the other two. In their view of the world, "different" could also mean "better."[5]

This aspect of challenging is especially difficult in a world that is running and changing faster than ever before. Consider the reality of shorter life cycles for both products and ideas. Business executives once spent much of their time looking for sustainable competitive advantage; unfortunately, given today's realities, competitive advantage is ephemeral. And so engaging in competition is more like guerrilla warfare: there is no "front" to move or defend.

OUR EMOTIONAL SELF

The skill of challenging is clearly one of the Prepared Mind skills that is closely linked to our emotional self. It's easy to intellectualize the skill from the point of view of what has to be done and what tools can be used. But when you look at leaders who are actually good at challenging, you see a set of requirements that go beyond tools and techniques. We see five basic requirements:

- Courage to step out of the mainstream
- Commitment to values
- Curiosity about their opportunity space
- A desire to improve
- Self-awareness of strengths and weaknesses

Our view of leadership is that you have to be willing to go beyond the strict confines of your job description to take advantage of opportunities for your organization. For most organizations, this requires a considerable amount of courage and a willingness to put up with resistance from those who see you moving onto their turf.

If courage were in plentiful supply, we would not continue to see disgruntled managers and workers talk about the silos in their organization. Process orientation and cross-functional teams would be the norm, not the exception. If courage were in plentiful supply, we would see overflowing suggestion boxes. We would have more good ideas than we could implement; consequently, part of management's time would be spent on prioritizing and acting on the best ideas. Unfortunately, these seem to be the exception and not the rule. And yet in times of emergency, whether it's a business, moral, or ethical dilemma, values make the difference. To learn about this, we sometimes have to look beyond business leadership to the world at large. Mahatma Gandhi led India into independence though his commitment to nonviolent resistance. Martin Luther King Jr. emulated Gandhi's practices and changed the racial picture in the United States through his commitment to equality.

Children are great at challenging us; their "weapon" is their curiosity and the word that they use with great effectiveness: "Why?" You were that way once, but the quest for "the answer" has driven a lot of your curiosity out of you, and, consequently, many of us have forgotten the power of "Why?" If you were really curious about your work environment, you might ask plenty of questions that would challenge the organization: Why do we keep running this report? Why have we lost so many customers in the city? Why can't we be best? Why should we outsource? Why shouldn't we outsource? And so on. Real curiosity always causes us to challenge the status quo, and that just might prevent us from succumbing to the trap of active inertia.

The desire to improve themselves is found in all great performers, from athletes to artists to business leaders. And the desire to improve is found in the challenges we create for ourselves. Lance Armstrong is the six-time winner of the Tour de France and could have retired years ago as a great cyclist. However, he continually challenges himself by riding higher and steeper hills and racing against younger, stronger riders. Likewise, you often hear of a stage actor who feels he has not proven himself until he plays a lead in one of the great Shakespeare plays. What challenges will you set for yourself in your quest to improve?

"Know thyself" has been an enduring piece of advice since the ancient Greek philosophers. The self-awareness that comes from challenging ourselves, knowing our strengths, and going beyond our weaknesses is fundamental to the topic of leadership. None of us was born a leader, and none of us has all of the knowledge and skills needed for the leadership challenge before us, whether we are individual contributors or heads of organizations. However, all of us have the capability for self-reflection, and when that is coupled with a desire to improve, we are capable of being greater than we are now.

We believe that if we are not challenging, we are not leading. Leading with a Prepared Mind requires our knowing why, at its foundation, challenging is so difficult and building our skill on that foundation.

ANCHORING CONCEPTS OF CHALLENGING

We find three core concepts are critical to understand and use when learning and exercising the skill of challenging: (1) cognitive dissonance, (2) dialectical thinking, and (3) perspective taking.

COGNITIVE DISSONANCE

When Leon Festinger proposed cognitive dissonance theory in 1957, he used it to explain the attitude change that often takes place in a person after he or she has performed an action inconsistent with one or more of his or her attitudes or beliefs.[6] It is believed that people generally do not like dissonance or inconsistency between their attitudes and actions. Since it is difficult to change an action and its consequences after it has been performed, people sometimes change their attitude about the action in order to reduce the dissonance.

Coping mechanisms after the fact, such as rationalization and even parts of Karl Weick's idea of sensemaking,[7] are ways to align actions and attitudes by changing the attitude or perhaps reframing the action so it does not seem so inconsistent with the attitude. But if we are willing to take a hard look at the inconsistencies and decide about future actions (that is, learn) or attitudes, then moments of cognitive dissonance become what educators call teachable moments.

In terms of challenging, most parents have helped their children face these teachable moments when they debrief with the child after the child has acted in a way that is inconsistent with their attitude, or with the attitude and values in formation and desired by the parents. The same teachable moments happen in business. Someone makes a decision or takes an action that is inconsistent with his or her own attitudes, values, and norms or those of the company, and there is tension until the situation is confronted or swept away through positioning, scapegoating, rationalization, or other human defense mechanisms.

Prepared Mind leaders know how to challenge their employees, challenge themselves, and invite others to challenge them so they surface these inconsistencies and figure out how the inconsistencies came to be.[8] Perhaps the attitude of the leader is not shared by the employees. Perhaps the company's professed attitude (often seen in policy) does not match its true attitude and actions.[9] Perhaps "mistakes were made," and if those involved had it to do over again, they would not choose the action they did.

Although we live in litigious times, cognitive dissonance is not about legal responsibility. Cognitive dissonance is more fundamentally about how humans cope when their actions and attitudes do not match.[10] Prepared Mind leaders address this very real human condition through the skills of challenging, learning, and enabling before they ever get to the courts.

What is not addressed by cognitive dissonance theory and its research but is a practical implication tied to the theory are strategies for enabling people to admit when a behavior was out of line with the desired attitude and take responsibility for their actions and mistakes. We often see this enablement discussed in management books as "creating a culture of trust." The problem is, "How?" The answer lies in people, especially in leaders, who model the behavior they expect and even put themselves at risk by letting themselves be challenged and by admitting bad decisions and actions from a business point of view and also from a social and moral point of view. The key comes in not stopping at what went wrong, but in holding the action in relief to the larger principle or goal at stake.

In John Steinbeck's novel *The Short Reign of Pippin IV,* the king is rebutting those who feel that the citizens and their country as a whole cannot change.[11] Pippin says, "People want to be good, just as long as they can be. That is why I resent it when goodness is made difficult or impossible for them." Granted, Pippin is an idealist. However, his point is that when people are feeling dissonant or nervous and looking for scapegoats and ways to pass the buck, they often need to be reminded of their larger common goals and ideals in order to focus on constructing the future rather than avoiding their past.

Think of people in your life you have seen exhibit leadership, especially in times of stress. Weren't they the ones who focused attention on the big picture rather than letting people focus on getting out of trouble? The tie to cognitive dissonance is that those moments of dissonance can be used to bring people back to their core ideals, values, and goals so they have a focus for their actions and attitudes. These leaders are also good at rewarding people for these behaviors of looking more deeply and more widely and making the learning more important than what could be construed as the original mistake.

The idea of cognitive dissonance provides strategies before deciding and acting. While cognitive dissonance has almost always been used to explain attitude change and coping after an action has been taken, Prepared Minds do not wait. They play out scenarios before they happen and practice comparing attitudes with potential decisions and actions. If they feel dissonance before acting, they know to stop, gather more data, and consider a different option. The phrase, "I had a gut feeling that it was a bad idea," does not describe the magical intuition of leaders. It describes their using cognitive dissonance in combination with the skills of imagining, reasoning, challenging, deciding, or any of the other skills that lead to action.

Cognitive dissonance theory also challenges conventional approaches to change management. For change to be internalized and sustained, often it is the attitude that needs to change to match the needed decisions and actions to move a person or an organization to an opportunity space. A singular focus on a change of behavior, without really accounting for the underlying attitude, will often lead to compliance but not to innovation or to people learn-

ing to think on their own. One underlying assumption of the Prepared Mind is that those who lead are always interested in the increased thinking ability of those around them, as well as their own
ability. Enabling people to develop Prepared Minds requires helping people work through cognitive dissonance and learn, often
with the help of challenging them to really look at their past or intended actions and attitudes from new angles. This is not easy, but
the world requires people who can think through ambiguity and
paradox and synthesize opposing points of view to come to a new
view altogether. That is why the next core concept for challenging
is dialectical thinking.

DIALECTICAL THINKING

Dialectical thinking has its origins in philosophy and refers to the
classic cycle of thesis-antithesis-synthesis. More recently, the ability
to hold two seemingly paradoxical ideas in one's mind and find an
integrating "third way" that rises above the two opposites yet reflects points made in each has been labeled the hallmark of adult
thinking and maturity.[12]

   The need for this method of thinking comes from the fact that
we live and work in a world full of paradox, ambiguity, and con-
tradictions, sometimes even within ourselves. These conditions of
paradox and uncertainty require us to make trade-offs and decisions, using our best judgment with incomplete information. However, these conditions also suggest that if instead of choosing to live
in a world of either-or, we choose to live in a world of both-and, we
will likely find and invent more opportunities that integrate aspects
of prior, seemingly opposing views. One example of an application
of dialectical thinking is the win-win approach to negotiation that
has become a norm across industries. Another is found in the
music industry, which, for a short time, saw itself as a business in
which customers either buy CDs or lift free music off the Internet.
Through the struggle of MP3, consumer demand, and creative
business models of sales and distribution, what emerged was a
both-and model of buying single tracks cheaply off the Internet
and giving the profit to the music industry while providing a customized, affordable product to the consumer. Now, Starbucks and
other cafés are making this business part of their business model:

we can download music cheaply and legally while we sip a latte in Starbucks.

The point is that if you challenge your own thinking or challenge others' thinking with an eye toward synthesis, you will likely see a wider opportunity space for both of you, and you will likely find a productive way to deal with differences, conflict, dissonance, and other deal busters. And while the skill of challenging and images of dialectics are often envisioned as a social interaction, they can occur within our own minds. Breakthroughs or "Eureka!" experiences occur when synthesis is reached in our own minds or within a group.

The skill of challenging Prepared Mind style in part rests on the ability to engage in dialectical thinking and challenge ourselves, and those with whom we work, to find the higher, common ground around which to synthesize. As previously implied, dialectical thinking is a hallmark of maturity and adult thinking, and that comes from perspective, not age or even experience. Perspective taking is its own foundational core concept for the skill of challenging.

PERSPECTIVE TAKING

Most of us have had the experience of being challenged or challenging others out of our own self-interest and worldview. Often our biases are unconscious, and we feel so committed to our own perspective that it is difficult to see the need to stop and consider what the other person's perspective might be, as well as how our particular view relates to a larger whole. Yet for other major competencies of leadership—skills in sales, persuasion, communication, inspiring, strategic partnering, even strategizing—perspective taking is a given. We learn to take the perspective of our customers and the competitive environment in order to know how to brand and position our products and services. We learn to take the perspective of our shareholders and the market sentiment in order to know what sort of balance and trade-offs they will accept between things like reinvestment and dividends. We learn to take the perspective of our strategic alliances, along with market demand and core competencies, when we negotiate roles, ownership, and rules of engagement. In the moment of challenging, whether of ourselves or someone else, the ability to take perspective and communicate our consideration of the other person's interests and the big picture adds credibility to our challenge because it shows we have truly thought through the different angles of the situation and declared that we want to arrive at a view that takes into account the different angles of an issue.

Perspective taking is a skill and a way of thinking that comes from the human ability to think in wholes, or what psychologists call *gestalts.* These theories suggest that we look for patterns of coherency, for whole structures or systems, and that we even organize our mental maps based on these whole chunks of information and relationships between them. When we ask ourselves or others questions about cause, effect, implications, or examples, we are seeking ways to place the current situation in a larger whole. Challenging with perspective taking is often a matter of seeking to find a coherent whole from which to base decisions and actions. When a military general makes a decision about whether to attack, his training has taught him to consider the whole in terms of strategies, contingencies, conditions of the environment, even future plans. A decision then falls into perspective under a larger attempt to win the war and not just the battle. Public companies often battle with the tension between the short-term, quarterly perspective and the long-term strategic growth perspective. The most successful CEOs are those who can deliver on the short term in service to a long-term strategy.

Perspective taking, particularly as it relates to human relationships in business or any other context, also comes from the human ability to have empathy, that is, the ability to identify with and understand another's situation, feelings, and motives. One CEO we know was often praised for his ability to communicate with his employees all over the globe. Even his general e-mails that were blasted to thousands of in-boxes received recognition and praise from employees, consultants, and the company's board of directors. When asked how he crafted such brilliant communication, he replied, "I simply remember what it was like to work in a cube, and I know what I would have wanted and needed to know from the CEO." In this case, his perspective taking came from his experience of having been there himself.

We can also have empathy and take perspective by searching our mental maps for similar situations (remember the power of analogical thinking discussed in Chapter Five), emotions, motives, and connections that seem present in the current situation and or in the perspective of the other person and we can, in a sense, walk in their shoes. This is another instance where the power of observing (meaning listening and seeing things that are not obvious) is vital to the skill of challenging.

Think about times when you have challenged someone without taking this person's perspective or acknowledging a bigger picture you and the other person share in common. Didn't you notice her eyes staring, muscles tensing, and tone ranging, or perhaps you heard a superficial acknowledgment and then a change of subject? Whether your challenge was legitimate or not, it didn't work. Now think of a time when you challenged with perspective. Did you notice people leaning forward, cocking their head, asking questions, engaging in dialogue? In this case, the challenging worked to bring both you and the other person to a new level of understanding or at least curiosity.

CONNECTING TO THE CONCEPTS: ANCHORED EXERCISES TO IMPROVE THE SKILL OF CHALLENGING

FIVE WHYS

Asking people to articulate the "why" behind their ideas or opinions is one of the most commonly used techniques for the skill of challenging. It may provoke cognitive dissonance if people start to stumble over their logic as they try to articulate the why. At the very least, it challenges them to think things through. By the same token, hearing the whys of others can open us to their perspective, which is necessary if we are going to challenge them with graciousness and respect.

ASSIGN A DEVIL'S ADVOCATE

Even the term *devil's advocate* provokes dissonance and unease in people. Assigning the devil's advocate role to our teams guarantees that cognitive dissonance will be provoked and at least keep people open to the challenge of their ideas. In terms of dialectical thinking, the devil's advocate represents the antithesis. Looking at the opposing view and the reasoning behind it can have the effect of challenging and improving our own awareness and thinking. In transformational change initiatives we have been a part of, we have noticed that the skeptics are listened to. The skeptics are different from the cynics, who are committed to new ideas' not working. Skeptics, like devil's advocates, can ensure we are thoughtful and prepared.

AROUND THE TABLE

In any sense–make sense–decide–act scenario, there will always be individuals who offer more than others. The danger is the lack of challenge from the quieter participants. One way to practice the skill of challenging and being challenged is to make sure everyone around the table is specifically asked to voice their perspective. If we find ourselves as the talkative types, it is wise to ask others to speak and sincerely listen and consider their perspectives, especially if there is challenge in what they say. If we are the quiet types, we can promise ourselves to voice our perspective at least once in a meeting at a time that offers a new view. Perhaps we can take on the role of synthesizer.

TRUE TO THE PRINCIPLES? TRUE TO THE EVIDENCE?

When we want to challenge ourselves or challenge others, we can do so on two levels, both of which encourage dialectical thinking. One level is the level of principle. If we know what we stand for or the principles at play in a situation (such as decision criteria), we can constructively challenge by asking, "Are we being true to our principles?" At another level, we can challenge reasoning by asking, "Are we being true to the evidence?" If the answer is no, we realize we have some form of antithesis or at least a different perspective on the table. It is then our job to reject that view or synthesize it into a higher, more integrative perspective. This comparison to some external standard (principles or evidence) takes the personal sting out of challenge and challenges based on more external criteria.

SYNTHETIC THINKING

At least two of the anchoring concepts for the skill of challenging, dialectical thinking and perspective taking, are addressed in the practice of synthetic thinking. Synthetic thinking takes the concept of dialectical thinking (thesis, antithesis, and synthesis) and speeds up its effects. Synthetic thinkers are creative innovators. They do not necessarily have to be presented with a thesis and an antithesis to merge them into a new idea. The general process of synthetic thinking is as follows:

1. Consider a variety of perspectives; then cull out the essence of each. (Culling out the essence means looking for an abstract idea or concept that is common to or is an underlying aspiration of all of the perspectives presented.)
2. Use this essence to articulate a higher, more integrative idea. This is a nuanced version of the skill of challenging because the integrative idea challenges people to think higher or think more deeply.

Synthetic thinkers are terrific at making sense and moving decision makers to action based on a compelling idea. Synthetic thinkers inspire. We often call the practice of synthetic thinking "wisdom." Granted, wisdom has other attributes, but the ability to give attention while remaining detached, do analysis while looking for the big picture, is a sign of wisdom. If we look at the conversations and interactions of such historic greats as Aristotle, Jesus, Thomas Aquinas, Abraham Lincoln, Mother Teresa, and our mothers, we realize that much of what set them apart was their practice of synthetic thinking.

We can improve our own ability to practice synthetic thinking by reading about these greats and looking for instances of synthesis. We can also discipline ourselves to lead by listening and looking for an integrative theme that incorporates but is not limited to the perspectives being presented. Pausing and offering the theme in a concise statement or phrase like, "It sounds as if what we are talking about here is tapping potential," or "It seems to me we are circling around the idea of spinning off a business," gives people a new idea to consider that taps into something they said and yet challenges them to think bigger.

THE CYCLE OF CHALLENGING

Obviously there are times when we will need to challenge others. But in the long run, the ability to challenge ourselves is most important. Consider the questions posed in Figure 6.1 as a starting point.

FIGURE 6.1. THE SENSE-RESPONSE CYCLE OF CHALLENGING

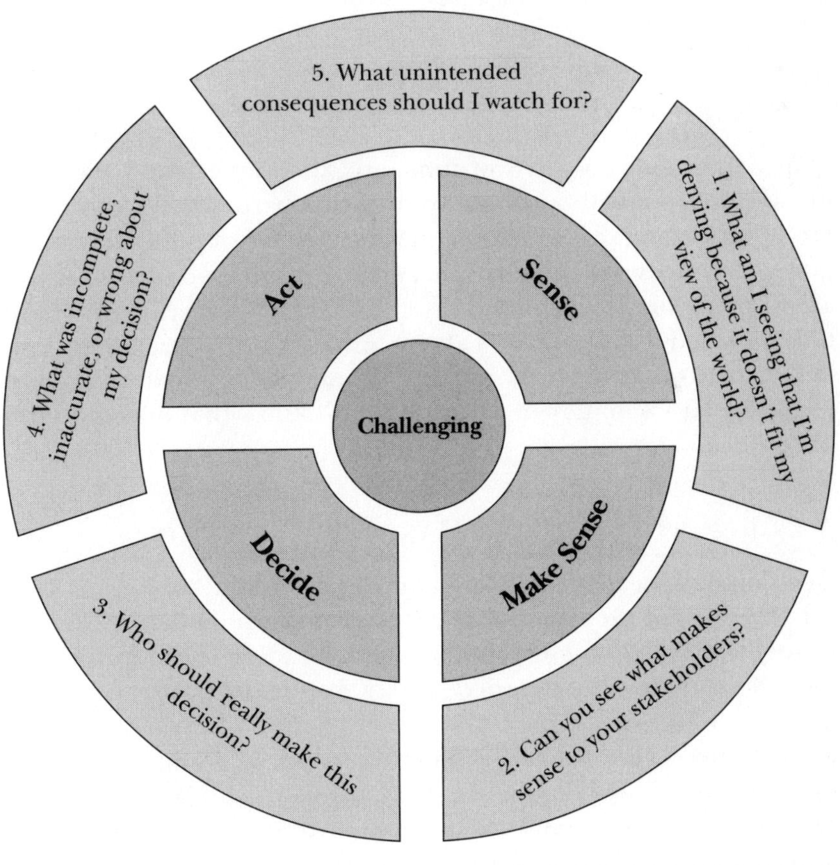

1. WHAT AM I SEEING THAT I'M DENYING BECAUSE IT DOESN'T FIT MY VIEW OF THE WORLD?

We need to challenge our view of the world for accuracy and completeness and remember that *our* view of the world is not *the* view of the world. Do you see your product as state-of-the-art? Ask a former customer who has shifted to a competitor. Do you see your organization as customer friendly? Ask an unhappy customer. Do you think morale is just fine in your organization? Go to a local restaurant and listen to employees discuss work with their coworkers. All of us want to feel good about ourselves and our organizations; we just need to remind ourselves every now and then to lift our heads and take an objective look at the world.

2. CAN YOU SEE WHAT MAKES SENSE TO YOUR STAKEHOLDERS?

Our mental maps ossify over time, and the longer you have been in a position, or with a company, or with a particular industry, the greater the danger is of having inaccurate and out-of-date mental maps. If we toss out the term *cell phone,* what do you picture if you are fifteen years old? Thirty-five years old? Fifty-five years old? How old are the decision makers at the telecom companies? Are they in tune with their user base? Sometimes it's not a matter of what you know; it's a matter of what you don't know that makes all the difference.

3. WHO SHOULD REALLY MAKE THIS DECISION?

Decision making is being turned on its head in the twenty-first century because of the "need for speed" and the relentless evolution of technology. If you are the boss, ask yourself these questions. First, do you have the knowledge to make the decision, or is someone else better suited? Second, is the decision important enough to be made at your level in the organization, or should it be delegated down? Third, is this the best use of your time? There are times we feel that we must make the key decisions; some of us need to develop the will to let go.

4. WHAT WAS INCOMPLETE, INACCURATE, OR WRONG ABOUT MY DECISION?

It's during the enactment of a decision that we have the best opportunity to learn from our mistakes and improve our decision-making process. Unfortunately, many of us miss this opportunity. We bury mistakes so as to not look wrong, even though the people around us can see the failure. As we are forced to run the Sense-Response Cycle faster, we will inevitably make more mistakes, not just in execution but in the process of making decisions themselves. It's a shame that many of us will not challenge ourselves and improve.

5. WHAT UNINTENDED CONSEQUENCES OF OUR ACTIONS SHOULD I WATCH FOR?

We've said this elsewhere in this book, but it's worth repeating since it's so important: *all* solutions bring about unintended consequences. We need to think about them in advance and watch for them before they cause real problems. The Sense-Response Cycle is never ending, and we would be foolish to think that anything is solved forever.

BENEFITS, RISKS, AND CHALLENGES OF CHALLENGING

Consider this starting list of benefits, risks, and challenges for developing and using the skill of challenging; then add to, subtract from, and modify to fit your reality.

BENEFITS OF IMPROVING YOUR SKILL OF CHALLENGING

Improving a skill takes time and energy, and before expending either, we need to be assured that the benefits are worth the effort. Consider the following points.

Teachable Moments

Challenging known truths within our organization can bring about teachable moments that move the entire organization to a new level of performance. The very act of challenging can raise interest and cause people to focus on the reality before their eyes. Your challenge may be right or it may be wrong, but getting an organization to think critically about accepted relationships and conditions can bring about deep learning that is rarely, if ever, found in the organization's training room.

Relationship Building

In finding a third way, we have the opportunity to turn past adversarial relationships into partnerships. We see this happening all the time in organizations that have taken their supply-chain relationship beyond the technology. Companies and their suppliers spent most of the twentieth century in conflict. Prices were contested, inventory levels were contested, and lead times were contested. When supply chain participants work on collaboration rather than competition, they have the ability to build, not destroy, value through the relationship.

Enriched Point of View

When we challenge our understanding of any situation (and remain objective), we inevitably develop a richer picture of the whole because we are forced to consider multiple points of view. The answer to the question, "Why is this so?" is found by considering the larger context of the situation.

RISKS OF CHALLENGING

An overemphasis on a newly developed skill can result in experiencing downside risks. Consider the following points.

Alienation

You may work in an organization where any challenge gets you labeled as nonteam player. There are times when a team is so focused on solving a problem or resolving a situation that they do not even want to hear anything other than positive comments. Unfortunately, when this happens, the team often denies itself the very information or point of view that is needed for a good resolution. However, using the skills of reflecting and enabling, with a good dose of interpersonal communication skills (for example, asking the person for permission to challenge them) will raise the true value of the challenge and lessen the perceived sting or need to be defensive. Exposing your own reflection that brought you to the point of cognitive dissonance, synthetic thinking, or some other need to challenge will give those you are challenging context and invite them into their own reflection and dialogue. Inviting others to challenge is a key to enabling them to think and show develop their minds.

Limiting Focus

We may empathize so deeply with another point of view or with another constituent, for the sake of perspective taking, that we may dull the needs and point of view of our own organization. Companies that place service people on-site at a customer location sometimes find that these people have "gone native" and see the situation only from the customer's point of view. Where they were once objective, they are now biased. This is a case where it pays to balance the skill of learning what others think and incorporating that into our reflecting and reasoning rather than challenging or questioning ourselves or our company at every turn. It gets back to our core definition of Prepared Mind leadership that calls for adherence to a core and to individual and corporate integrity that does not change.

Jeopardizing Relationships

You may lose friends. Even within a culture of constructive challenge, you may rub someone the wrong way or be seen as questioning something about themselves they hold near and dear. While you may not be in business for the friendship, losing valuable connections in a social network is a risky business and social thing to do. Using the skill of observing to perceive others' reaction to your challenge and knowing when to back off or approach the challenge with another strategy is important in using this skill effectively.

CHALLENGES TO CHALLENGING

Why is challenging so difficult? We see five reasons:

- Time pressure
- Industrial age models of authority

- Fear of losing face
- Poor listening skills
- Fear of change

Time Pressure

The old saw, "We need it yesterday," does not suggest taking time to challenge things by asking questions like, "Do we need it at all?" "What is the 'it' that we need, and is it really what we want?" "We may need it yesterday but will we need it tomorrow?" In other words, the pressure of time can box us in to becoming order takers and not critical thinkers.

Industrial Age Models of Authority

We say we are in the knowledge era, with flattened structures of formal authority and millions of knowledge workers essentially acting as their own bosses and as collaborators across teams. However, the reality in practice is that most of us tend to defer to and not challenge ideas or practices we perceive as coming from someone with more authority than us. We may complain and disagree, but often we either fear what might happen if we challenged the boss or we do not accept challenging as our responsibility.

Fear of Losing Face

Even if we are not afraid of losing our job if we stop the train of decision making and action and challenge those around us, often we are afraid to take the risk of opening our mouth and being perceived as wrong, as a squeaky wheel, as not adding value to the team. We remember from Abraham Maslow that most humans have needs for affiliation and for esteem. When we challenge others and create dissonance for them, we risk losing that affiliation or their esteem for us. This is very much akin to the risk of losing friends.

Poor Listening Skills

The Prepared Mind version of challenging is not about convincing or talking people into submission. But most of us, when we are calling something or someone into question, want to rush in with our version of what we think is right. Sometimes we even literally interrupt other people so we can make our point. People who are focused on their own way or getting their point across do not listen

Applied Challenging: The Talent Problem

Consider these illustrative questions and activities of Prepared Mind leaders working on the problem of acquiring, developing, and retaining the right talent from the challenging point of view:

- An executive might challenge herself by asking if the organization's goals are tough yet achievable. More important, do the workers consider the goals achievable? Stretch goals are certainly a test of everyone's abilities. Has she made sure that everyone knows and understands the mission of the organization so that they can put these goals in context and perspective?
- A middle manager might have to be blunt with a peer about poor performance and then explain it in the light of the organization's mission and goals. It's always amazing to compare the performance of the organization to the ratings that are given through the performance management system. Often you see a company that is falling behind in its industry, yet the executives and managers are all getting above-average marks on their performance review. *Something* is not going right, but we fail to take the challenge of looking at our role in the problem.
- An individual contributor might ask for tougher assignments or more freedom. He might consider his attitude toward risk and take a chance on a riskier assignment. However, during lean times, we tend to hunker down and hope that we can stay out of sight until times get better. Some of us trade off perceived safety for the opportunity to improve.

well for the truth in the other person's statement. This is difficult in personal relationships, and it is certainly difficult in work relationships, especially in highly internally competitive or low-trust cultures.

Fear of Change
If we challenge other people or they challenge us, it means someone is going to have to change their minds and change the actions

and outcomes they may have already imagined. This disrupts the pictures we have of ourselves and of our worlds and may throw us into confusion amid what is already a pretty confusing, high-pressure, time-sensitive life. Who wants that?

BUILDING YOUR SKILLS

Here are some more ideas for developing the skill of challenging.

MEET THE CHALLENGES OF CHALLENGING

Here are some tips for dealing with each of the challenges of challenging.

Not Letting Time Pressure Keep You from Challenging

Set an agreed-on time and process for testing ideas and creating new alternatives through dialectical thinking. We set time and processes for strategic thinking and planning, for tactical thinking and project updates, even for creative thinking in the form of brainstorming sessions. Dialectical thinking is certainly as important to making sense and deciding on a plan of action as any of these other common business practices. If you establish and teach the process for doing this kind of thinking and adhere to time guidelines, that is, time-box the time allowed for it, it will become a habit.

Overcoming the Industrial Mind-Set

This is where the formal leader, the person with the most authority, can use that role to encourage, not discourage, challenging. In other words, leaders can use the skill of enabling to encourage the skill of challenging. They can ask questions that require people to challenge conventional thinking, questions like, "All the data say we should undertake this project, but give me three reasons why we should not." The formal leader can also invite her boss, a consultant, or a trusted colleague in to challenge. How the formal leader responds to the challenge will provide a model for the rest of the group. The leader can even express any dissonance she is experiencing but frame it as a positive and a real opportunity to learn. This will help people grow more comfortable with the discomfort brought about by challenges.

Challenging Without Losing Face

The formal leader can invite challenge and praise it when it happens. The team can set ground rules for challenging that, for instance, insist that everyone around the table take a different perspective so the discussion is guaranteed not to fall into groupthink. Even if you are not in an authority position, you can enable others and help them learn how to challenge by telling people you are going to challenge constructively and why you think it will help the group and show them how it can be professional without being personal.

Applying Better Listening to Challenging

One of the oldest listening skills in the book applies here. Repeat back to the person talking what you heard him say and call out a good point in his perspective. It shows literally that you are open to perspective taking. This provides a positive motivator for the speaker to keep offering his perspective, models how to hear and affirm another perspective, and forces you to consider other perspectives by repeating them and intentionally looking for a good point on which to build. This enables others to learn how to hear the challenge in a friendly way, without blocking out the challenge with defense strategies.

Overcoming the Fear of Change Brought On by Challenging

Be up front about the three core concepts of cognitive dissonance (expect it), dialectical thinking (here's how to do it and what it will result in), and perspective taking (agree to do it) before the challenging conversations even begin. This will put everyone on a level playing field and give them tools for challenging (perspective taking and dialectical thinking) and tools for coping with the discomfort of challenge (cognitive dissonance). After awhile, it will become part of the expected culture, and you will not have to make a point to call these things out anymore—until a newcomer joins the group. Then you have to help the newcomer learn by observing her and enabling her to join in the challenge by modeling how the group does it and explaining why it is beneficial.

THE FUNDAMENTALS

Knowing a few techniques to improve your challenging skill is not enough; you will not suddenly become better. Like all other skill building, it takes some underpinnings and some practice. Consider the following as starting points:

- *Know your values.* What are your espoused values, and do your actions support your espoused values? Ideally, this should not be a problem, but it often is. Here's the nasty issue: many of us talk about the importance of good work-life balance, yet we miss too many opportunities to spend time with our families because we have to be at work.

- *Break rules that no longer apply.* Drive around your town, and we're sure you'll see a house that has multiple additions. It's ugly because the owners kept adding on to meet a need at the time. Many organizations have rules and policies that were added on to meet a need that no longer exists. Both need to be challenged and remodeled—by first tearing something down.

- *Challenge yourself to improve.* Kids have fun because they constantly challenge themselves; they get bored when there's nothing new to challenge them. All of us are like kids to some degree: we need to do new (and hard) stuff to keep us fresh.

- *Ask great questions.* Great questions are those that shake up the organization and cause it to move in a new direction. Great questions are those that are asked before the competition asks them. Great questions separate the leaders from the followers. Face it: we can find answers to really hard questions; somebody, somewhere can figure out the answer. But we will never get an answer to the question we don't ask.

- *List your assumptions, and visit them on a semiannual basis.* Assumptions are wonderful in that they act as shortcuts to our thinking and deciding. However, just as high blood pressure is the silent killer of the circulatory system, bad assumptions are the silent killer of strategy.

MORE QUESTIONS TO CONSIDER

- **History lessons.** The telegraph and telephone changed the impact of distance on the lives of people and companies. Photographs and phonographs extended the concept of time.

Distance and time were both fundamental constraints and barriers to early life and business.

> List the constraints imposed on your business. Who has already dealt with these constraints? What did they do, and what could you do?

- **You know the rules.** Many innovations come about by breaking the rules that everyone else is following. Rules often take the form of assumptions or industry truths.

  > Name some rules that you follow. What would be the benefit of breaking any of these rules?

- **Illegal, immoral, unethical.** Brainstorming sessions often stop after the group exhausts all of its ideas. Fire up the group by asking for illegal, immoral, or unethical ideas. Take some of these ideas and "bring them back" into the legal, moral, or ethical world. In one of our workshops, for example, the concept of "kidnapping" customers resulted in further discussion about making them so happy that they would never leave.

  > Try making a list of outrageous notions to trigger more useful real-world ideas. How could you cheat without cheating? Steal without stealing? Spy without spying?

GO FORTH AND CHALLENGE

Reflect on the concepts and skills presented in this chapter, and try some of the exercises suggested. Start today by challenging your own challenge-proof assumptions in innovation, decision-making, and problem-solving situations in your world.

You cannot solve a problem with the same level of thinking that caused it.
—Albert Einstein

The Prepared Mind questions the world to stimulate next-level thinking and surface powerful new possibilities. Such questions come in clusters, never alone. World-changing questions come in threes: questions designed to uncover facts, illuminate assumptions, and constructively challenge assumptions to see new possibilities.[13]

CHAPTER SEVEN

DECIDING
Choosing with Consequences in Mind

In 1992, IBM lost $5 billion on revenues of $64 billion. Most of the "experts" had declared IBM to be old and nearing death and saw the breakup of the company as its only chance for survival. The outsiders saw this as inevitable, and the people on the inside had already started to make plans to dismantle an American icon.

In a fascinating story of decision making at its riskiest, Lou Gerstner, a decidedly nontechnologist, takes the helm of the world's most famous technology company in April 1993 and within his first hundred days makes four critical decisions:[1]

- To keep the company together because, as he sees it, the industry needs an integrator, and that integrator should be IBM
- To change the fundamental business model from selling high-margin "iron" (mainframes) to lower-margin products and services
- To reengineer how IBM does business to keep costs under control
- To sell underproductive assets because the company is running out of cash

In some cases, Gerstner had hard data to support his decisions; in other cases, he had a view from the field.

DECIDING AND DECISION MAKING

Decision making is its own critical step in the Sense-Response Cycle, and, as expected, it is supported by many of the other Prepared Mind skills. But when you look at the skill of deciding in isolation, you see a skill that transforms cognitive agility (quickly sizing up a situation) into decision-making agility (turning thought into action in a timely manner).

Deciding is the process for committing to a particular course of action. How leaders turn thought into action depends on how they come to understand or make sense of the situation. And once they have decided on a course of action, they have to find ways to communicate it effectively, engage the stakeholders, and enable those who will be called on to execute the decision.

We often assume that decision making is a rational process that requires a sort of calculus or economic modeling explicitly or within our heads. Most textbooks depict a decision tree with which we describe the paths we might take and assign probabilities to the success of each path. We assume that people will decide on the action that optimizes their best interest and is within the odds of attainability. We assume that by taking a very rational approach, we can determine the one "best way." This view of decision making is very rational and takes an economic and probabilistic approach to decisions. However, is that the science we really use to make decisions? No. Research and experience tell us there are simultaneous social, emotional, and cognitive processes at play during real decision making. As is the case with so many other things, the approach we take defines the type of outcome we get.

DECISION MAKING: FIVE METAPHORS

In the history of decision-making research from a social science perspective, four metaphors have emerged to explain the limitations found in the process of deciding.[2] We think that there is a fifth metaphor to use when considering the role that the skill of deciding takes among the eight skills of the Prepared Mind. The metaphors are:

- The Economic Actor
- The Satisficer
- The Intuitive Decision Maker
- The Emotional Decision Maker
- The Prepared Mind Decision Maker

THE ECONOMIC ACTOR

The assumption behind what has become known as the "economic actor" or "corrigible rationalist" model is that people are fundamentally rational, but that they make mistakes in decision making because of a myriad of idiosyncratic reasons that involve the context as much as the person and his or her rational thinking. This prescribed, optimized, and rational approach is similar to some merger and acquisition decisions that wind up falling apart because less rational factors, such as incompatible cultures, were not taken into account. They couldn't quantify the differences between two cultures, so they ignored them. Decision makers may scratch their heads at the failure and say, "This doesn't make sense," but indeed they may not have considered multiple kinds of data in the making-sense process. When it comes to merger and acquisitions activities, the numbers tell only part of the story.

On an individual level, this approach describes the person who, when buying a car, lists his criteria with an explicit weighting system, collects data from *Motor Trend* and *Car & Driver* as to how different cars meet his criteria, and then finds that the car he wants to buy is unavailable for three months due to a dockworkers' strike that prevents the car from being unloaded. Sometimes the key to the success of the decision is found in the larger context of the decision, like reading the paper and considering the real impact of a dock strike.

The issue here is that quantification is very appealing, but it is rarely enough when it comes to dealing with complex decisions. We hear executives deriding the "soft stuff," but in reality, the soft stuff is the hard stuff. One of us has extensive experience in running projects and for the past few years has been facilitating workshops focused on project leadership. The introduction to the workshop is an exercise called, "Best of Times–Worst of Times," and in this exercise, the participants (generally seasoned project managers at large companies) are told to recall the best project they have ever been part of and the worst one. The question then is, "What made the project so good or so bad?" The answers are invariably grouped around the larger context and the people issues that arose but were not addressed.

THE SATISFICER

Another view is that people satisfice or take shortcuts, rational-ize, or do not try as hard as they otherwise might due to lack of time and resources. Sometimes we fall into this because we "know" the answer, and sometimes we succumb to the pressure of a real or imagined sense of urgency. For example, during the dot-com boom of the 1990s, one of the mantras was "ready, fire, aim." Decision makers moved through the Sense-Response Cycle so quickly that they seemed to skip the make-sense phase because of the time pressure and venture capital pressure to decide and act. What was lacking at times in their decision-making consid-erations were basic economics and organizational infrastructure. Another example is the company that decides on an off-the-shelf technology tool for quick installation, not considering the work process of those who will use the tool or its compatibility with other systems, initiatives, and organizational factors competing for attention and the environment's ability to incorporate the new tool into the regular routine.

One of the most dangerous shortcuts leaders take is when they grab the first workable solution to a nagging problem. You can al-most hear the collective sigh of relief that *any* solution has been found, and there is often great hesitancy to explore further and see what other solutions might be tried. And once they have a so-lution, it quickly becomes *the* solution. Now it would be very con-venient to label those who satisfice as lazy or incompetent, but the reality is that the vast majority of managers are time-starved. It's natural for them to want to get on to the next issue.

THE INTUITIVE DECISION MAKER

The third metaphor, the "error-prone intuitive," moves through sense and make-sense so quickly, or seemingly so unsystematically, that one wonders if the decision making is data based or, more likely, hunch based. Decision making by hunch was common in the dot-com era when money was flowing and decision makers took a flyer on anything that felt personally right to them. One of us re-calls two partners of a prestigious consulting firm cashing in their stock and six-figure salaries because they had a hunch that people would buy mustard over the Internet. The reason? They liked mustard and were sure that others did as well.

Real experts often describe their decisions as intuition, but more often than not, they are basing their decision on subtle patterns they detect or mental simulations that fly through their heads.[3] Unfortunately, not all of us are real experts, and we often put too much credence on a hunch.

THE EMOTIONAL DECISION MAKER

The fourth decision-making metaphor, known as the "slave to motivational forces," says that people employ faulty decision-making processes because they are emotional and stressed. Unlike Economic Actors, Emotional Decision Makers bypass their brain and make decisions based on feeling. These are the people who fire employees on the spot when they are under pressure to make their numbers. They don't want to consider options; they just want to "do something."

Daniel Goleman, the author of the best-seller *Emotional Intelligence,* refers to this as "emotional highjacking."[4] This might be considered a cute phrase to describe a person who buys impractical fashion attire or kids who succumb to the appeal of the latest school craze. However, when you consider all of the managerial fixes that have gone into and out of the lives of many executives, this is a serious issue. Reengineering was going to eliminate waste, so companies pursued it with a vengeance. But it turned out to be a shortcut to cutting head count. Six Sigma programs are valid, but too many companies have "decided on Six Sigma" without really understanding what it takes to make it effective over the long haul (that is, once all of the "low-hanging fruit" has been picked). Any time you see a managerial fad on the rise, you can assume that emotions are preceding thinking.

THE PREPARED MIND DECISION MAKER

What would the Prepared Mind metaphor be? Perhaps it would be called the meta-macrocognition metaphor.[5] More plainly, it might be called "the big picture" metaphor. The implication of the big picture is being mindful of economic, social, organizational, and psychological factors they we use in any given instance to make up our minds. It also implies being aware of our own decision-making processes, including our heuristics and biases,[6] and constantly reviewing them for improvement. The things that go into decision making and affect the big picture outcome of decisions certainly include rational things like goals and risks and probability of achievement. However, they also include less rational things like preferences and values, other initiatives in the system, and emotions toward prior similar decisions. These irrational things are the stuff that unintended consequences are made of, both positive and negative, and we have no choice but to take them into consideration.

Prepared Mind leaders combine the skills of imagining and learning to assess what is in the environment and what the impact on the environment might be as they are deciding. We call this decision-making approach *meta* because, like the scientific term *metacognition*,[7] it is getting above the situation to see what factors of thinking and deciding are at play. We call it *macrocognition* because it looks at not only what is going on in individual minds but also in their real-world environments. This includes the interaction with people, places, and things around them that affect what is sensed, how sense is made, how decisions are made, and what actions are accepted in the environment. Finally, we call this approach to decision making "prepared" because it takes a multi-angle lens to many factors at play, and it considers the intended and unintended actions and making sense that might occur as a result of any particular decision.

ANCHORING CONCEPTS OF DECIDING

It will come as no surprise to any reader that a lot goes on below the surface of any decision. We have chosen three anchoring concepts to introduce as a means of understanding the cognitive complexity of decision making and improving your skill of deciding. The first concept, *schema,* is likely unfamiliar if you do not hang out with cognitive and learning scientists. However, we think it is important enough to devote some extra time and space to because it underlies all of the skills of the Prepared Mind and is a more formal way of describing what we are referring to as a mental map: the content and connections in our minds, including what we know, how we know it, and why we know it and use it the way we do, which has emotional implications as well as pure cognitive ones. The other two anchoring concepts, *criteria/rules* and *commitment,* are likely more familiar to you, and we will touch on them briefly.

SCHEMA

In offering this anchoring concept, we are purposely using a word not found in most business books. The word *schema* is often confused with the term *mental model.* However, we believe that *schema* belongs in your lexicon because it is the major determinant of what and how we think. It reveals the relationships between mental models, not just individual mental models. Complex problems draw on these relationships. It gives us more things to tap into when we are trying to understand other people, including values, beliefs, and the way they process information. Mental models are somewhat static, but understanding schema is akin to understanding the blueprint of how they work with one another.

By definition, *deciding* means "making up your mind." One of the characteristics of human cognitive ability is that we make up our minds by adding to or changing the content of what is already in our minds, or we change how we process the content. What is already in our minds and how our minds tend to process information is known as *schema*.[8] Schemata are even deeper than mental models and have many functions that strongly influence our future thinking by drawing what has already been committed in our minds. These schemata direct perception and therefore determine what we sense. Schemata also make making sense or learning and comprehension possible.

Schemata aid recall, which supports the process of searching our memories to see if we have been in similar decision scenarios before and, if so, how we might reuse what we did before. For instance, if you have the schema that leadership is about making financial decisions, you will make different decisions than if your schema is that leadership is about developing people. In the Prepared Mind view of leadership, both the financial outcome and the human process and outcomes are important.

Schemata are powerful influencers of the entire Sense-Response Model of cognitive and leadership agility, and Prepared Minds are aware of what goes on in their own minds when they are in the act of deciding. Another advantage to this awareness is that knowing one's own schemata and mental models makes it easier to change and develop them as needed. Prepared Minds need many interconnected bundles of knowledge and processing tracks in their minds so they can be flexible in what they choose to apply in dynamic, fast, and high-risk situations.

The ability to think fast is at least in part the result of having a wide repertoire of robust schemata in one's mind. If our repertoire of schemata developed through experience, learning, and reflection is deep but not wide, we are likely better decision makers around a narrower band of issues within our expertise. If our repertoire is wide but not deep, we are likely better at many kinds of decisions but need help when the decision requires deep technical knowledge. Prepared Minds know their strengths and weaknesses and make wise decisions about how they will go about making any given decision.

CRITERIA/RULES

The concept of having criteria against which to weigh alternative decision options makes intuitive sense. Criteria-based decision making can be learned as a process. The tricky part is that sometimes, in the midst of everyday decision making, we are not so clear, even with ourselves, as to what our criteria or even our goals are. One way to become better at articulating criteria and making decisions informed by those criteria is to think like a designer. One of the first things designers do, whether they are designers of homes, educational courses, software programs, or cell phones, is to gather user requirements or criteria that the designed thing must meet. Imagine going into a serious decision-making session on your own or with a group and coming to agreement around the goals and criteria of the decision and the rules for making the decision. This is more than writing down a pro and con list. This is more in keeping your decision making in line with larger goals. Of course, you as an individual or as a group may choose to override the criteria and rules, but they at least provide a good common ground for reasoning, imagining, challenging, learning, and deciding together.

Commitment

Commitment acknowledges the role of emotion in decision making. Without commitment to a decision, it will never become an action. Commitment can be applied to the decision itself. It can also be applied to the decision-making process and criteria in use. Good leaders of decision making will make the decision-making process, criteria, and rules clear. They will also understand what is already on the minds (or in the schema) of those making the decision and surface things like goals, agendas, biases, fears, and other challenges to decision making in a nonthreatening way. In terms of commitment to a decision, it is important to demonstrate it through consistent action.

One issue we hear from many leaders is that a group will appear to be on the same page about a decision and then go back to their business units and cave in or ignore the decision. It is clear that there was or is no real commitment. Commitment comes from tapping into motivation, be it yours or someone else's (motivation is discussed more thoroughly in Chapter Nine). However, two criteria for commitment are clear: (1) the decision must be tied to goals, values, and principles that people would spend extra effort in acting on, and (2) the decision makers and those charged with acting on the decisions need to see the link between what they can do and the intended consequence of the decision.

Connecting to the Concepts: Anchored Exercises to Improve the Skill of Deciding

Take a Class

Of all the skills of the Prepared Mind, the skill of deciding is the one that has been studied the most, debated the most, and taught the most. Its prevalence implies two practical things, and therein lies the good news and the bad news.

First, as the chapter suggests, there are many approaches to decision making and, second, there many contexts in which decision making occurs. For instance, there are approaches that are purely economic, where we spell out criteria and employ rational reasoning to get to some utility. There are intuitive and emotional approaches that teach people to rely on their gut instinct and a sense of what they can commit to when making decisions. There are many more approaches that could be compared and contrasted. This gives us many choices, and that is good news. However, this gives us many choices, and that is also the bad news. The news is not really so bad, though, if we know how to be a wise consumer of decision-making models, understanding there is not one acceptable best way. Besides learning all of these approaches, which is probably not necessary, you can benefit from learning good strategies versus error-ridden strategies within each.

Similarly, there are many different contexts for decision making—for instance, virtual decision making, online decision making, individual decision making, collaborative decision making, authoritarian decision making, consensus-driven decision making, and the list goes on. Each has its own benefits and challenges.

Most of us think that we usually do an effective job of decision making. However, we have found that decision making is one of those often-used skills like listening, where we do not realize what we don't know and "effective" is relative. There is a lot of knowledge in the world about decision making, readily available through formal learning that we can take advantage of in order to improve our skill. Perhaps the best way to get an overview of what is out there in a real way and get practice in multiple approaches is to take a course or a workshop from a credible institution.

DESIGN CRITERIA

Decision making based on criteria or rules is the decision-making process that architects, product designers, learning designers, engineers, and all other designers use most often when they are deciding what to design and how. Usually they start with a problem to solve or ask users what they want the designed thing to enable them to do. An automotive engineer might be asked to design a new car, but she would be in the dark until told such criteria as number of passengers, mileage requirements, luxury or utility, and safety requirements.

Practicing our work as designers, where we begin with the end in mind and actually take into account our objectives and what our users need or want to be able to do as a result of the decision, is a great way to practice the skill of deciding.

Decision Matrix

A decision matrix is a helpful tool when we have multiple criteria and multiple choices. It is human nature to brainstorm solutions along with our brainstorm of problems. Here is a simple process for forming a decision matrix:

1. Brainstorm a list of possible solutions to the problem named.
2. Brainstorm a list of criteria the solution must meet.
3. Assign a relative weight to the criteria (for example, 1 = mildly important, up to 5 = absolutely necessary, or 1 = effective, 2 = achievable, 3 = effective but low achievability, 4 = low effectiveness but high achievability.
4. Draw a matrix. Put the criteria across the top and the list of choices down the left side.
5. Evaluate each solution against the criteria, using the weighted system.
6. Multiply each solution's rating by the weight. Add the points across the row for each solution. The decision may or may not be determined absolutely by the score, but the process can generate a robust, data-based discussion. In the end, you have to decide on something to which the group can commit.

Ideal, Acceptable, Nonacceptable States

Emphasizing the core concept of commitment is one way to improve practical decision making. By asking yourself or the group to generate decisions whose implications are ideal, acceptable, or nonacceptable, you can make a clear, high-level cut of what decisions to take out of the running (no commitment to unacceptable) and which decisions are likely to generate the strongest commitment (ideal). Seldom are decisions this clear, and trade-offs need to be negotiated. Naming the criteria embedded in the decision and where each criterion falls on the ideal-nonacceptable continuum is one way to get to a state of negotiation.

INTENDED AND UNINTENDED CONSEQUENCES

With discipline, we can name criteria we expect decisions to meet. This exercise of criteria naming helps us predict the future impact of the decision, at least the impact in the direction of our criteria. However, often we have blind spots about the implications and consequences of a decision that we did not select criteria for and did not plan. Often we are so committed to a particular decision for the criteria it helps us meet and the emotional appeal it has that we fail to look at more subtle impacts it will have on the system in which results of the decision will be released.

One way to sensitize ourselves to the reality and power of unintended consequences is to read about them or think about them in our own lives. We recommend to you Edward Tenner's *Why Things Bite Back: Technology and the Revenge of Unintended Consequences*.[9] Considering unintended consequences is not meant to freeze our decision making but instead help us overcome early commitments to a particular decision that may meet our stated criteria but may work in opposition to tacit criteria of long-term consequences. Anticipating consequences helps us prepare for trade-offs and risks.

THE CYCLE OF DECIDING

If we are going to be prepared for our future, we need to determine what is important and what is "noise." Furthermore, we need to make sense of important events and use this knowledge to constantly reposition ourselves in our business ecosystem. Consider the questions posed in Figure 7.1 as a starting point.

1. CAN I AFFORD TO IGNORE WHAT I HAVE SENSED, OR SHOULD I DIG DEEPER?

We are constantly bombarded with new offerings and have to determine if they affect us. For example, the advent of bottled water was simply competitive "noise" to many of the soft drink manufacturers in the early 1990s; Coca Cola initially dismissed it as unimportant (it made its money selling concentrate) and got into the bottled water business a bit late. The RCA video disk was a short-lived

FIGURE 7.1. THE SENSE-RESPONSE CYCLE OF DECIDING

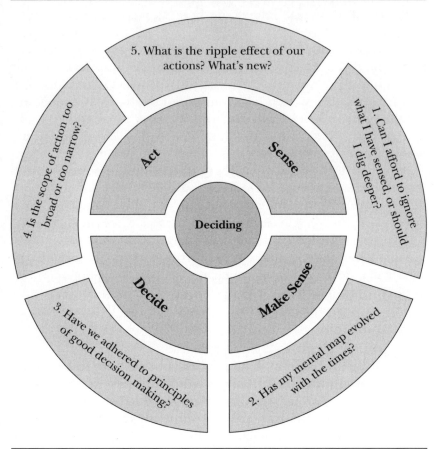

event in the electronic entertainment world, but the introduction of DVD changed everything. Hybrid cars were unimportant noise to the Big 3 automakers, but now they're playing catch-up because Toyota and Honda took the concept seriously.

2. HAS MY MENTAL MAP EVOLVED WITH THE TIMES?

All of us find comfort in stability, however short-lived, and, consequently, our mental maps are often a bit behind the times. We can look back over the history of business and criticize all of the times executives missed a fundamental shift in their business models and maps. Gee, the railroad executives must have been pretty blind not to see the impact of the interstate highway system. And GM must have been looking the other way when the Japanese auto companies came onshore. And how did all of those blind retailers miss the impact of the Internet? What are *you* not seeing because it's not important to your existing mental map? We can easily see all of these changes after the fact, but it takes a conscious effort to challenge our mental maps and decide if they are (slowly) misrepresenting reality.

3. Have We Adhered to Principles of Good Decision Making?

Only time will tell if our decisions have good or bad outcomes, and, quite honestly, some of the results of our decisions are out of our hands. But we do know that there is such a thing as a good decision process and that, all things being equal, it will lead to consistently better outcomes. Do you consider multiple points of view? Do you shut down the naysayers, or do you listen to them? Do you have clear criteria? Do you take the time that's needed? We realize that there are all kinds of extenuating circumstances as to why we shortcut the decision-making process, but we have to be honest with ourselves that when we do so, we risk experiencing a less than desirable outcome.

4. Is the Scope of Action Too Broad or Too Narrow?

Business consultants and pundits have talked about silos for a couple of decades, and you would think that by now, all of our decisions would take a cross-functional perspective. Not so. We still see information technology "solutions" that are focused on the technology but ignore the people affected. We still see outsourcing of manufacturing that neglects the impact on design engineering. We still see massive efforts to implement Six Sigma programs without considering all of the other programs in play in the organization. Sometimes these are simply trade-offs that we accept. But sometimes we have neglected to look at the scope of the decisions we

have made and how they interact with all of the other demands
we have on company time and resources.

5. WHAT IS THE RIPPLE EFFECT OF OUR ACTIONS? WHAT'S NEW?

Enacted decisions always have a ripple effect, sometimes good and
sometimes bad. New incentive systems make some people happy
but demoralize others. Streamlined supply chains cut costs, but
also eliminate old sources of know-how. New products keep customers happy but at the risk of old inventory write-offs. We owe it
to the people in our organizations to watch for these ripples, make
sense of them as fast as we can, and, if needed, modify the decisions we have put in action. Big organizational decisions often have
a ripple effect on morale and organizational confusion. We ignore
the downside of these effects at our peril.

BENEFITS, RISKS, AND CHALLENGES OF DECIDING

Here is a starter list of the benefits, risks, and challenges associated
with the development and use of the skill of deciding. But the most
important list is the one that is specific to you. So don't assume that
we have given you a comprehensive view. Add to, subtract from,
and modify this to fit your reality.

BENEFITS OF IMPROVING YOUR SKILL OF DECIDING

Deciding is a process, not an event, and the process can be used as
an opportunity for discovery.[10] As we improve the process skill of
deciding, we have an opportunity to reap benefits beyond the outcome of the decision itself.

Bigger Picture
If we use the process for discovery rather than the imposition of a
preconceived idea, we have the opportunity to refine and expand
our mental maps to get a bigger and more comprehensive view of
the situation. Through the discovery process, we will have an op-

portunity to understand and communicate the "Why?" of the situation as well as improve our understanding of the many relationships in play.

Better Alignment

Leaders are charged with obtaining results in both the short and long terms. We can impose our will on the organization in the short term and achieve short-term results, but we need the organization's backing to achieve long-term results. A good decision-making process helps those below us learn "how it's done" and ensures alignment through the organization.

Greater Commitment

By allowing dissent and debate, we build buy-in of the decision outcome. People in our organizations want and need to be heard. Once they have had a voice, it is much easier for them to rally behind the decision that has been made. People are more inclined to support a decision in which they have had input. They want to be heard.

Risks of Deciding

The benefits described are aligned with the concept of decision making as a discovery process. However, this process takes time if done comprehensively. Like so many other things in a leader's life, there are trade-offs.[11]

Time Invested Sooner or Later

Decision making under time pressure may mean that we have unheard constituencies. The risk is that since they were not involved in the process, they will not buy into the end result and may drag their feet. It's faster to make the decisions ourselves, but we often have to pay for that in the time it takes to get the decisions implemented.

Potential for Failure

We may be associated with a bad result. Face it: using a good decision process does not guarantee a good result, and, depending on the organization, having your name associated with a bad result may hurt your career. One of us worked as a consultant to an international aerospace firm in the early 1990s, and this firm believed strongly in decision made by consensus. However, the firm was not very forgiving of bad outcomes. It was fascinating to sit in a meeting, watch the team come to a consensus decision, and then watch some of the individuals line up their excuses as they left the meeting, just in case the decision didn't meet with management approval. It may have been a "team" decision, but the individuals always wanted an out in case the results were poor.

Endless Debate

Controlled dissent and debate are hallmarks of a good decision-making process. However, the risk is that the debate gets out of hand and instead of a healthy give and take, we end up with warring camps. All you have to do is watch Congress debate an issue, and you can often see the bad use of a good process.

CHALLENGES TO DECIDING

It is almost impossible to determine the quality of a decision as it is being made. However, there are a number of traps into which decision makers typically fall. Awareness of the traps in front of you is one way to avoid falling into them.

No Existing Schema

A situation with profoundly new data, or one that requires a different mental decision routine, is difficult because we don't have a schema for it. However, as humans, we do not want to leave things ambiguous and unknown. We also do not want to look dumb or admit that we do not know how to solve a problem. Therefore, we often try to make new situations fit old ones so we can at least build an understanding of the new situation. Sometimes, however, we go overboard in seeing situations as similar or familiar when they are not. We want to place a new situation in an old, familiar bucket so we know what and how to think through it. This can result in deciding on the wrong question or on having the same set of decisions for every kind of problem.

At the same time, if we admit that we do not have the prior knowledge for the situation at hand, we can suffer from analysis paralysis or fail to make a decision at all because we subconsciously think we think we have the capacity to address it as something new. With no new decision, or with a decision that may or may not map to the problem at hand, the action or inaction may result in disaster, or at least in being left behind the competitors who were prepared to make up their minds and act.[12] Currently, Motorola struggles with its competency of being an exceedingly good engineering company with a strong attention to quality. However, as Motorola's product development process tends to look at everything as a design or quality issue, it slows the market realities of needing to get the product out the door faster. Consequently, it has fallen behind in the cell phone industry, an industry it helped get off the ground with its early expertise. While "ready, fire, aim" may be a shortcut error of decision making, the flip side is to get stuck on getting ready or aiming and not pulling the trigger to fire.

Reusing Old Mental Models

Another common pitfall in decision making is failure to review old decisions and ask "Why?" This is why skills like learning and reflection are critical to do on a routine basis. They help us keep our decisions and our decision-making process fresh and relevant to the circumstances at hand.

During a study of turnaround companies, the researcher heard a classic tale of decisions that had outlived their usefulness but were still alive as company policy and driving current decisions.[13] During the bankruptcy period of one company, the policy was implemented that workers could not change positions until after they had been in their current role for eighteen months. The rationale was to prevent job hopping and lack of expertise buildup in any one job as employees were trying to move regularly to jobs they felt stood the least chance of being eliminated. Two years later, when profits were flowing and the company had clearly turned around, the CEO was walking the shop floor and happened to ask one of the workers how she was doing. She reported that she was frustrated: she was unable to apply for a job she really wanted because she had been in her current job for only twelve months. The CEO was shocked and said, "That's the dumbest rule I ever heard. Who decided that?" The worker's reply was, "You did." Sure enough, when he checked with the vice president of human resources, he was reminded of an entire set of decisions he had made to fit the temporary situation that had lived on after the reason was no longer relevant. In fact, now it was getting in the way of worker satisfaction and talent management.

Rationalization

The judgment of decision quality has an after-the-fact review element to it that can be rational and based on clear criteria. For instance, did that investment decision pay off in greater-than-average returns? We can also be less objective after the fact. Sometimes we make sense of past decisions like a revisionist historian, leading to reverse engineering of our decision process, explaining what we did and why in order to justify the outcome. It is like walking backward through the cycle of sense and make sense. We begin with an action, or more likely a result of an action, and we rationalize why we did what we did.

One of the problems with rationalization is that it makes it difficult to learn from bugs in our decision-making process and improve our decision-making ability because we are so busy defending the particulars. This is especially when we need the skill of challenging (ourselves or having trusted friends and colleagues who will challenge us) to keep us from rationalization. Remember high school math when you got as much credit for showing your work as you did for the answer? To improve the skill of deciding, you have to be cognizant of the process you are using and "show your thinking," not just rely on the result. You also need to be open to being challenged.

OTHER COMMON ERRORS IN DECISION MAKING

The traps mentioned above are some of the deeper ones we fall into, but they are not the only ones. Here is a handful more to consider and to use as a checklist:[14]

- *Partial consideration of critical information.* Recall the decision to launch the *Challenger* space shuttle in 1986. There were sufficient data to explain the problems with the O-rings, but not all of the information was taken into consideration.

- *Not considering relationship of decisions to other decisions and processes in the environment.* When you study the reasons for the many failures of enterprise information technology systems, you consistently see that not enough time was spent on dealing with the human interface. The system could be installed, but it was not implemented.
- *Different decision models at work in people's minds around the decision table without explicit acknowledgment of those differences.* One of Ellen Langer's hallmarks of mindful behavior is that of using multiple points of view.[15] Functional silos in many organizations prevent using multiple points of view.
- *Not considering both quantitative and qualitative information.* We do this all the time when we run the numbers but forget to talk to the people.
- *Not articulating how and why a decision was made.* This gets in the way of adoption and therefore intended results. One of the solid findings from the past twenty or so years of "change management" is that people don't resist change very much when they know why it's important to do so. Most organizations overprescribe and underexplain.
- *Making a decision based on a symptom versus a root cause.* This is the classic case of "make the pain go away." Symptoms are easy to see, so we go after them, but we don't dig deep to find and fix the real reason.
- *Identifying a decision scenario as something familiar.* We believe the scenario is one we have seen before and use old or favorite heuristics to reach a decision when, in actuality, the decision scenario is different. This is the problem with having a lot of experience; we use history as a substitute for thinking about the future.
- *Simply going along with the group decision to maintain cohesion.* This error is so dramatic that it has its own name: groupthink. Sometimes we overemphasize the importance of the team and underuse the view of the individuals.

In the twenty-first century, we can be sure that increasing complexity, limited time, and the accelerating pace of change will continue to confound good decision making. Even with reliable decision support tools to supplement our human processes with statistical data, we still struggle.

Applied Deciding: The Talent Problem

What kinds of questions and what activities might Prepared Mind leaders consider as they think about the talent problem from the deciding point of view? Consider the following:

- An executive might need to consider the role and expense of people in both the short-term survivability and the long-term success of the organization. Chasing short-term profit by instituting layoffs might help the short term at the expense of talent needed for the longevity of the organization. All decisions have trade-offs, and this is one of the nastiest to deal with.
- A middle manager might have to decide on her role in the success of her team and the entire organization. Development of her team means more than spending allocated training dollars. She has to consider the developmental activities for her team in the light of the bigger needs of the organization.
- An individual contributor needs to take responsibility for his own development plan and not wait for a boss to provide opportunities. This turns out to be a rather contentious issue in many organizations. Sometimes it seems as if the boss is abdicating responsibility for taking care of his workers when he says, "It's your career, so take care of it." On the other hand, he may feel as if people are waiting to be spoon-fed and doesn't consider that to be part of his responsibility.

BUILDING YOUR SKILLS

Here are a few more techniques leaders at all levels, in any contexts, can use to improve their skill of deciding.

CHECKLIST FOR EFFECTIVE DECISION MAKING

In spite of all the things that can go wrong in decision making, research and experience show a series of factors that contribute to effective methods for deciding. Try running through this check for effective decision making:

Have you:

- Shown a clear link to root issue?
- Canvassed a wide range of alternatives?
- Been aware of the process for decision making and shared it with other decision makers if the decision is collective?
- Made a clear link to the full range of goals and the value added implicated by the choice?
- Weighed the values of the alternatives?
- Considered possible consequences of each alternative, both positive and negative?
- Searched for new information relevant to the decision?
- Assimilated new relevant information, even if it did not support the course of action you initially preferred?
- Involved input about and from those affected?
- Included a plan for adoption and contingency plans?
- Challenged outworn decisions?

TRY A DECISION SCORECARD

Try improving the quality of your decisions by keeping track of them for a month. Evaluate your "scorecard" and see how often you are following a good process. What did you do that got you your successes? What caused your failures? Look at problems from another person's point of view, and then develop a plan from that perspective (for example, what would you do if you were the union shop steward and you were preparing for the contract negotiation?).

EXPAND YOUR REPERTOIRE

Explicitly learn the different models of decision making, and apply them to various cases, perhaps to decisions that have already been made. Assess the outcomes to help choose what method to use under what conditions. Most bookstores have books on different approaches, such as consensus decision making, building decision criteria matrices, and multivoting. One book we have found particularly helpful in terms of tools for decision making and other tasks aligned to the Prepared Mind is *The Quality Toolbox* by Nancy Tague.[16]

BE EXPLICIT IN PRACTICE

When making a group decision, make the process of decision making and the definitions of the issues and terms clear so everyone is considering similar information. To prevent groupthink and encourage critical analysis, assign roles to the decision team so they can formally introduce different perspectives to the decision. This helps everyone show their thinking.

USE A DECISION ADVISER

Have an outsider come in to watch your decision making, especially group decision-making process, and analyze with you how you go through it and what it leads to.

REMEMBER THAT TWO HEADS ARE BETTER THAN ONE

If you face an unfamiliar situation that requires a decision, try for a convergence of ideas and experiences from many different perspectives. You may want to make rules for advising and decision making explicit at the outset—for example, who will have the final word, what questions you want the group to answer, what perspective you want each person to take. All of this will prevent groupthink and confusion and bad affect over the process. The idea, though, is for a group of good minds to converge on an issue and, with a healthy dynamic, come to possibly a new way of viewing the situation and well-thought-through decision.

REVIEW OLD DECISIONS

Few organizations we know of have a mechanism or rule in place for revisiting old decisions, old assumptions, and the status quo as a matter of routine. Those who design for continuous change and innovation, however, usually include a regular assessment piece in their process that looks at what was decided and why and whether the same reasons exist later. Some people have a rule that they do not buy any new clothes until they go through their closets and pitch or give away those clothes they no longer wear. You might devise a similar rule for sorting out the closet of old decisions before packing new decisions in on top of them. Besides keeping insights fresh, it might also help to reduce information overload.

OVERCOME RATIONALIZATION

When we think of commitment in decision making, we usually think of commitment to a particular decision. In fact, sometimes we become so emotionally committed to a decision that we rationalize and defend it even if it turns out not to work very well. To help yourself and others overcome this tendency, consciously commit yourself to the decision-making process, not just to the decision and its results, and model that commitment for others. This may mean teaching people different methods for decision making and requiring them to "show their work" for reasons of understanding and coaching rather than for reasons of catching them in error. In this respect, the skill of enabling can help overcome a common error in decision making by helping people think beyond the immediate decision and fine-tune their skills of reasoning, observing, imagining, and whatever other skills may improve their process.

MORE QUESTIONS TO CONSIDER

- **Bug list.** What bugs you, or your customers, or your employees? Find them, list them, and fix them.

  List ten bugs that, if eliminated, would increase your value to your customers. List ten bugs that you have about your suppliers or customers. Jot down potential solutions to the bugs you have described.

- **Now you've done it!** One of the premises of systems thinking is that every solution brings about its own set of new problems. (The insecticide DDT was a solution; chlorofluorocarbon refrigerants were a solution; inner-city housing projects were a solution.)

  Write down the potential long-term consequences of a problem you recently solved. What might happen, and did you take that into consideration?

- **Old dogs and new tricks.** Study companies and industries that changed (GE today is not the same as GE in 1930, for example).

Study other companies that did not change (Railway Express). What's around; what isn't? Why? What new tricks does your company have to learn? Keep a list of things you'd like to change some day.

GO FORTH AND DECIDE

Make a commitment to leave this chapter prepared to apply the skill of deciding, even if it is with just one strategy in mind. The strategy could be to add structure to your process, which could mean clearly defining and framing the decision, identifying plenty of alternatives, and using different techniques to decide among them. The strategy could be around overcoming the reuse of outdated mental models. Or the strategy could give you practice in developing commitment to the decision-making process, not just to the decision itself.

No sensible decision can be made any longer without taking into account not only the world as it is, but the world as it will be.

—*Isaac Asimov*

Prepared Mind leaders have a flexible and influential decision-making style. They adapt decisions to the emotional and political constraints around them. They also influence decisions objectively by adding structure to the process. Structure ensures quality assumptions, robust alternatives, and solid criteria for selecting among them.[17]

CHAPTER EIGHT

LEARNING
Keeping a Developmental Mind-Set

Learning is like rowing upstream; not to advance is to
drop back.
CHINESE PROVERB

This chapter is a bit different from the other skill chapters in that
we are going to launch our discussion of the skill of learning
around a history question. The reason is that the process of learning that ripples across our mental maps and ignites the Prepared
Mind to consider new opportunities and relationships that it didn't
consider before is, almost always, set off by a question that intrigues
us and is not easily answered. With that in mind, here is the question: Which two of the founding fathers of the United States died
on July 4, 1826?

U.S. history buffs or Trivial Pursuit champions may want to skip
to the next paragraph. However, most of us do not know the answer to that question, but we do care enough to read on and learn
the answer, don't we? Why? What would make a question like that
interesting to you, a business leader? Does it have much to do with
your life, your values, or your business? Maybe it does not, on the
surface. However, finding the answer to a question like this one
sets off processes that are very similar—in fact, are the processes
you go through when you are trying to find or construct an answer
to a business issue. This chapter will show you how a common concept like learning is actually a complex, rigorous enterprise for
building knowledge, which is the underlying lifeblood of business
in the twenty-first century.

DEFINING LEARNING

When one of the former justices of the U.S. Supreme Court was asked how he defined pornography, he answered, "I know it when I see it." The definition of learning is a lot like that. All of us know learning when we see it or experience it, but we are often hard-pressed to say exactly what it is. Some have said that learning is a change in behavior. To that we would say that a change in behavior is a potential result of learning. However, haven't you learned something that did not cause an immediate or direct change of behavior? Some have said that learning is the storing of knowledge in long-term memory. To that we would say learning sounds a lot like remembering, and, in fact, storing and recalling knowledge from our mental maps is a necessary part of the learning process. Some have said that learning is a change in thinking. To that we would ask if it is a change in *what* we think and know or in *how* we think. The answer, by the way, is probably "both."

For purposes of the Prepared Mind, we will define learning as a process for changing the content, and the connections between the content, of one's mental map, expanding capacity and capability for a variety of actions.

We know there has been much written about the concept of organizational learning in the past twenty years. The question as to whether organizations can learn, in the way we think of the process of learning, is still under debate. The Prepared Mind will focus on individual learning, while acknowledging that there is some similar process that occurs for collectives to develop and change their mental maps and cultures.

SEVEN C'S OF LEARNING

Since learning is a process, there are factors that occur to activate and enable the process. We will use our history question to illustrate these factors, which we call the seven C's of learning at work. The seven C's are:

- Compelling questions
- Conscious discontentment
- Content

- Connections
- Confidence
- Construction
- Capability building

COMPELLING QUESTIONS

Go back to our opening question and ask why this bit of American history trivia might be compelling. If we are American, and even if we are not, what Alexis de Tocqueville called "an experiment in Democracy," in speaking about the United States, is familiar to our minds, resonant or dissonant with our values, and intriguing to our implicit curiosity of wondering what the men who put the whole thing together must have been like. Even if we are not fascinated by the history of the United States, most of us reading the question are struck by an irony embedded in it. We know that July 4 is the birthday of the United States and is the only national holiday named after its date. The anniversary of the country's birth is also the anniversary of the deaths of two men who gave it birth. There is mystery in that. Humans accept mysteries as often unanswerable or unexplainable, but we still try to figure them out. This particular question, since it points to coincidental life and death, even has an air of the metaphysical to it, and most of us are curious to know that which we cannot know by our five senses, that which is beyond the physical. It is human nature to want to know about irony and mystery greater than ourselves, whether that something bigger has to do with community, country, ideals, ideas (such as democracy), God, or what some people think of as "the great unknown."

While we tend to spend most of our time focused on the concrete, people, especially those who are interested in cultivating a Prepared Mind, are willing to entertain the abstract and see how they can make it real. The founding fathers of America had that capacity. Familiarity with what we already know, resonance or dissonance with our values, intrigue with mystery, and a sense of connection to something bigger than ourselves combine to make us feel discontent enough with our own state of knowing (or not knowing) to compel us to take the step to find new knowledge about it, to learn.

What are some of the compelling questions in your opportunity space? What are the questions that, if answered, would make a difference in your organization's ability to thrive? Consider the problems and opportunities facing your organization and see if you can separate the trivial from the compelling questions. If you need a starting point, consider the following questions that Peter Drucker asked in his 1992 essay, "Planning for Uncertainty":[1]

- What has already happened that will create the future?
- What changes in industry and market structure, in basic values, and in science and technology have already occurred but have yet to have full impact?
- What are the trends in economic and societal structure? And how do they affect our business?

CONSCIOUS DISCONTENTMENT

In order to be compelled to learn, we have to feel a conscious discontentment with our current state of affairs. It could be that something we want to know is not currently answerable unless we take the trouble to learn. Or perhaps achieving some goal or solving a problem is unattainable unless we take the trouble to learn. In other words, we have to be discontent with not knowing, and we have to be willing to consciously do something about it that might possibly change our minds.

Call to mind the times when you have been uncomfortable with not knowing an answer or not understanding a situation at work. Was there something about the situation that was familiar, even vaguely so, yet not an exact match to what you already knew? Did the situation bump up against your values and beliefs, in either resonance or dissonance? Was there something about the situation that seemed ironic or paradoxical with what you already knew and considered to be normal? Was there something about the situation that connected to something bigger than yourself that you cared about connecting to? How did the discontentment of not knowing or not understanding make you feel? What did you feel was at stake by not learning? What did you imagine was possible if you did learn and come to see the situation differently?

Whether it was fear, anger, sorrow, curiosity, passion, or competitiveness that drove you, there was affect in your motivation to learn. Even emotional responses are stored in our minds and are part of our mental maps and learning process. Most of us have emotional responses prepared and ready to pull out and use when we realize that we are in the dark and learning is required. Human beings do not like to live in uncertainty and the unknown, especially when things like money, time, reputation, people's jobs, and business opportunities are at stake. We will go to great lengths to fill in the blanks of the unknown by pretending that we do know and rush to decide and act. Or, if you are Prepared Mind leader, you will admit the need to learn from and with other people, realizing that your learning may lead you to construct an answer where one does not currently exist. However, no leader is content to just let the world happen to them without making some attempt to learn and adapt with it.

At times, this may require learning new content. At other times, it may require making new connections between content. Often it requires both.

CONTENT AND CONNECTIONS

Our minds are like our organizations or, more accurately, our networks of business relationships and transactions. They are complex and often messy but nevertheless full of things that weave themselves into an organizing scheme where we can recognize, retrieve, and add to them quickly. It is artificial to separate the content in our minds and the connections between the content, because the two are continuously working together in an inseparable web of cognition, all in service to our knowing more than we did a moment before.

Think of all of the things that are in your head: expertise, models, memories, standard operating procedures, storage, rules, files on people, hot links and buttons, communication channels, outcomes of various degrees of value, structures that vary in their degree of hierarchy, evaluation systems, rewards and punishments, stories, labels, and all the other things that help us know who we are, where we are, and where to put new incoming information in our minds. In the business world, we tend to call this collection of content and how it works together "the corporation," "the firm," "the organization," or even "the culture." In the world of learning, we tend to call this content in our minds "schema." In other words, our minds have organizing schemes, just as our businesses do, and everything we do is determined by the content that already exists in our minds and the connections between that content and the incoming new information. In the Prepared Mind, we have broadened the use and visual imagery of the word *schema* and instead have chosen to refer to mental maps. Our maps give us direction as to which way to travel with our train of thought and suggest to us what we might expect to find and where. If we are in entirely new territory, we turn to cues on our maps like directional diagrams and landmarks to help us make up new routes. We do the same things in our minds.

The content within our mental maps is declarative knowledge, or the kind of things we can say that we know that are real facts or seem real or factual to us. Examples of declarative knowledge include dates, numbers, names, directions, principles, beliefs, and other things we take as fact that we have acquired through our prior use of the skills of observing, reflecting, and learning.

The connections are the well-worn paths or paths we form that move between chunks of content and incorporate new content. We think of this as procedural knowledge or "know-how" and conditional knowledge, "know-why" and "know-when." Connecting knowledge includes things like rules, decision-making processes, if-then conditions, procedures for processing and storing information (learning, remembering, reflecting, representing things mentally, imagining, making metaphors and analogies, reasoning, and other skills and processes that are included in the Prepared Mind).

In the spirit of Malcolm Gladwell's *The Tipping Point,* Prepared Minds are great mavens (collectors and sharers of content) and great connectors (mentally and socially).[2] Have you ever noticed that those you consider as having Prepared Minds seem to have a lot of knowledge (random and otherwise) that other people don't? They also seem to see and make connections between knowledge (especially between old and new) that other people do not. Why is that? The answer to that question lies in our fifth, sixth, and seventh C's: *confidence, construction,* and *capability building.*

CONFIDENCE

In the world of knowing what makes people tick, motivation theory and learning theory are closely related. One of the leading theories of motivation is expectancy theory, which says, in a nutshell, that in order for people to be motivated to act (which includes learning), they need four things:

1. *Valence,* or an imagined future or outcome that represents, in their minds, something of value to them.
2. *First- and second-level outcomes.* This means that humans quickly reason that if they take a specific action (for example, go to a search engine about that gnawing founding fathers July 4 death date question). The first-level outcome, a search, will lead to a second-level outcome (for example, giving information listing the founding fathers of the United States and their death dates or even an article with the two names in it).
3. *Instrumentality,* which is related to the first- and second-level outcomes. That is, we have to believe that doing the first thing will lead to the desired second thing, and that will get us closer to the ultimate value we are trying to create for ourselves by learning.
4. *Expectancy.* We have to have confidence and expect that the whole process that we undertook will lead us to our answer and deliver the value in it for us.

In order for us to prepare our minds by learning, we have to be confident that the answer can be found or constructed. We plot a route in our mental maps that tells us that if we take certain actions, they will lead to certain outcomes that will eventually lead us to an answer for our question.

CONSTRUCTION

In the industrial era of the late nineteenth and early twentieth centuries, the dominant theory of learning and motivation was behaviorism. Behaviorism focuses on what can be observed, not what goes on in the mind, and it explains learning as conditioned responses to rewards and punishments for exhibiting specified behaviors. There are still a lot of behaviorist assumptions present in business practice and business books today. How do you recognize it? You may see learning defined specifically as "a change in behavior," and that it is cultivated through feedback loops to the behavior. Many people think that individuals and organizations learn this way. Whatever you get rewarded for by the external environment, you will keep doing. Whatever you get punished for or ignored for by the external environment, you will quit doing (or you will do it to get attention because, to some people, negative attention is better than no attention at all). We have heard the mantra that "people will do what they get rewarded for." This is partially true. However, this is not the whole story of human behavior, including human learning, and it is not enough of an answer to motivate human learning and behavior in a service, knowledge business where there is often no one best behavior to reward and punish, and the feedback loops are not controlled by an immediate boss or holder of rewards. If we want people to act freely, quickly, and wisely, we need to attend to what is on their minds and how they work, so they have a platform on which to build a wide repertoire of appropriate decisions and actions.

Think of the Prepared Minds you know. Isn't there something of a self-starter characteristic to them? They are motivated to think, do, and learn beyond, or even in spite of, what their immediate environment tells them to do. And what if the reward is delayed or uncertain? Don't the Prepared Minds you know seek to learn and understand anyway? They construct responses and knowledge on the spot, based on what they already know and the demands of the presenting situation. The content and connections we already have in our minds, our mental maps, in interaction with data we have coming to us from the outside, and the data we believe come from somewhere deep within our hearts and souls (for example, beliefs), determine things like what we observe, what we challenge, how we reason, how we make decisions, what we imagine, how we feel and go about enabling others, and what and how we learn. Our ability to spontaneously construct meaning on the spot and figure out a plan of action based on that meaning is uniquely human, and is more and more what is being called for in today's leaders and workers at all levels.

The Prepared Mind is always under construction, building on and renovating its content and its connections, searching for meaningful connections between what it knows. Like a building under construction, the Prepared Mind has scaffolds built in it that span a wide range of knowledge domains (for example, history—we have not forgotten the founding fathers question—economics, art, and so on) that we use to stand on to make new meaning. Leaders also help others build those scaffolds so they too can build their capability to stand and learn and think on their feet and act intelligently in the midst of uncertainty. When we hear a leader tell a story, reference a sports metaphor, or recall a moment in the company's history, they are providing a scaffold for people to stand on so they can make meaning out of something new by relating it to what they already know.

Capability Building

The seventh C stands for *capability building,* a primary goal of the Prepared Mind leader, linking together the skills of learning and enabling. The result of a continuously improving capability is that you get better and better and faster and faster at things that not only look difficult but are difficult. One of the unique capabilities of a leader with a Prepared Mind is that he or she learns to sense, make sense, decide, and act more quickly and with better alignment between core values and environmental changes, resulting in leading the way versus reacting to others' actions. Prepared Minds have a greater capability for innovation, because innovation is about knowledge creation, and that is what learning does. This capability to think about the same situation from many different angles, seemingly at once, and understand the meaning from these multiple perspectives is the key to mental agility and a sure sign of someone who has a prepared mind. Like physical agility, you do not gain mental agility unless you discipline and prepare yourself by working out. You have to learn how to prepare your mind. In fact, you have to learn how to learn. Underneath the definition of learning and the seven C's are the anchoring concepts of experience, prior knowledge, and transfer. Understanding these will equip you better for acquiring mental agility and the ability to learn more deeply and more quickly.

Anchoring Concepts of Learning

Underlying the seven C's of learning are experience, prior knowledge, and transfer, all of which anchor the abilities to learn and make use of learning across situations.

EXPERIENCE

In the world of work, there is an implicit assumption that the more experience a person has had, the more the person knows. It is why we ask for resumés and work histories. Yet experience alone does not lead to learning and knowledge. Experience is the way we describe the meaning we attach to a cluster of closely related events, interactions, or knowledge cues. It makes sense that if learning is, in large part, the construction of meaning and connections between information we receive, then the way we describe that meaning will suggest what, if anything, we learn from it and how we use it going forward. If we have a negative experience with our boss and we let it mean simply that the boss is a jerk, we might feel better but will personally not learn much from it. If, on the other hand, we have a negative interaction with the boss, and the meaning we attach includes an assumption that we could have perhaps managed the interchange of ideas more clearly, we may learn better how to interact with the boss and have a different, preferred experience. Experiences give us information that we can choose to let fall by the wayside or that we can process and turn into a bank of knowledge for the future. That is what learning does: build our bank of knowledge capital. Experience gives us the impetus for learning and the content of our learning.

Experiences can be directly related over time, as has been the traditional case of professions. If, for instance, I have multiple experiences of one type, I am a doctor. If I have experiences of another type, I am a lawyer. The experiences, however, that the various professions are having are now more varied and require them to learn new things, like how to do business as well as practice medicine and practice law. In this case, experience is an impetus for learning.

We know from the world of adult learning that indirect experiences can also bear on our learning and performance at work. We know one executive who requires his employees to volunteer at a local food and homeless shelter. Besides being a generous thing to do, he wants them to have the experience of seeing that most of the world does not have job security. He hopes that they internalize the experience to think about work differently and translate that into being more proactive and less complacent at work. However, as a leader, if he wants his hope to become a reality, he will need to help them practice the skills of reflection and learning so the experience takes on more meaning than charity or just something the boss wanted them to do.

Experience needs to be combined with the skill of reflection in order to be internalized and take on meaning that can then turn into principles, attitudes, skills, and ideas to be used and reused later. Also, experiences do not happen to a blank slate. Experiences in part take their meaning from what we have already learned from previous experience. New experience is affected by prior knowledge.

PRIOR KNOWLEDGE

Prior knowledge is the content and connections of our mental maps and can be classified in three ways: knowledge that (declarative knowledge), knowledge how (procedural knowledge), and knowledge why and when (conditional knowledge).

When we have a new experience and take in new data from our environment, if we attach any interest and importance to this information at all, we search our mental maps for a place to put it. We ask ourselves if our new information looks like anything else we already know or believe or declare to be fact. If the new information from experience requires us to do something, we ask ourselves if we already have the know-how to do the job (procedural knowledge). If the new information or experience is ambiguous or challenging or seems to have a lot of interdependencies attached, we ask ourselves if we know why it is important and if we know when and where to use it. Helping people learn to develop conditional knowledge is a huge and imperative task for Prepared Mind leaders in the knowledge era, given all the ambiguity and complexity most of us have to deal with on a given day. It helps to focus our energy and knowledge if we know why something is important and when and where our contributions might be important to the outcome.

When experience mixes with prior knowledge, three levels of learning can occur: assimilation, tuning, and restructuring.[3] Level 1 is simple assimilation. We knew something before, and we know more of it or more about it now. The next level is tuning. We knew something before, but the new experience does not quite fit it, so we have to tune our mental maps with new categories or skills in order to be able to retain and use the new experience. A lot of training is aimed at this level of learning. Failure to observe or see changes in the environment as different or affecting us often comes from our wanting to do assimilation or tuning when deeper, more difficult learning is required.

The third level, restructuring, is the most difficult and often the most necessary in times of intense change. It means we have to create entire new categories and or a series of new connections on our mental maps in order even to think about the new situation. We literally have to change our minds and see things in new ways. For those searching for opportunity space, the ability to learn at the level of restructuring is imperative. The Prepared Mind consciously restructures itself, not necessarily throwing out the old but being more agile and open about new content and new connections.

TRANSFER

Let's say we combine our prior knowledge and experience and use the seven C's effectively to create new knowledge for ourselves. The ultimate benefit of learning occurs when we can take what we have learned and transfer it to different situations. If the new situation is the same context as before, this is easier to do than if the new context is different. Have you ever followed CEOs from company to company who diagnose the same problems and employ the same solutions at each company? Maybe they are even known to be great turnaround artists or whatever the set of complex skills is that they employ across companies. They are transferring what they learned in one company to another. The danger is if the context really is not the same.

If we acknowledge differences across situations, some small and some big, we are still faced with knowing what and how to transfer our knowledge to the new situation. Educational scholars have not figured this out to their satisfaction. However, one thing they do know is that you have to look below the surface of similarities for deeper indicators of what is the same and what is different. You have to do due diligence to know what prior knowledge to use and what new things you are going to have to learn. The first hundred days of many CEOs' lives in a new company are about doing this due diligence up close and personal. Another thing research tells us about transfer is that we have to reflect on any learning experience to pull out general principles and concepts to test and apply across situations. We have to make sense and make meaning by forming categorical take-aways. That is why learning in organizations is so difficult. We are so focused on doing that as soon as one project is over that we go on to the next without real time for reflection or consideration as to where to store and how to share what we learned. Yet this is key to turning learning into a true capability builder for your company.

CONNECTING TO THE CONCEPTS: ANCHORED EXERCISES TO IMPROVE THE SKILL OF LEARNING

PREVIEWS, IN-VIEWS, AND REVIEWS

As we mention in other parts of this book, after-action reviews, as developed by the U.S. Army and now used in many corporations, are a useful tool for reflecting backward and learning from experience. We have built on that method and worked with companies to do previews, in-views, and reviews before, during, and after action.

Learning is goal directed, so it makes sense that we would review goals before we make a decision or act and preview or imagine the experience we would like to have to meet our goals. Keeping our goals in mind reminds us what we want our pending experience to look like and why we want to engage in the first place, based on our personal, professional, and practical business goals.

During an experience or action, we do well to take a breath and ask ourselves how well our goals are in view, given our current experience. We do well to ask ourselves or others, "How are we doing?" "Are we on track for our goals?" "What do we see happening that we did not expect?" "Does what we see happening remind us of anything we have experienced before [capitalizing on prior knowledge]?" "What, if anything, should we do with this new information?" This taking a moment to stop, check, compare, and internalize our status is learning and suggests to us how we can proceed more effectively. We can employ a version of the Daily Examen, suggested within Chapter Ten, as a method for learning in action or doing an in-view check.

After-action reviews help us learn from the immediate past, as long as we have enough feedback to tell us what happened as a result of our action. Did our experience meet our expectations?

Combined, we see previews, in-views, and reviews as a powerful way to learn with experience.

READ WIDELY

Reading well is one of those habits most of us take for granted as a good thing. From our earliest days of childhood, learning to read is set as a common priority within our culture. Why? Reading builds our bank of prior knowledge, including the building blocks of knowledge such as language, which we can then transfer across domains. Prepared Minds read all kinds of books and weave the influence into their work through word use, examples of great leaders, strategies used by ancient warriors, or ethical principles, for example. Prepared Minds are interested minds, and minds that read.

PULL OUT THE PRINCIPLES

Whether it be in reading or interactions or events, whenever we have an experience, we do well to learn from it by stepping back and pulling out the principles learned that can be generalized and applied in other situations. This pulling out general principles is key to learning transfer. Is this the same as best practices? Not at all. Best practices do not always pull out the principles—the why and the what. They often pull out the how. Principles can be gathered by asking questions: "What did we see as a success factor that we have seen play out time and time again?" "What is the underlying theme that summarizes your theory about why it did or did not go as planned?"

SEEING THE FAMILIAR

Whenever we are in a new situation, we have to be open to its being new. Yet we learn quickly if we can ask, "What about this have I seen before?" Consultants and new executives who can walk into

a company and figure it out quickly are relying on the familiar—
on their prior knowledge from other situations that at least gives
them clues as to what to look for and how to act.

PERSONAL RESEARCH QUESTIONS

If you are an academic or a scientist, you are always walking around
with a mental or literal sheet of interesting questions you would
like to research if you had the time. Successful businesspeople do
the same thing. They notice phenomena in the market or in the
company that others do not see, and they ask questions to try to
hypothesize or explain them. Even if they do not find the answer,
the process of asking the questions, collecting data, and playing
with ideas teaches them more about the situation than they would
have known before. Keep a list of three to five personal research
questions going at all times. You will start learning more in your
day-to-day work and employing the other Prepared Mind skills in
service to answering your question.

THE COMPANY WE KEEP

We are never too old or too big or too powerful for mentors. The
people we keep around us, formal mentors or not, should be people with experiences and prior knowledge different from those we
have had who can challenge us, enable us, and help us learn. Prepared Mind leaders seek other prepared minds for the company
they keep.

THE CYCLE OF LEARNING

Experience is a good teacher, but not the only teacher. Consider
the questions posed in Figure 8.1 as a starting point to trigger your
learning journey.

1. WHAT DON'T I KNOW ABOUT WHAT I'VE SENSED?

There are problems and opportunities in our opportunity space
that sometimes just seem strange. The danger we face is that we
might be tempted to ignore them because we don't know anything

FIGURE 8.1. THE SENSE-RESPONSE CYCLE OF LEARNING

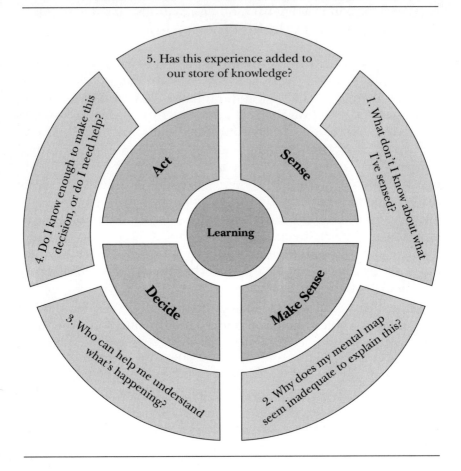

about them or, worse yet, force-fit them into our existing mental maps.

2. WHY DOES MY MENTAL MAP SEEM INADEQUATE TO EXPLAIN THIS?

In our attempt to simplify the world around us into clear cause-and-effect relationships, we often oversimplify our mental maps and disregard the complexity of the world in which we live. Peter Vaill coined the term "permanent white water" in an effort to provide a meaningful metaphor for today's business and social environment.[4] He also identified five conditions that point to a need for robust mental maps:

- Permanent white-water conditions are full of surprises.
- Complex systems tend to produce novel problems.
- Permanent white-water conditions feature events that are messy and ill structured.
- White-water events are often extremely costly.
- Permanent white-water conditions raise the problem of recurrence.

Do your mental maps allow these conditions? If not, what do you have to learn to increase their robustness?

3. WHO CAN HELP ME UNDERSTAND WHAT'S HAPPENING?

Connections happen in our head and in our social networks. Who do you know who can help you understand the situation, especially if you are faced with a white-water situation as described above?

4. DO I KNOW ENOUGH TO MAKE THIS DECISION, OR DO I NEED HELP?

Even if you can develop a conceptual understanding of the situation, do you have enough knowledge and experience to make an informed decision? There is nothing sadder than to watch an executive make a decision when the people around him realize that he does not have the requisite knowledge and should not make the decision.

5. HAS THIS EXPERIENCE ADDED TO OUR STORE OF KNOWLEDGE?

Mortui vivos docent: "the dead teach the living." Just as the body of medical knowledge is expanded through the use of autopsies, businesses can and should increase their body of knowledge by reviewing past decisions and actions. Whether the result was more or less than expected, there is always something to learn. Unfortunately, most organizations do a dismal job of learning from past decisions. If things work as planned, we move on. If things do not work as planned, we forget and then move on.

BENEFITS, RISKS, AND CHALLENGES OF LEARNING

All of the Prepared Mind skills have benefits, risks, and challenges associated with their development and use. Here is our starting list for the skill of learning; add to, subtract from, and modify it to fit your reality.

BENEFITS OF IMPROVING YOUR SKILL OF LEARNING

Improving a skill takes time and energy, and before expending either, we need to be assured that the benefits are worth the effort. Consider the following points.

A Richer Opportunity Space
The more you know, the more you see. People with wide-ranging views and knowledge of the world are in a better position to see obscure problems and opportunities.

Richer Networks
Specialists can have a great conversation with other specialists, but they rarely develop networks outside their field. Deep generalists, in contrast, are capable of conversations across a range of specialties.

Up-to-Date Experience
You have to answer this question for yourself. Does a person with twenty years of experience have twenty years of experience, or one year of experience twenty times over?

Better Capability and Capacity
You are better able to learn, to work through the sense–make sense–decide–act cycle, with a richer store of knowledge to pull from and the ability to go more quickly and with greater ease.

Developmental Mind-Set

Never settle or grow stale. You are always poised to learn and improve and to encourage those around you to do the same.

RISKS OF LEARNING

An overemphasis on a newly developed skill can result in experiencing downside risks. Consider the following points.

The Potential to Be Considered a Dilettante, a Dabbler

Some of us are so fascinated with the world at large that we scurry about learning a bit of everything, but without developing expertise in anything. The Prepared Mind, though, moves us to decide and act so our learning has a purpose.

Dilution of Relevancy If Technology Shifts Rapidly

Engineers with deep knowledge of analog circuits found themselves suddenly obsolete as digital circuits took center stage. Sales representatives with great relationship-building skills found themselves moved aside as technology-based supply chains came to the fore. Learning more than one thing and how to apply expertise in different situations is imperative for staying relevant. Many of the other Prepared Mind skills, such as observing and reflecting, are not about technical knowledge but help us learn to be strategic as well.

Frustration When You Cannot Apply All You Know

Sometimes the timing, the culture, or the leadership around us do not allow us to use all we have learned, and that can be frustrating. But by using the skills of challenging and enabling, we can help cultivate the environment so it is riper for learning.

CHALLENGES TO LEARNING

We know that we should improve our skills; however, we are all faced with barriers and obstacles. Consider the following points.

It Takes Time

As organizations have focused on getting lean, they have intentionally or unintentionally added more work to do for the people who remain. Unfortunately, company-sponsored learning events have taken a back seat. Interestingly, Toyota Corporation has *added* training facilities while most of the rest of the industrial world has reduced capabilities. Especially if we develop the skills of observing, reflecting, and reasoning to go along with learning, we can learn in the midst of doing and even be gathering and creating knowledge as we are deciding. Also, learning is not necessarily training. We can learn anytime, anywhere we are weighing new information against what we know and are open to reconsidering what we know or how we know it. Learning, for many Prepared Mind leaders, is a way of life.

It Takes Effort

True learning comes from effort, which is the normal avenue for organizations' view of learning. What we have noticed is increased interest in events that focus on thinking processes rather than the acquisition of predigested "knowledge." Learning anchoring concepts like metacognition and other Prepared Mind skills such as reflecting helps us consider how we think, not just what we think. Observing how others process information and asking them to talk out loud about their thinking can give us models for thinking through things in new ways. We can also apply the skill of challenging to ourselves. If we are resisting something new, we may ask ourselves, "What could we be learning from this?"

BACK TO THE OPENING QUESTION

The two founding fathers featured in our opening question appear to have been Prepared Minds and used them wisely across domains in their lives. Who are these men?

As a way of showing you the power of constructing new answers by integrating new questions and information with prior content and connections, let us help you figure out the answer. The first tip uses the internal mental process known as analogical reasoning (looking for similarities to what we already know) as a way to tap into *prior* knowledge. Here are a few clues. What presidents of the United States fondly refer to each other as 43 and 41? If you answered George H. W. Bush and George W. Bush, you would be right. Now if they are the second father-and-son team to become presidents of the United States, who were the first? Answer: John Adams and John Quincy Adams. As you can see, if you are using the Prepared Mind skill of reasoning, specifically analogical reasoning in this case, you can figure out that at least one of the Founding Fathers who died on the same day was John Adams or John Quincy Adams. In addition, you remember the original question refers to founding fathers. In that case, John Adams must be part of the answer because John Quincy Adams was not part of the signing of the Declaration of Independence. You are continuing to construct meaning around the different pieces of information you have, with the expectancy or confidence that you can put the pieces together and solve the mystery. Great! You have half the answer.

But what other founding father shared John Adams's death date? Let's go back and tap into your working memory, or that part of your memory you just used in your reasoning. We are speaking of the use of the 41 and 43 to refer to recent presidents. In the spirit of using numbers associated with the order of presidents, what if we used 2 and 3 to refer to the presidents in our question? For those who have a good content store of American history in your minds, this new information from the environment, combined with your prior knowledge, might be enough to figure out the answer. What if you do not have a rich store of American history in your mind and do not know who the second and third presidents of the United States were? What if you had another trigger given to you? What connection would the word *Monticello* bring to mind? Or what if we gave you just one more piece of information about the person's special role in the founding of the United States (author of the Declaration of Independence)? By now, almost everyone has figured out the second person is Thomas Jefferson. So John Adams and Thomas Jefferson both died on the same day: July 4, 1826. We are quite confident that this now learned fact will be retained in your long-term memory for potential use. Why? Because you went through the process of learning. Learning creates knowledge capital that grows with use to build more capital and cannot be taken away. Learning is the "stickiest" of the Prepared Mind skills in that what you learn sticks with you. The question is, are you open to learning and unlearning when necessary?

Applied Learning: The Talent Problem

Here are three examples of the kinds of questions and activities a Prepared Mind leader might consider as she thinks about the talent issue from the learning point of view:

- An executive should learn about what motivates the people in her organization. What would make this organization an employer of choice for the best talent in the marketplace? What problems and opportunities are entering the organization's opportunity space?
- A middle manager might need to learn the basics of the new technologies that help improve communication and knowledge sharing.
- An individual contributor should learn enough about the issues, tools, and techniques of cross-functional team members. She'll need this knowledge if they are to have meaningful conversations.

BUILDING YOUR SKILLS

One of the easiest ways to learn and refine skills is to use experiences from your own life as the basis for reflection and practice. After you "test" the skill in your own life, then you begin applying it to other situations. Look for consistencies across situations, as well as nuanced tweaks of the application that need to occur with changes in context. With that in mind, we offer you strategies for practicing the skill of learning.

YOUR TURN

Reflect on your formal education—what you studied and why you studied it. How do you incorporate it into your life and vocation now? Do you have a personal philosophy that guides your action in business, governance, relationships, and more? How do you learn from others you agree with and those you do not agree with? How do you take time to write and reflect? In what ways do you take time away from the action to question your own preparedness and recharge your batteries before reentering the messiness of doing business? How do you deal with paradox and remain balanced and true while negotiating with rivals?

Navigate the Seven C's

Knowing and following the Seven C's of Learning are the best way we know to keep your Prepared Mind skill of Learning effective. In addition to these tips, we encourage you to build tips and learning strategies of your own by taking the three anchoring concepts—experience, prior knowledge and transfer, and engineering strategies—to navigate the seven C's.

- Compelling questions. Start your day with a compelling question, and record how many events of the day directly or indirectly address the question. For example, you could ask yourself, "How did my day add to or detract from progress in my opportunity space?"
- Conscious discontentment. Write down a few things that keep coming back to make you wonder or bug you. These are pointers to areas ripe for learning.
- Content and connections. Map part of your mind's scheme (content and connections) around a certain issue or habit you want to understand better—something you are consciously discontent about. Trace why you think what you think and do what you do using a "talk-aloud method." This is better if done with a partner.
- Confidence. Map out your learning logic or line of sight. Begin with your end goal or value in mind, and work backward until you get to what you need to learn in order to enable you to do what you need to do that will then lead to what you want.
- Construction. List all the learning opportunities you have before you, and picture yourself as the architect of your learning. Which things will cause you to start from the ground up,

meaning you have little prior knowledge? Which things could you learn with a little help or scaffolding from others or from the tools in your environment? Which things are structurally sound but could use some trimming? Which learning opportunities would put you in direct access to a life goal? This might be a good way to do your performance and learning plan for the coming year. Another fundamental question to ask yourself, on top of all these practical questions, lies at the heart of the constructivist approach to learning: Which of these learning opportunities will be most meaningful to you, and why?

- Capability building. Start with a capability you want to build in your own life, and work backward as to the five steps you could take where you would expect to learn and develop that capability. Choose steps you can really do.

MORE QUESTIONS TO CONSIDER

- **Déjà vu?** 600 percent growth! Hackers! Concern about financial transactions! The Internet? No. These were problems that the telegraph industry faced in the mid-1800s. You may be able to see part of the Internet future by understanding the history of the telegraph.

  Look at your current business or life situation. List possible historical technologies, practices, or events that might provide insight. Now go learn about the future by studying some history.

- **Listen to the experts.** During World War I, Henry Ford retooled to manufacture submarines. The venture was not successful, partly because he was too arrogant to listen to navy experts. Swallow your pride.

  Go to three people you should be listening to but don't because of your pride. Document their comments regarding your problem.

- *To Engineer Is Human.* This is the title of a wonderful book written by Henry Petroski in the mid-1980s. In it he writes, "No one wants to learn by mistakes, but we cannot learn enough from successes to go beyond the state of the art."[5]

  List some failures from your past. What did you learn from them?

GO FORTH AND LEARN

Leadership often means facing new situations that don't have a ready-made answer or strategy in our mental storehouse of experience. While we don't know, for instance, what new technologies will be important to an individual business's future, we can learn the underlying patterns of technologies and the principles of how things work. This calls for deep learning, for digging under the surface of what is observable (though observation is a key partner skill to learning), and using skills like imagining and reasoning to understand the transferable principles that underlie everything from nanotechnology to human behavior. This level of learning also requires changing our mental models of the way things work or even in terms of what is possible, in order to make room for the impact of change and use it to our advantage.

Consider the lilies of the field, how they grow; they toil not, neither do they spin.
—Matthew 6:28–29

The Prepared Mind makes full use of prior knowledge by transferring ideas and skills learned for one domain to other domains. The result is that our mental maps become vibrant and dynamic, and learning becomes a continuous process of making meaning by applying prior knowledge to new situations.[6]

CHAPTER NINE

ENABLING
Exercising Leadership
from the Outside In

> No man is an island, entire of itself;
> every man is a piece of the continent, a part of the main.
> If a clod be washed away by the sea, Europe is the less,
> as well as if a promontory were,
> as well as if a manor of thy friend's or of thine own were.
> Any man's death diminishes me because I am involved in
>   mankind;
> and therefore never send to know for whom the bell tolls; it
>   tolls for thee.
> JOHN DONNE, "MEDITATION XVII"

John Donne's meditation spoke of all of humanity. It expresses sadness at the loss of a single person and the view that the whole is diminished whenever this happens. Your job as a leader is smaller in scope but no less noble: to help others to succeed. Enabling is the active consideration of what it will take to help those around us achieve their own level of leadership. You can look at this from two points of view. The first might be the "Gee, isn't that nice" point of view: we enable those around us because it's nice to do. The more hard-nosed point of view is that running an effective operation is hard work, and we need to surround ourselves with effective people.

The truth of the matter is that when you consider operating the Sense-Response Cycle and all of its inherent work, you can't do it alone. To paraphrase John Donne, "No leader is the company unto himself or herself." You may be able to sense changes in your opportunity space, but that space is only a small part of the space available to the entire organization. And when it comes to acting on the decisions you and others reach, you need help. The best way to get help in any organization is to enable those around you.

Defining Enabling

Enabling, from the point of view of the Prepared Mind, is designing opportunities for others to develop their Prepared Minds and apply them in practice. Enabling is about helping others to experience, know, and do things differently. It is what we do when we want to help other people learn and develop. Our specific application of enabling is to enable others to lead with Prepared Minds. Of the eight skills, enabling is the most focused on other people's development. That is the good news and the bad news. The good news is that enabling fits with many common conceptions of leading others and proposes that people can learn to lead because enabling is a learnable skill. The bad news is that when you focus on other people's development, you have to learn what makes them tick, and this can be tricky—but not impossible.

When you investigate the meaning of the word *enabling* and the actions behind it, you find a proverbial three-legged stool of knowledge, opportunity, and means:

• *Knowledge.* You enable others when you provide them with relevant knowledge to understand and perform their job. You enable your boss by providing new market insights. You enable your subordinates by sharing the short- and long-term goals of the organization.

• *Opportunity.* You enable others when you provide them with the opportunity to do their job to the best of their ability. A friend of ours is a human resource executive who likes to find "dumb rules" inside organizations and then see what happens when they are eliminated. Typical dumb rules have to do with the number of signatures required to hire someone for a budgeted position. A supervisor is empowered when her signature brings the person on board. For her to have to get additional signatures takes away her opportunity for responsibility.

- *Means.* You enable others when you provide them with the means to accomplish their job. We would never expect a carpenter to build a house for us using only a hammer. So why do we deny people in our organizations the tools they need to get their job done?

But what does this three-legged stool of enabling look like in practice? Consider the comments that came from an experienced project leader with a reputation for accomplishing tough assignments. When we interviewed her, we simply posed the question, "How do you enable your team members?" Without much hesitation, she listed seven items that embodied enabling in her world of multimillion-dollar projects:

- Sharing the vision of project success (knowledge)
- Sharing the "why" behind the project—not necessarily for approval or acceptance but for understanding (knowledge)
- Engaging in dialogue about the pros and cons of the project (opportunity)
- Giving the team members boundaries, but not telling them how to operate within the boundaries (opportunity)
- Explaining and discussing her expectations of the person in the role (opportunity)
- Removing roadblocks (means)
- Engaging the sponsors and key stakeholders on behalf of the project (means)

Notice that there was no proclamation: "I've empowered you." Rather, she leads through a number of small enabling acts that in the end result in a more enabled team of people.

Now consider a couple of these actions from the team members' point of view. Sharing the vision behind the project and program and the underlying reasons gives the team, those who have to accomplish the vision, an insider's view of "why we're doing what we're doing." Sometimes executives defend not doing this by saying things like, "They'll never understand" or "They're not interested." The fact of the matter is that "they" understand much more than we give them credit for and are interested in the reasons behind our actions as leaders.

Engaging in dialogue and giving boundaries but not explicit instruction allows the team members an opportunity to take responsibility for not only their own actions, but for the success of the project or program as a whole. Some people thrive on having more responsibility; others would rather not have it. However, all of us at least want the opportunity, even if we turn it down.

LOOKING FROM THE OUTSIDE IN

The skill of enabling is unique among the eight Prepared Mind skills in that you cannot exercise this skill without looking at your leadership abilities from the outside in. This is the skill in which the other point of view and your reaction to it are all that count. We can't enable the people around us unless we know what reality looks like from their point of view. You can't enable your suppliers unless you see your company from their point of view. You can't enable your business partners unless you see advantages and risks from their point of view. You can't enable employees unless you see the things that tap into their intrinsic motivation, the things that will bring out their expendable effort and desire to learn and contribute in different ways.

Enabling means to "make able," and from the perspective of Prepared Mind leadership, this means to make those around us better able to develop and use their Prepared Minds. Consider this from the workers' point of view in any organization. When we consider the three aspects of enabling—to provide knowledge, opportunity, and means—we have to understand their particular needs.

KNOWLEDGE

When we look at enabling others by providing knowledge, the question becomes: What do the people in my organization need to know? Consider the following as a basic list; the real list will not be formed until you ask the people in *your* organization. As a start, we know they need:

- *An honest evaluation of where the organization stands.* They don't need or want a cheerleader to make them feel good; they need the truth. In the words of Jim Collins, they need the "brutal facts" so they can face them.[1]
- *A sense of where the organization is headed.* You may call this your mission, or you may explain long- and short-term goals. Or you

may just give them a sense of direction. No matter what, they deserve to know.

- *A road map.* They need to know how you or other leaders in the organization plan to move from your current position to where the organization is headed.
- *The role that they are expected to play in the transition from today to tomorrow.* The Marine Corps refers to esprit de corps as a binding force of the organization, and a critical part of that sense of pride is knowing that every person counts: each has a job that is important to the success of the mission. How many people in your organization collect a paycheck but have no sense of pride of their role in the organization?
- *Most important, the values that drive the organization.* This means more than words on a plaque or a laminated card. People watch the actions of the leaders and quickly figure out their *real* values. A mismatch between espoused values and actions leads to cynicism.

OPPORTUNITY

When you look at enabling others by providing opportunities, the question becomes: What opportunities do people in my organization need? In general, they need the opportunity to:

- *Try new things and learn from both successes and failures.* If experiments are not tolerated and failures are met with crushing criticism, you can bet that people do not have a sense of being enabled.
- *Be heard and valued.* Once again, actions speak louder than words. Is your door really open, or are those the words you use to fool yourself?
- *Challenge and give input to decisions.* The opportunity to ask questions in public and private settings goes hand in hand with enabling the skills of challenging and deciding.
- *Work with a variety of people.* This means working not only with people across a wide range of functions and geography, but also with people who can serve as mentors and coaches.
- *Teach others.* You enable them to enable others with what they know and do well.
- *Develop their skills.* This includes providing ways to systematically learn new technical skills and knowledge through formal and

informal education such as getting an M.B.A., special projects, coaching, and reading.

MEANS

When you look at enabling others by providing the means to develop and enact leadership, the questions again revolve around the people who work with you. If they are to work and contribute from their Prepared Minds in an enabled sense, they need:

- *Time to think.* One of the terrible by-products of the "lean and mean" downsizing of the past decade is the crushing amount of work left for those who remain. Time is a precious commodity for the Prepared Mind, and it's often in short supply.
- *Systems that eliminate non-value-added work.* Put good people in a bad system, and they will fail. The activities and processes associated with most jobs need to be revisited.
- *The means by which they can build their own knowledge and skills.* We see this clearly when we look at people who have been tagged as "high potentials." What do they get? They get advanced education, job rotation, and, most important, the attention of management.
- *Appropriate tools and technologies.* They need ready access to information to do their work more efficiently and to know when and how to use available tools and technologies.
- *Clear pathways for growth and development.* These means need to be supported by those around them through continuous coaching and checking in.
- *A voice.* They need to share their thinking, including the rationale for decisions, out loud so they can use others' skills to build their own strategies for leading and deciding.

"ARRANGING DOINGS" AND "ARRANGING KNOWING"

When asked how to help others transform their practice, Louis Gomez, a professor of learning sciences at Northwestern University, recently shared a phrase that is as interesting in its implications as it is in its word choice. He said that leadership is about "arranging doings." In other words, one way to provide leadership and enable others to perform differently is to give them different sets of things to do. It is in the arranging of these doings that the design element of leadership comes into play.

For instance, if we want to help someone become a better public speaker, we give her opportunities to speak publicly. If we want to help someone become a better designer (say, of software), we give him things to design and support in his environment to coach him and support his practice. The argument here is that it takes practice to change practice. Therefore, if we give people things to do that we believe will lead them to a more desirable state of performance and give them tools to support their performance, their performance will increase; understanding and beliefs will eventually follow. The trick to making these obvious enabling strategies work is that we have to figure out what things people can do and will do that will enable them to reach a desired outcome. We also have to be able to figure out what tools they need, give them the tools, and teach them when and how to use them. In many respects, this strategy mirrors those used in large-scale work process redesign and technology implementation projects. Give people new tasks with the right tools, and in theory, they should work better. As most of us have experienced, sometimes this strategy works, but often it does not. Sometimes, we would argue, you need to give people things deeper than "arranged doings" and tools to support them.

Behaviors, actions, and techniques are necessary to consider, but so are underlying patterns, strategies, plans, concepts, and theories to help enable people to develop and use their minds in a more prepared way. Our premise is that understanding and action have a reciprocal relationship. Repeated doing may lead to new understanding and belief. However, understanding and belief also lead to action. In a world that is uncertain and often unpredictable, we cannot ask people to wait for us to specify what they should do. People often have to figure out and orchestrate their own doings by applying what they know from beneath the waterline.

Somewhat less obvious when it comes to developing the skill of enabling is to study the five main approaches to learning: (1) behaviorism, (2) cognitivism, (3) social learning, (4) humanism, and (5) constructivism. If enabling is about helping people learn, understanding and selecting strategies from these five approaches to learning can help you, and those you are enabling, select methods to use when learning each of the eight skills, suited to the person and the condition. For instance, humanism stems from a belief that we have everything we need in us, and it is the role of the enabler to bring out this latent talent and motivation. We might apply strategies from humanism to high-potential employees and self-directed learners through use of the Socratic method or by giving them a special assignment. Behaviorism in its most basic form is about rewards and punishments. If we want to motivate someone to try something new, one option is to reward this person for performing the new task in the way we envision the performance. There are many performance and compensation systems based on this approach to learning.

The social learning approach starts from the premise that we learn by watching other people, particularly those we admire. For example, if we want to enable one of our employees to become more observant, we might assign him to a formal or informal mentor who is a good observer and is well liked by the person we are enabling with the skill of observing. The point is that sometimes the best tool we can provide someone in order to enable him is the tool of understanding different approaches to enablement and when and how to use them. To enable others, we often have to "arrange doings" and "arrange knowing."

ANCHORING CONCEPTS OF ENABLING

Three core concepts are necessary to understand if we really want to become expert at knowing when and how and why to develop and use the skill: (1) motivation, (2) design, and (3) scaffolding.

Even if we believe our job as a leader is to "arrange doings," we are far better at it if we understand what motivates people to do things (or not do things) we arrange for them to do. Being strategic and systematic about "arranging doings" and "arranging knowing" points to the need to understand how to design things, including how to design meaningful work and learning situations. Finally, while it is one thing to say, "Give people the right tools to do their jobs," it takes understanding and applying the concept of scaffolding to help people use the right things in their environments (including tools, people, structures, policies, and opportunities) as scaffolds or ramps that help them build their skill and proficiency so eventually they can stand on their own when using the eight skills of the Prepared Mind in combination.

MOTIVATION

As we work to enable those around us, we can provide them knowledge, opportunity, and means—yet still fail to enable them. If they are not motivated to use the knowledge, accept the opportunity, or work with the means provided, all of our efforts at enabling are for naught. We first have to do our homework and understand what motivates them to change, learn, develop, and grow in general and in the specific skill and situation that is the focus of our enabling strategies. If we provide only the things that motivate us, we are guilty of self-referencing, and that is often a formula for failure. And remember that motivation as a core concept for the Prepared Mind is not unique to enabling. Learning, challenging, and deciding also rely heavily on the concept and theories of motivation.

Motivation may well be one of the most studied tools of business while being one of the least well applied. Still, we cannot enable you to understand and use the power of motivation without enabling you to study the main theories of motivation and what those theories will allow you to do. Psychologists and organizational behaviorists in the past century gave us four ways for understanding motivation and organizing its theories. Generally what we know about motivation is categorized into content and process theories and into intrinsic and extrinsic motivators. As you read through this overview of motivation theories, reflect on which ones you use and see being used by default. Then ask yourself which ones you could leverage more in your goal of motivating and enabling others to develop their Prepared Minds.

Content Theories Overview
Content theories of motivation talk about motivating factors such as needs. The most famous content theory is Maslow's hierarchy of needs, which says that we are motivated by lower-order needs like food and safety until they are satisfied.[2] Once they are satisfied, our behavior is motivated by higher-order needs like esteem and for a

small segment of the population (approximately 5 percent), motivation comes from the need to self-actualize. If you apply Maslow's theory, then you would not ask your team to develop themselves into a high-performing work team if they are awaiting word about the next layoff (remember that safety needs are more basic than esteem and self-actualization needs).

Another famous content theory is David McClellan's Learned Needs Theory.[3] This theory proposes that we all have a blend of the need for power, the need for achievement, and the need for affiliation. As a leader attempting to enable others to develop their own Prepared Minds and act in a world of opportunity space, it pays to understand the needs of those you are enabling and how to link the opportunities and suggestions you are giving them to those needs. So, for example, if you are working with a sales force that has a strong need for achievement, it is more motivating to present them with opportunities (say, new prospects) that they believe will lead to achievement than with opportunities for affiliation or power.

Process Theories Overview

As intuitively appealing as the content or need theories are, understanding needs is not enough to lead and guide the attention and behavior of others. You need to understand the dynamics of what people do to meet their needs in order to enable them through the resources and opportunities you can provide them. Another category of motivation theories, known as process theories, attempts to explain the dynamic connections between thought and action.

Process theories suggest ways managers and leaders can enable those they lead to make decisions they believe will result in actions that will, in their minds, meet individuals' needs and the needs of the organization. In Chapter Eight, we briefly explained expectancy theory, which basically says that people take action based on their belief that the action will lead to some outcome related to what they want or value.[4] The nice thing about expectancy theory and other process theories is the possibility that leaders can affect behavior by changing the factors of the environment that connect to what people want to do to get what they want and value. B. F. Skinner's operant conditioning model claims that we can control behavior by controlling the rewards and punishments a person gets as a result of the behavior.[5] The problem is that in the knowledge era, where many environmental factors are dynamic and out of control of the boss, you have to rely on the knowledge worker to be self-motivated, that is, intrinsically motivated.

Intrinsic and Extrinsic Overview

In addition to content and process theories, intrinsic motivation and extrinsic motivation are the other ways to view motivation. Extrinsic motivation comes from being rewarded (being given something by the environment to meet your needs) in exchange for appropriate behaviors. This assumes that someone in the environment knows what the appropriate behaviors are, has the power to reward them, or has built feedback, rewards, and punishments into an organizational system or process, and that the person acting knows that he or she will be rewarded as a result of performing a certain behavior. That works for some of the people some of the time, and some of the requirements of work and business some of the time, but not for all of the people in all situations all of the time. Also, it may not be the most effective means for enabling people to act and reward themselves using their own Prepared Minds.

Intrinsic motivation occurs naturally as a result of simply engaging in a behavior and does not rely on some external agent to judge the behavior and give a reward. Frederick Herzberg wrote one of the most popular *Harvard Business Review* articles to date, "One More Time: How Do You Motivate Employees?"[6] He found that motivating factors like achievement, the work itself, responsibility, and growth are often intrinsic to the work. One of the implications for leaders who wish to enable others is to design tasks, assignments, jobs, and learning experiences that allow those they lead to experience these intrinsic motivators in their work. More recently, with an emphasis on "full engagement" (that is, tapping into people's commitment and expendable effort at work), leaders and managers are looking for ways to help their employees become more engaged, more self-directed, more growth oriented, more committed, and more willing to expend effort beyond the narrow constraints of their traditional jobs. In many ways, this is implying that there is a focus on building leadership from within—within the organization and within the individuals. The strategies around full engagement tap into the insights of intrinsic motivation.

A major concept of what we know about motivation is that when it comes to the skill of enabling, it is advisable to design experiences for those you lead to meet their aspirational needs that also serve the future of business. This is easier said than done, though what we know from the worlds of design and of learning and development give us some ways to strengthen the legs of the three-legged stool of knowledge, opportunity, and means.

DESIGN

The idea that leaders are designers and that just about any aspect of business can be thought of as a design problem is relatively new to business thinking—new but powerful.[7]

To think like a designer with the purpose of enabling others means imagining the future in which those you lead are themselves leading with Prepared Minds. Let's be clear that design also involves emotion. Don Norman and others point to the power of emotion for a designed thing to be adopted.[8] Think of moments when you have been in Sharper Image or one of the other creative appliance stores and felt compelled to buy something because it just seemed cool as well as useful. The designer had the emotional aspects of user motivation in mind, as well as the functional aspects. Or think of the last time you were moved by a speech or something you read. The writers designed the words, images, and structure to appeal to your heart and your head. This is very related to motivation. Needs like esteem, belonging, even self-actualization have a strong element of emotion in them, and the process for meeting them needs to include thinking and doing things that are emotional. This is one reason that, for instance, influential leaders who are known for enabling others often use rituals and symbols as part of their leadership language, rituals, and symbols that resonate with deep values and aspirations. We have worked with CEOs who transformed their organizations in part by appealing to values and needs around family, around being empowered, around being innovative. Of course, the leader using these emotional symbols and ideas needs to sincerely believe them, or people see through it and become skeptical and cynical.

To tap into emotion, functionality, and adoption, it is powerful to involve those you lead in the design of solutions or in ways of adopting them so they themselves become designers of their own futures. The design team, be it two people or twelve people or more, must use the skill of reasoning to decide what knowledge, opportunities, and other means will enable them to reach that vision. This is tricky because often people want to jump to surface solutions or, as one of our clients calls it, "Band-Aid" solutions. Leaders who enable others challenge those they lead in a positive way to stretch and dig more deeply to realize what one or two key things could really move the person and the group to a higher level of analysis, synthesis, and ambition.

The way to get to this level varies from group to group, which is another reason that formulas and techniques are not by themselves helpful to those who lead with Prepared Minds. We have worked with some groups that required total restructuring, and they did this work themselves. We have worked with other groups where beer together on Friday nights, and what occurred during those Friday night conversations, met their needs for affiliation and creativity and lifted them to the next level of commitment and understanding the business they were in. When enabling an individual or a group, the key is not to design something in isolation (for example, a job) and give it to them with no support, no regard for their emotion, motivation or current capacity, no vision. The key is to envision the opportunity space and design ways for the people you are enabling to make a difference in the space—for their own good and for the good of the organization. Like most other designed things that work, you often have to test them and adapt them before they are fully used. The same is true for people and the opportunities they have. Let's say you are enabling someone by giving this person a new role. She almost always has to tailor the role to fit what she can do now, what she can learn to do in the near future, and where she sees herself going in line with the strategic direction of the company. Part of effective enablement is allowing that local tailoring, within the bounds of acceptable practice.

Sometimes, however, there is a need for more explicit support to enable others to perform their new work. You don't build a building from standing on the ground and jumping to the top. You need to stand on scaffolding and work your way up. The same is true for people who are learning—people whose growth you are enabling.

SCAFFOLDING

Scaffolding is a great metaphor, used in learning, for building supports (for example, knowledge, experiences, resources, tools, and coaching) to help people perform and build new skills and new mental maps. Traditionally, providing scaffolding might suggest the strategy "send them to training." In some cases, training may be the appropriate scaffold, or one of them. However, more often than not, especially in a fast-paced, dynamic, global environment, scaffolding has to occur in the midst of performance, with a learning-while-doing mind-set. Leaders who coach and mentor, those who rotate their team through different tasks to widen and deepen their mental maps, and those who model and explain their own decisions are just a few examples of leaders enabling others in the midst of doing.

Imagine a Prepared Mind leader who deliberately and explicitly walked through the sense–make sense–decide–act cycle, using the eight skills and talking out loud to those who work with or for him to demonstrate how he uses the Prepared Mind. This would be a tremendous example of enabling behaviors. Furthermore, imagine the leader enabling someone else by asking her to talk through the cycle using the eight skills and coaching her along the way. These talk-aloud techniques are associated with an apprenticeship method for teaching, learning, and leading.[9] The role of the leader is to support people during their exploration and execution of opportunity space, not just test them and punish them if they do not measure up after the first few tries.

Motivation, design, and scaffolding are foundational concepts to the skill of enabling. Understanding where people will put their expendable effort, if given the right tools and scaffolds, and then designing those scaffolds is a primary role of a Prepared Mind leader committed to enabling others to build and use their talents and to develop their own Prepared Minds.

CONNECTING TO THE CONCEPTS: ANCHORING EXERCISES TO IMPROVE THE SKILL OF ENABLING

STRETCH ASSIGNMENTS

Through our consulting and research, one of the most consistently used methods of enablement by people considered great leaders is that of giving those around them stretch assignments. Choosing an assignment that (1) builds on someone's strengths, (2) exposes the person to new issues and opportunities that require the development of knowledge and skills she can use in her professional and personal life, (3) being clear about why she was chosen for the task, (4) providing expectations and boundaries in terms of time lines and desired outcomes, and (5) making clear links to support systems all speaks to the Prepared Mind leader as designer and motivator.

To achieve the desired outcomes of stretch assignments, leaders have to assess the requirements of assignments and the abilities and potential of people. They have to strategize ways to enable the person for the long term so the assignment is a development opportunity and not just an end in and of itself. They have to design the assignment, its success criteria, and its support structure so the person taking it on has curbs to operate within and knows he is being set up for success. Coaching, mentoring, and other forms of scaffolding and support from the leader and others may be necessary during the implementation and adoption of the assignment. And evaluation with an aim of helping the assignee learn, and learn with them, is absolutely essential for this type of enabling strategy to work and requires each step of the design process be enacted.

Stretch assignments often have the following characteristics:

- They are not part of a usual job.
- Their products and outcomes have medium to low risk but high payoff. Often these are the assignments that everyone would like to see completed but no one seems to have the approach or time or scope to set aside to do them.
- They require interaction with multiple stakeholders and sources of data.

- They have milestone moments where the leader can give feedback on a regular basis.
- There are people in the organization or in social networks outside the organization who can help the person doing the assignment acquire the knowledge and skills needed.
- They have a mix of tasks that draw on strengths of the person doing the assignment and clearly require the person to develop other areas of strength.
- The person receiving the assignment is open to coaching and sees it as a development opportunity.
- The leader allows the person the flexibility and struggle to make it her own, coaching without doing it for her.
- There are a clear beginning and an end, with explicit deliverables.
- There are opportunities to reflect on and debrief throughout the assignment and after.
- The leader clears the path of any unnecessary obstacles that would prevent the person with the assignment from doing it.
- The person who receives the assignment is motivated because of the challenge of the assignment and because of the faith and investment shown to her by the leader.

Cognitive Apprenticeship

A specific method for scaffolding learners, or those being enabled, the cognitive apprenticeship method was designed for novices learning from experts.[10] As it pertains to the Prepared Mind, experts in different skills of the Prepared Mind who employ them in practice can enable others with their own Prepared Minds by using cognitive apprenticeship. The basic steps are as follows:

1. The expert models a particular behavior or method to the novice and talks aloud about what she is doing and why she is doing it in a particular way. She provides context, principles, and tips that go into her thinking and action.
2. The novice engages in his own problem solving, decision making, or behavior and talks aloud to the expert about his thinking.
3. During the novice's engagement in the task, the expert coaches the novice on the actions he is taking and how he is thinking

through them, correcting errors, giving tips, and praising good approximations.

4. The novice engages in a similar task, and this time the expert stands back and offers advice only when the novice asks for it.
5. The novice masters the task and talks aloud about his process and thinking.
6. The novice and master debrief and make explicit the principles of the task and process that can be used in other domains and on other problems as well.

These steps may occur in the matter of hours if the task is very behavioral (such as practicing a speech) or may go on over weeks or months if the task is complex and multilayered in its subtasks and the thinking required.

THE SOCRATIC METHOD

The ancient Greeks have given us many exercises for improving our Prepared Minds that at once motivate, teach, challenge, and inspire us. One of the most famous is the use of the Socratic method, which is a good method to develop the skills of challenging, reasoning, reflecting, and learning as well as enabling. There is no formula for doing the Socratic method well, except to say you must be committed to enabling others by patiently asking them deeper and deeper questions that help them peer into their own prior knowledge and ways of thinking and enable them to see the logic or the erroneous assumptions of their ideas, knowledge, and beliefs. There are well over 100,000 references to the Socratic method on the Web. There are a great number of books that explain how to use the Socratic method in law, teaching, selling, and counseling. Here we share with you "rules" for asking good Socratic questions based on the work of Rick Garlikov.[11] The questions you ask must be interesting and intriguing (that is, motivating) for the one you are asking:

• The questions must scaffold the learner by leading with incremental and logical steps that reference the learner's prior knowledge.

- The questions must be seen as leading to a conclusion, not just making an isolated point.
- The questions must be designed to get the learner to see particular points that can point him to the logic or error in his thinking.
- Questions can be logically leading, which requires the learner to understand underlying principles and concepts of an idea. Questions can also be psychologically leading, which allows the learner to follow clues in the questions that take him on paths that lead to conclusions.

Be especially cautious in using psychologically leading questions, for they may motivate the learner to simply reflect back to you what he thinks you want to hear or cause him to feel as though he is being manipulated.

If you are serious about wanting to learn and apply the Socratic method, we suggest reading more about it and paying attention to leaders and teachers you know whose questions have caused you to say, "That's a good question. You know, what your question is helping me realize . . ." They may not be using the Socratic method in full, but you can certainly learn by reflecting on their models of good questions.

Participatory Design

Throughout the Prepared Mind, but particularly in this chapter on enabling, we have discussed the importance of leaders' thinking like designers. Among its many benefits, design requires imagining the end state and the end user, based on the assumption that we want to enable end users to do something better than they did before, with the help of whatever we design for them or with them.

More and more designers are catching on to the importance of really understanding and involving the end users in the design process itself. Whether it be a new information technology system, a new policy, or a new product, involving those we count on to adopt and use what we design enables them to understand the design and the thinking behind it and motivates them to embrace it.

It also enables the leader-designer to understand where end users may need scaffolding in terms of use and benefits.

In a nutshell, participatory design means including end users with all different perspectives in the design, implementation, adoption, and evaluation of something new. They are responsible for gathering information and for decisions and they are enabled to speak up and have their views heard, while being encouraged to see the problem and potential solution from multiple perspectives. Participating in the design of change is a great "stretch assignment" for enablement. It also enables leaders to share their thinking with many others and to consider multiple perspectives that they might not otherwise have access to. Ironically, while the act of participatory design seems fairly democratic and a flattening of power, in order to catch on in organizations, we have found that a leader with power has to enact it. They have to knock down the roadblocks and model good listening so people do not get trapped in old roles.

EXPOSURE

We have found that one of the simplest ways to enable others is to expose them to all kinds of knowledge that is interesting to them and can be associated directly or indirectly with their growth. We have seen Prepared Mind leaders enable their people to appreciate the wider world through volunteering together once a month at a homeless shelter. Others are avid readers of all sorts of books and pass them along to their mentees to read and consider. Taking those you want to enable on trips and to meetings with you, giving them a task, and debriefing after is a great way to scaffold them to go solo and motivate them to learn. Some companies we have consulted with and researched motivated their executives to see the need for change by insisting they go out and talk to customers. After getting an earful, they changed their minds about what needed to occur.

ASKING, LISTENING, AND COGNITIVE STRATEGIES

We enable others by asking them good questions and really listening to their answers, without imposing our own answers. This motivates them to share, take risks, and open themselves to mutual learning. By building off their ideas and ways of seeing the world, and by their building off ours, mutual enablement occurs. If we are in a role of enabling others more than they can enable us at the moment, the use of images, examples, and metaphors (that is, cognitive strategies) can help bridge them to a new or deeper level of understanding.

Cognitive strategies are great ways to scaffold others, especially if we are using them to learn with others and not just teach. We have specific memories of being enabled by a mentor who listened to our perspective and then graciously said, "Think of it this way. Now how do you see it?" We also remember being told a meaningful story or having someone draw a two-by-two matrix to explain how he saw critical factors relating to each other. These cognitive strategies can be designed and become part of the natural way we teach and enable and check our own understanding. In fact, we have found that leaders who have Prepared Minds tend to rely heavily on the use of story, metaphor, analogy, imagery, matrices, chunking categories, and other organizing and memory devices to store and share knowledge and information. One of the best ways to learn how to use them naturally is to read and listen to how others use them naturally and then practice them when communicating in presentations and one and one.

SHARE YOUR STRUGGLES AND TIPS

There is a bit of the Golden Rule in the skill of enabling. "Do unto others as you would have them do unto you" suggests that to truly enable others to develop their own Prepared Minds, we do best when we are humble. Sharing our struggles with those we are enabling, how we thought through them, lessons we learned, and tips we have gained for handling those same situations more effectively can do wonders to prepare others for the tough and constant work of preparing their minds and using them in decisions and actions.

THE CYCLE OF ENABLING

Knowing that we can only set the conditions for an enabled workforce, we have to look at this skill from their point of view. Consider the questions posed in Figure 9.1 as a starting point.

FIGURE 9.1. THE SENSE-RESPONSE CYCLE OF ENABLING

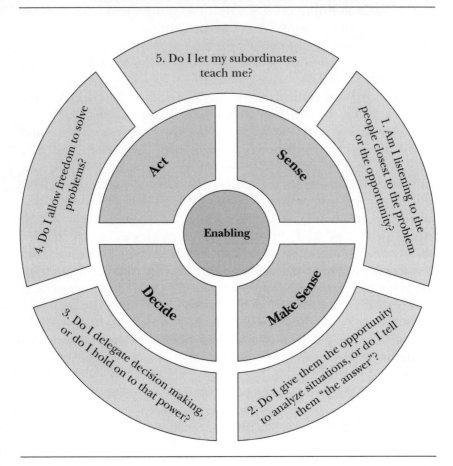

1. AM I LISTENING TO THE PEOPLE CLOSEST TO THE PROBLEM OR THE OPPORTUNITY?

Do you give people the opportunity to be engaged? Too few of us realize that communication takes place only with a two-way interchange of ideas and information. We expect those who work for us to listen to us, but all too often, we don't take the time to listen to them. Think back to when you were new in your job or in your company. How many times did a boss miss out on a good idea because he or she would not take the time to listen to you? If you are like many other people, you stopped trying to communicate good ideas because "no one listens!" Now the question you have to ask yourself is if you are guilty of the same behavior you so disliked as a new employee.

2. DO I GIVE THEM THE OPPORTUNITY TO ANALYZE SITUATIONS, OR DO I TELL THEM "THE ANSWER"?

Being in charge can be frightening, especially during times of rapid change. Sometimes we find comfort in our knowledge and experience and want to show the rest of the organization that we still have what it takes. And so, at times, we are tempted to skip the make-sense phase of the Sense-Response Cycle and fall back on experience. Unfortunately, this can have two negative side effects. First, we might be wrong, and nobody will tell us because we made it clear that we are not to be challenged. Second, and more damaging over the long run, we stifle the problem-solving abilities of the people in our organization. They don't have to think because we do all the thinking for the organization. Even if this works in the short run, it is hurtful in the long run.

3. DO I DELEGATE DECISION MAKING, OR DO I HOLD ON TO THAT POWER?

Most of us have been exposed to the concept of situational leadership espoused by Paul Hersey and Ken Blanchard years ago.[12] We learned that there are times when we should be directive and when to delegate. It's our experience that many managers and executives know the theory but neglect to use it in practice. Delegation is risky in that "they" may not take the same actions as we would take. Even worse, "they" may make a mistake. But how will anyone improve her skills if we don't give her the opportunity to succeed or fail on her own?

4. DO I ALLOW FREEDOM TO SOLVE PROBLEMS?

Once we have arrived at a decision, by direction or delegation, the organization has to act on the decision if the Sense-Response Cycle is to progress. However, as we all know, problems happen along the way. Do we provide the knowledge, opportunity, and means to those who have to solve the problems? Or, like some managers, do we "play the hero" by making them come to us for problem resolution?

5. DO I LET MY SUBORDINATES TEACH ME?

Role reversal is a powerful tool in enabling our workforce, and one of the best approaches is to let the student become the teacher. Give your subordinates the opportunity to make the presentation to the board. Or let them make the pitch to the prospective client (because they know the material better than you do!). Or debrief a significant project, and let them tell you what they've learned and how you might improve your performance in the future.

BENEFITS, RISKS, AND CHALLENGES OF ENABLING

All of the Prepared Mind skills have benefits, risks, and challenges associated with their development and use. Here is our starting list for the skill of enabling. Add to, subtract from, and modify it to fit your reality.

BENEFITS OF IMPROVING YOUR SKILL OF ENABLING

Improving a skill takes time and energy, and before expending either, we need to be assured that the benefits are worth the effort. Consider the following points.

Bench Strength

Because of the tough economic climate in the opening years of this century, we see many organization that have slowed hiring at the same time they have "right-sized" the organization. The dilemma that many leaders are faced with now is the reality of a weak "bench" when the economy becomes more robust. Some of the usual means of building the strength of our subordinates (advanced training, job rotation, stretch promotions, and so on) are not available. Enabling our workforce to take on more responsibility is one good way to ensure solid backup to leaders.

Building Trust

We can put up banners about teamwork and can give speeches about how we are a company "family." Nice words, but will your people believe you? If you want to show people that you trust them, let them take on responsibility and give them the authority to accomplish activities that are significant to them, to you, and to the organization. Think back to when you were young and got your driver's license. How did you know your parents trusted you with the car? They let you drive. How do your employees know you trust them? When you let them "run the business."

Increased Supply of Intellectual and Social Capital

If the claim of the knowledge era that people are the greatest asset is true, then enabling them to develop and share their assets, especially in the form of Prepared Mind skills at all points in the organization, is good business sense.

Learning from Enabling Others

It has been said that if you really want to learn something, teach it. The same can be said for enabling. In the act of demonstrating, explaining, delegating, coaching, or other things that enable people, we very likely learn something about the task, the content, and even about ourselves. Sometimes we learn it is difficult to let go.

RISKS OF ENABLING

An overemphasis on a newly developed skill can result in experiencing downside risks. Consider the following points.

Insecurity

We may develop people who are better at our job than we are. If we are in any way insecure in our position, the possibility of developing superior talent may be a real risk. We would love to be able to tell you that real leaders surround themselves with talent and that doing so is a mark of your leadership ability. However, the reality for some executives with whom we have worked is that enabling the talented people around them is truly a risk. We suggest that you take the risk. Although we may find it beneficial to learn from enabling others, we often have to check our own motivation when we find it hard to let go or things do not go exactly the way they would have if we had done the task. The skills of challenging, learning, and reflecting can help us learn about ourselves and separate ourselves from the tasks, goals, and people involved so we can be fair and open leaders and not project our own insecurities onto the situation.

Loss of Control

People might go beyond our ability to control their actions. Sometimes we worry about people who will not accept responsibility; however, there are times when employees will "run amok" when they get some freedom. A lesson from President Reagan might apply here: "Trust, but verify." We have seen leaders enable others successfully by building in a check to reasoning in the task. For instance, sending someone off to design something is one thing. Asking the person to explain her logic and giving her criteria to consider helps her practice reflecting and thinking through multiple sides of an issue.

CHALLENGES TO ENABLING

We know that we should improve our skills; however, we are all faced with barriers and obstacles. Consider the following points.

Letting Go

It's hard to let go. Some of us are very hands-on leaders, and we like it that way. However, that may not be best for the organization. One of the toughest challenges for many executives is the challenge of letting go. Go back to the metaphor of driving: How did it feel to sit in the passenger's seat the first time your own teenager drove *you* someplace? The same feeling hits many executives when they hand over the wheel of the business to some of their junior associates. As mentioned as a benefit, if we can frame letting go as a way for us to learn, then it can make it easier to enable others so we can learn from them and be free to learn other things. There is also a difference in totally letting go and in scaffolding. Learning how to scaffold is a delicate art and science. It can breathe a whole new rationale into enabling others that serves your own learning and leadership as well as theirs.

Fear of Failure

It's painful, but we have to let people make their own mistakes. Some of the best and most enduring lessons we learn in life come from the mistakes we make. When we attempt to enable those around us, we have to let them make (some) mistakes; otherwise they miss a valuable opportunity to learn and improve. Helping people learn and practice the skills of learning and reflecting while enabling them is important. We can feel more secure about their own eventual ability to think ahead and self-regulate if we help them learn how to learn from mistakes, being honest that everyone makes them.

Applied Enabling: The Talent Problem

Consider the following questions and activities Prepared Mind leaders might consider as they think about the talent issue from the enabling point of view:

- An executive needs to keep people informed about the real condition of the company and the industry. You may be tempted to protect your employees from the bad news, but that is not giving them the opportunity to help you and take an active role. Give supervisors more freedom to do their job. Keep development budgets and activities in place during tough times as a strategic priority.
- A middle manager might focus on giving her peers honest feedback and coaching. All of us need, but may not want, a balanced review of what we are doing right and where we need improvement. In addition, she could offload some of their work so as to give them time (again, that precious commodity) for development and improvement.
- An individual contributor could tell the boss what he needs to be more effective in his job and why he needs it. Most bosses are not uncaring people, but they are very busy and may not see your needs until you point them out.

Building Your Skills

Here are a few more ideas to add to the anchoring exercises to build your enabling skills.

To-Do List

While making your to-do list, identify one specific idea or technique you want to teach. Pick something small but important. Also identify who you want to share it with. For example, you could introduce a new speed reading technique during a staff meeting. The key is to pick something you can teach and make sure you do it.[13]

More Questions to Consider

- **Batman's belt.** Batman comic books, TV shows, and movies have kept many of us enthralled over the years. Batman's utility belt always seemed to have the right gadget for the dilemma he was trying to overcome.

  What tools might you devise to help your people do their job better? List some tools that don't exist, but, if they did, would make work much easier.

- **Who ya gonna call?** We are all part of work and social networks. Yet we often feel as if we have to handle problems alone. Think of the song from the old *Ghostbusters* movie: "Who Ya Gonna Call?"

  Make a list of your friends and acquaintances. What expertise can be found in the list? Are you tapping into the base of expertise? Are your employees on the list?

- **Talk about not listening!** In 1876 Alexander Bell offered to sell the telephone to Western Union. They couldn't see the value in his "toy" and turned him down.

  List the people in your life or organization who are currently not important enough for your attention. Are there any names that should be removed from the list?

GO FORTH AND ENABLE

Prepared Minds and great scholars we have known in the corporate world, at the university, and on the global stage have told us that if they really want to learn something, they teach it. Making our minds up to teach just one thing during the day can enable others through the teaching and enable ourselves to be more attentive and more sensitive to our interactions and the way we think about and use our knowledge. Everybody wins.

It is by teaching that we teach ourselves.
        —Henri Frederic Amiel

Prepared Minds embrace the value of teaching and sharing knowledge. Having the discipline to share a little knowledge every day builds relationships, deepens your own knowledge, and expands the capability of those around you. In short, it produces a threefold return. This discipline starts with adding a small but relevant teaching goal to your daily schedule.[14]

CHAPTER TEN

REFLECTING
Looking Backward,
Forward, and Inward

By three methods we may learn wisdom: First, by reflection,
which is noblest; second, by imitation, which is easiest;
and third by experience, which is the bitterest.
CONFUCIUS

Reflecting is noble? Maybe it was twenty-five hundred years ago, but what about today? Why would anyone say this, and how does it relate to the leadership pressures of the twenty-first century? Hold that thought for a page or two while we use our recent past to position the need for leadership reflection in today's world.

GLANCE AT THE REARVIEW MIRROR

Leadership in the twentieth century was considered the domain of the heroic leader who, by force of style and personality, could focus a nation or an organization on a goal, noble or destructive, and its achievement. People followed their lead, and he or she was declared "a leader." We saw Winston Churchill, Adolf Hitler, Mao Zedong, Tom Watson, Golda Meir, Margaret Thatcher, Benjamin Graham, and J. P. Morgan focus their followers and achieve, at least for some time, greatness. Having a vision (good or bad) and rallying people around that vision is what they were good at. So who needs reflection? It might only bring doubts into your mind. Or, we contend, it might make you a better leader.

We revel in the stories of past heroic leaders, but we wrestle with the issue of leadership in our own organizations. Do we need bigger-than-life leaders to address our realities today? Maybe we do for nations but probably not for business. We need leadership of a different sort: leadership that is attuned to the business realities we are facing, the realities of speed and change. Moore's Law, once a descriptor of the evolution of the microprocessor (the doubling of the number of transistors on a chip every eighteen months), had become a self-fulfilling prophecy until we ran into the physical limitations of microprocessors. Globalization, which once had a dampening effect because of the buffer of time zones, has faced up to the reality of 24/7 operations, enabled by integrated systems and distributed operations. Product and service life cycles have been compressing for at least twenty years, and competition is relentless. Nothing stabilizes because we don't let it stabilize. We argue about the madness of change, but we know that competitive advantage is only temporary, and therefore we bring even more change down on our organizations.

This brings about an awareness of another reality: command and control, the dominant management style of the twentieth century, was sure, but it was also slow. (And it is not even sure anymore as more and more work and productivity rely on changing knowledge and human interaction in uncertain environments.) But it was built on the premise of leaders with direct reports, which is less important in today's world of independent knowledge workers and organizations with matrix, network, and project structures. The style doesn't fit the needs of today's climate.

We need organizational greatness, but we can't wait for the single leader to build, rally, and command an organization. We need leadership distributed throughout our organizations. Steep hierarchies have given way to flat, distributed organizations. Furthermore, we need these distributed leaders to possess an understanding of the organization's goals and to have the skills to move their part of the organization toward those goals in this environment of speed and change. We need leaders who can move their organization in an agile fashion within the bigger picture and toward the bigger goals. We need leaders who know their own strengths and weaknesses and can work with others who supplement those strengths and offset those weaknesses. This kind of deep learning and self-strategic awareness cannot exist without the skill of reflecting.

There should be no doubt that leadership is a hot topic. When we searched for "leadership" on the Amazon.com Web site in early 2005, we obtained more than fourteen thousand hits. So, going to the popular press and looking for "the" answer may result in more confusion rather than less. There are books based on academic studies, personal experience, and company-specific data. There are books that purport to offer the secrets of historical or current leaders. There are books that attribute specific skill sets to leaders, but we know that these leaders were formed by their unique environments as much as they changed the very environments in which they worked. There are too many books, and we have too little time, and there is no one solution that works every time. Like it or not, we will have to figure out the answers on our own. And in the work involved with figuring it out, we need to reflect on our role in the successes and failures we have brought about.

So why is reflection noble? The answer is in the explanation of the word *noble*. This old word relates to some very specific needs of the twenty-first century: moral character, honor, courage, and generosity. These are the very attributes needed in a leader dealing with the problems of this century, and leaders need to understand their positions about the issues they face. Reflection is noble because we can develop these attributes only if we know ourselves. And this is the point: we reflect in order to learn from past successes and failures, weigh options for our future against some underlying principles that rarely change, and use this knowledge for the betterment of our organization in the future. We use reflection to understand why things happened or could happen the way they do. And we use reflection to build and adhere to our integrity as leaders and organizations.

DEFINING REFLECTION

Reflecting is one of the most powerful skills for guaranteeing and applying a Prepared Mind. It helps us hold our mind, heart, values, and circumstances up to a mirror and see the whole picture: if they fit together, how they fit together, and even why they fit together. Albert Bandura says that it is reflective capacity that gives us the ability to think about what is going on in one's own mind and with one's own feelings and interior stirrings, and study oneself.[1]

This definition may make reflection sound like the skill of self-absorption, and what is practical about that, especially in an active, results-oriented environment? Actually, reflecting is one of the most practical and potentially socially influential skills because it is the skill that makes sure the center holds in the midst of change. Reflection is the skill that builds integrity. Here, integrity means the tight integration of who we say we are, what we say we want, and what we actually do. It is also the skill that shows us distortions in our self-image, thoughts, feelings, and behaviors. Reflection helps us look backward. Reflection helps us look forward. But most of all, reflection helps us look inward for the balance between our inner world and the outer worlds we create.

REFLECTION IN DISGUISE

Acts of reflection look very much like acts of learning, imagining, and even challenging. The skills are interdependent, with reflection typically being the integrator of what we learn, what we imagine, what we challenge, what we believe, and who we are. When a Prepared Mind is in reflection mode or helping others reflect, you will see a lot of questions being asked—open-ended questions that often do not have a right or wrong answer in the objective sense, but questions that provoke the person reflecting to weigh his experience (or imagined experience) against his standard or image of what he thinks should happen or what he wanted or expected to happen. After-action reviews used by the military, project lessons-learned sessions, formative evaluations, talk-aloud techniques (when someone walks you through a task by talking about her choices and reasoning each step of the way), and essays at the back of most popular weekly news magazines are all observable examples of reflection. They open the door to questioning.

Underneath these actions are patterns, models, and applications of reflection that are often captured under the titles of "organizational learning," "team learning," and "reflective practice." These terms are usually used to describe the application of the skill of reflection to actions and outcomes that have happened in the past or perhaps in recent moments (as when a physician, for instance, "reads" how a patient is taking the news of a diagnosis and steps back to reflect and consider what the patient needs at the moment besides information). Individuals who are good at reflecting in practice are often those we think of as thoughtful and professional. We often attribute their ability to compassion and good interpersonal skills. However, applying compassion to good interpersonal skills requires the ability to reflect in the moment. Patterns, models, and applications of reflecting forward usually get attributed to decision making and reasoning, particularly ethical decision making and moral reasoning. However, it is really reflection that helps us make choices and proceed along some particular path of principles, values, and goals, and it is reflection that tells us if we are on or off the path we have chosen.

Decision and reasoning are more about rational thought. Yet the calculus of the mind would not produce decisions and answers that made sense to the minds and hearts of people in complex situations, filled with all kinds of competing information and agendas, unless the skill of reflecting against some standard had occurred. This standard includes not only individual values but also the imagined consequences of different alternatives on ourselves and others and how those alternatives map to what we know and believe and judge to be in our bounds. Reflection helps us recognize our bottom lines of value.

Decisions and reasoning about things as large scale as going to war, as personal and poignant about leaving someone on or taking him off life support, as ordinary to business as whether to outsource all require leaders to reflect ahead of time and know why, in their hearts and in their minds, it is a good decision. We may not always agree with them, but leaders who reflect generally have our respect and respect themselves. They have addressed the question of "why."

REFLECTING IN ACTION

As we consider the eight skills of the Prepared Mind, we see reflecting as the quiet skill that keeps us honest. It is the skill wherein we ask ourselves the uncomfortable questions: "Why?" and "What was my role in this?" Our jobs go well—or not so well; our attempts at navigating our individual and organizational opportunity space are sometimes successful and not so at other times. But progress and continued navigation require learning and improvement, and this comes from good reflection.

Henry Petroski, the author and engineering historian, wrote a fascinating book about twenty years ago entitled *To Engineer Is Human: The Role of Failure in Successful Design.*[2] Surveying the history of technology and using stories of faulty bridges, fragile railroad trestles, and imploding airplanes, he reinforces the point of his research: that great improvements in design come only after failures have been understood and corrected. As he puts it, "No one *wants* to learn by mistakes, but we cannot learn enough from success to go beyond the state of the art."[3] His stories are technical and engineering based, but his conclusion is valid for leaders in any organization. Our successes are wonderful and comforting, but we learn best when we spend time reflecting on and analyzing our failures.

As you read the leadership literature, you come to the conclusion that great leaders, in addition to all of their other traits and attributes, know themselves. And "knowing yourself" requires a well-developed skill of reflecting. Mezirow writes of the three functions of reflection as it applies to adult learning:[4]

- To reflect as a guide to action
- To reflect to give coherence to the unfamiliar
- To reassess the justification of what we already know

REFLECTION AS A GUIDE TO ACTION

How do we make reflecting a practical skill that gets used daily in our organizations as a guide to action? Consider these four questions:

1. What did I/we expect to accomplish?
2. What, in fact, did I/we accomplish?
3. Why are the answers to questions 1 and 2 different? (Notice that the question is not, "Who's to blame?")
4. What actions do we have to take to make sure this does not happen again? In other words, what did we learn?

Consider the power of these four questions if they are used regularly and objectively in any organization. Questions 1 and 2 are straightforward and should be answered as completely and objectively as possible.

For example, I may have hired a new director of sales and expected to see sales rise within six months of her coming on board.

It's now six months later, and sales have not risen at all. At this point, I may be tempted to put the blame on the new sales director, but that would be foolish until I spend the time to reflect on the third question: Why? Maybe the answer is obvious, like a downturn in the entire economy, or maybe the answer is subtle, like a shift in R&D priorities that will bring out a "killer application" and the entire customer base is simply waiting. Until I do a good job of thinking about the third question, I cannot even begin to answer the fourth.

And then there is always the hard part of answering the third question: maybe I did a poor job of hiring the right person for the position, or maybe I put a good person in a bad system and no one, not even a sales superstar, could have succeeded. Reflecting may mean looking "out there," but it must include some time looking in a mirror.

Reflection to Give
Coherence to the Unfamiliar

Giving coherence to the unfamiliar is found when we review the results of past actions and see how they should be used to modify the mental maps we referenced when we decided to act.

Consider, for example, the reflecting that should have been going on in early 2005 at some of the major automobile companies that had succeeded in maintaining unit sales growth for the past three years based primarily on incredible financing terms for the purchase or lease of new cars. The mental maps that show a strong relationship between new sales and great financing are starting to fray. What worked in 2002, 2003, and 2004 is starting to falter in 2005. These companies have a great opportunity to learn from the successes and, now, diminishing returns of a car sales strategy built on financing. Part of their reflection should most certainly consider the unintended consequences on the mental maps of the average buyer: financing incentives are now a given and have changed the whole concept of sticker price and its real meaning.

A clear-cut signal of when we need to engage in reflection is when we find ourselves surprised by unexpected business results. Peter Drucker writes about this in his essay "The Theory of Business" when he identifies the signs of crisis in an organization's theory of business: rapid growth, unexpected success, and unexpected failure.[5] It could happen to our own organization or to another organization in our industry. But the simple fact that we were surprised means our mental maps are not coherent. Our lay of the land was wrong, and that often means our concept of our opportunity space does not reflect reality.

REFLECTION TO REASSESS

This third function of reflecting, to reassess the justification of what we already know, sits at the heart of thinking critically about all of our plans and strategies and strikes at the most subtle of managerial weaknesses. At the heart of our plans and strategies are the assumptions we make about all of the players and relationships in our business ecosystem. Assumptions save time since we do not have to get everyone aligned. But for that very reason, they are not evaluated and discussed on a regular basis. Our weakness as managers is that we are generally quite poor at dealing with slow change—and assumptions often change slowly, not in a single cataclysmic event. Consider the evolution from analog to digital in the telephone industry. We now see it as having been "fast" and yet, at the time, the urgency to shift built slowly.

And so it is the third function of reflecting that allows us to look for failed assumptions of the past, but requires that we engage in forward reflecting as we consider the future of our job and organization.

Ask yourself what assumptions your latest plan is dependent on.

ANCHORING CONCEPTS

At the deepest level of understanding are three core concepts and processes on which the skill of reflection relies. They all involve thinking about our thinking, being able to act with a higher and deeper level of awareness, monitoring our own consistencies and inconsistencies, and making what are often fuzzy assumptions, logic, or intuitive hunches clearer so that we can hold them up to the mirror of our consciousness and reflect on them. The three anchoring concepts underlying the skill of reflecting are:

- Metacognition
- Tacit, implicit, and explicit knowledge
- Self-regulation

METACOGNITION

Metacognition is thinking about our own thinking. The products of this process are knowledge and beliefs about our own activities of the mind. This awareness then serves as a strategic tool for building and managing the content and connections in our mental maps that bear on our choices and behaviors in the future. Metacognition helps us know what is on our minds; how it is organized and stored as knowledge, skills, and beliefs; and the various processes and tools we use or can use to create or reorganize our knowledge. Metacognition sets the stage for people's strategic thinking in decision making, planning, and acting. Reflection is one of the most powerful cognitive strategies known for increasing awareness and performance, and it relies on our ability to be metacognitive.

For instance, if we know that we tend to overemphasize the risk inherent in choices (as compared to other peers), our strategy may be to gather or require a lot more data before making a decision than our colleagues who rely on their gut reaction, so we feel better about our decisions. Or we may arrange our social environment in a form that ensures there are others on our decision-making team who have various levels of risk aversion and can offer various levels of data, logic, vision, and ideas to balance our own cognitive tendencies. An even simpler example of the potential power of metacognition is that if we know we are a slow reader who gets lost in details, we may ask for an executive summary of reports. If, however, we want to improve our skill of detailed analysis, we may recruit an expert to walk us through her reading of reports, explaining what she focuses on and why, and then gives us feedback as we practice detailed analysis within a specified time frame. As you can see, metacognition often precedes self-directed learning, another skill of the Prepared Mind.

Most important, metacognition has a reciprocal relationship with the skill of reflecting. In order to activate metacognition, we have to stop and take the time to look inward and examine our own cognitive patterns and how they fit our visions for ourselves and our goals. At the same time, metacognitive processing and knowledge gives us the content for our reflection. One point worth noting is that while cognition does not strictly acknowledge emotions in a practical sense, we know it does, and we assume emotions to be included in metacognition.

TACIT, IMPLICIT, AND EXPLICIT KNOWLEDGE

Moving to and from tacit, implicit, and explicit knowledge is a close cousin to metacognition, and it is also a critical underlying process for the skill of reflecting. *Tacit knowledge* is what we know and believe but cannot articulate, often because it has become so deeply ingrained in our minds that we cannot separate it from who we are. *Implicit knowledge* is what we know and believe and can articulate if prompted by aids in our own thinking (such as a stirring memory) or, more often, by a prompt from the environment (for example, a good question like, "Tell me how you do that"). *Explicit knowledge* is what we know and believe and can articulate without prompting (for example, "Let me show you how I calculate net present value").

Taking the time and effort to reflect implies that we want to take something that is tacit or implicit and make it explicit to ourselves or to others so we can shine a closer light on it, study it, and perhaps discuss it. For instance, in the 1980s, many companies had an implicit understanding and policy of no layoffs. Yet when global competition accelerated and these companies fell behind, they took that implicit understanding and made it more explicit so they could examine its feasibility in the light of changed market conditions.

Reflection can also take us in the other direction, comparing what is explicit to what is more implicit or tacit. For instance, we know an organization that explicitly solicits sponsorship and support from various industries and is under financial pressure to do more of this kind fundraising. At the same time, the organization has an explicit mission to fight heart and lung disease. In terms of reflection, its leaders weigh their needs and their sponsorship-getting ability against the sponsor's affiliation with the tobacco and alcohol industries. If there is an affiliation, they do not take the money. However, the reflection grows even more important when their pending sponsor is seen as having a potential self-interest in selling to the members. Is it the organization's role to guard members? Is the concern really about selling? What is wrong with selling? Is it conflict of interest or acceptable mutually beneficial interest? These are questions the leaders have to ask themselves again and again because there is no clear right answer. Moving back and forth from what is internalized into tacit and implicit and what is externalized into explicit is a common exercise that occurs when we reflect. It is the studying of oneself from inside out and outside in.

This movement from tacit to implicit to explicit knowledge is critical when it comes to applying another Prepared Mind skill, the skill of enabling. We enable people when we provide them opportunity and give them the knowledge and means to make use of the opportunity. If we never shift our own knowledge from the implicit to the explicit, we can never truly enable those around us except by giving them experiences they have to catch on to themselves, and not have the benefit of learning from others' experience and reflection on that experience. So we reflect to enable ourselves to reason better and make more decisions grounded in integrity. We also reflect to enable others to learn with us from our experience and their own.

SELF-REGULATION

Our human capability to consciously regulate ourselves takes what we come to know through metacognition and, by traversing tacit, implicit, and explicit knowledge, then applies judgment to it. Underlying the process is our openness to changing our minds or behavior to meet the standards we have chosen as priorities within ourselves. We have heard a lot about self-regulation through the controversies in the accounting, pharmaceutical, and medical industries. For instance, professional societies that set up codes of conduct are attempting to have professionals in their societies regulate their behaviors according to some common norm, so, in theory, the government and other legal entities will not step in to regulate.

However, as it applies to individuals' developing and using Prepared Minds, self-regulation is the core aspect of the skill of reflecting, where we essentially ask ourselves, "How does what I can do or how does what I have done compare to my standards of practice?" Those standards can be ethical, moral, social, intellectual, or financial, but they provide the bottom line for our decisions and actions. That is one reason that the skill of reflecting is critical to do in the make-sense phase of the sense–make sense–decide–act cycle. We can, through self-regulation, think ahead about options compared to our bottom line of interior standards.

What if our interior standards are in competition or conflict? The answer often depends on how much we invest in reflecting throughout our lives. Typically, the more we reflect and examine ourselves, the more our interior standards align with each other. That is how we come to integrity and coherency within ourselves. Still, there will be times when our standards are in competition. Then the choice of standards against which to weigh our decisions and actions may be a matter of reflecting what really is the deeper standard within us. Other times, the choice may be a trade-off or compromise between standards. External monitors such as the law, advice from colleagues, and religious practices may all help form and test these standards. However, the Prepared Mind learns to take these external sources of standards and internalize them (or not) and take responsibility for our own choices after engaging in thoughtful reflection and self-regulation.

Sometimes self-regulation does not have such heavy implications. When we develop social sensitivities about what to say and what not to say to strangers, competitors, or new colleagues, for reasons of trust, protocol, or many other professional reasons, we are practicing the core skill of self-regulation. Often, reflecting and learning after prior instances where we perhaps did not get the reaction we expected, or after watching someone we admire handle herself socially, has led us to self-regulating habits and standards. Whenever we engage in review of our actions and interactions, whether large stakes or small, we are using the skill of reflection to refine our self-regulation capability. Also, this capability gives us the practical reason to reflect on and be open to change in ourselves, particularly in our decisions and actions.

CONNECTING TO THE CONCEPTS: EXERCISES TO IMPROVE THE SKILL OF REFLECTING

REFLECTING FORWARD AND BACKWARD

We often think of the skill of reflecting as being applied only after we act. Reflecting backward is important and draws on the anchoring concepts of metacognition, self-regulation, and making implicit knowledge explicit. One simple formula that individuals or groups can use consists of asking yourself these questions:

1. What was my goal or intention?
2. What happened?
3. How did what happened meet my goal or intention?
4. What else entered into the process and had an impact on the outcome?
5. If I had it to do over again, what would I keep? What would I change?

However, if what you want to develop is a Prepared Mind, it is good to develop the skill for reflecting forward as well. This requires the use of foresight as well as hindsight. Reflecting forward incorporates the skill of imagining and requires us to dig a little more deeply into our tacit and implicit knowledge before we act. This may delay action for just a little while (we can also employ self-regulation to the time we allow ourselves to think ahead so we do not risk overthinking and underacting), but it can often save us from unwise action and negative unintended consequences, and help us see risks and opportunities in the situation we did not see before. If we are open to being self-critical using our skill of meta-cognition, we can also detect our own biases and blind spots in what we know and how we process information, so we can call on other perspectives before taking action.

There are many ways to practice the skill of reflecting forward. The first method here is a variation on reflecting backward. Before you decide or act, ask yourself these questions (again, this method can be used by a group as well as by an individual):

1. What is my goal or intention?
2. What do I already know about the situation that could be used to improve the chances of my goal or intention?
3. What is the risk of acting? Of not acting?
4. What are various scenarios I see happening if I act? If I do not act?
5. Are they worth the risks?
6. What don't we know about the situation that we need to learn before we act?
7. What will I be content with seeing and hearing as a result of my action?
8. How willing and ready am I to be a leader of change that may ensue?

Another method for reflecting backward and forward is one we have seen practiced by both famous and quiet leaders we admire. It is a values- or principle-based reflection method:

1. Establish a short list (three to seven) of key principles or values you want to guide your day and all the decisions and actions you take on that day.
2. Early in that morning, look at the list and at your calendar and imagine how you see those principles being employed as a part of each of your tasks. Also be open to opportunities to employ them in spontaneous ways to events and interactions that are not on your calendar.
3. Review the list and your day at midday to see how well you are doing at employing your principles and where it was difficult to do so.
4. At the end of the day, use your principles as a checklist for reviewing the day. The areas that were particularly tough may point out areas in your life that could benefit from the skill of learning.

EXPLORE YOUR OWN MENTAL MAP

One way to exercise our human capability of metacognition within the context of reflecting, especially if you are a visual person, is to review visually one or more decisions or actions you have taken. By drawing your own version of a mental map that shows you how you got to a particular decision or action, you are employing a particular application of the cocktail napkin exercise discussed in Chapter Four.

Here is a short list of questions you can use to generate the contents of your map for reflecting backward or forward:

1. What were the key factors I considered when making this decision? List them.
2. How do I see these factors related to each other? Draw lines between them, or build a hierarchy or a network of the factors in relationship to each other.
3. Where do I see clumps, patterns, circular reasoning, or linear thinking?
4. What conclusion did this chain of relationships between factors lead to?

5. If I were to reorganize the factors and their relationship to each other, what other conclusions might I have come to?
6. Who do I know and respect who would look at the same decision and come up with a different set of factors or relationships between them? What conclusion did she, or would she, draw?

Ask for Feedback

Asking for feedback seems like an obvious step in developing the skill of reflecting. What feedback does, if it is honest, is make others' implicit reaction to your decision, action, or deliberation explicit to you. What we have found, however, is that asking for feedback is not as common as we would think. Why? It takes trust and the ability to risk, on the part of both the one asking and the one giving feedback, in order to be authentic and helpful. Also, many of us do not know how to ask for feedback in a way that makes it easier for the person giving the feedback to scope what they say so it is helpful. The question, "What did you think?" is limited in its usefulness because it is too big in its scope. Sometimes we just want to hear what is on others' minds in a general way. Usually, though, we want to focus feedback on particular aspects of our thinking and doing that we are willing and able to change.

Here is a short set of questions that focuses the feedback:

"If you were in my position, how would you think about this?"
"Tell me what important information you see me not considering or skimming over."
"What went right about what just happened?"
"How could we have seen the consequences in advance?"

Writing

Many of the great Prepared Minds in history were letter writers, note takers, and journal keepers. The personal reflections of Thomas Jefferson, Benjamin Franklin, Albert Einstein, great saints, and great explorers and ship captains, to name but a few, reveal their own thinking about their thinking. One of the important contributions that written expression makes to our thinking is that having to put ideas into language that can be understood by ourselves and others forces us to make our ideas clearer and make the implicit reasons behind the patterns of our thinking more explicit. Not only does this have the effect of having the receiver of our writing reflect on something in new ways, it also gives us pause as we write. Structuring our thoughts and committing them to paper and then sometimes reading them after can reveal things to us we could have never realized by just keeping it bottled up in our minds.

Writing regularly requires self-regulation and discipline. However, to be a true instrument for reflection, what we write must not be too guarded or planned. Find someone you trust to write your ideas to, or write to yourself in a journal.

Here are some tips for keeping a regular discipline of writing:

- Commit to a regular time each day to write.
- Find a regular, trusted readership for your writing.
- Record a few questions to write about every day. You can also ask new questions each day.
- Read journals and letters of leaders you admire to see if there is a structure they use that you could employ in your own writing.
- Keep a copy of the letters you send to others, and reread them on occasion.
- Reread your journal on occasion, and look for themes.

DAILY EXAMEN

The Jesuits are known for their intellectual rigor and reflective capacity, even in the midst of busy lives. They are not monks but contemplatives in action. In the 1500s, Saint Ignatius of Loyola, the founder of the order, developed a spiritual discipline called the Daily Examen that Jesuits and laypeople still practice.

The Examen is a simple, quick, practical way to work at self-regulation by stopping three times a day and reviewing your life from the time you did the previous Examen. As you replay the moments of your day like a movie reel, you ask yourself how you stay true to God and to your principles for relationships. You become conscious of where you want to improve and then move on to the rest of your day. It takes as little as five minutes. What is interesting is that when we have shared this model with businesspeople who wish to develop their skill of reflection, we find many of them realize they have mentors who do something similar, sometimes spiritually based but always principle based.

Whether you take a spiritual or principle-based approach, make explicit to yourself one or two deep values that you wish to practice across all domains of your life. Stop yourself three times each day and replay the day, asking yourself, "How am I doing against these values?"

THE CYCLE OF REFLECTING

If we are going to be prepared for a better future, we need to stay true through the entire Sense-Response Cycle. As we work the cycle, we need to reflect on the future, the present, and the past. Consider the questions posed in Figure 10.1 as a starting point.

1. WHY DO I IGNORE SOME OF WHAT I SEE?

As human beings, we have dozens of biases and blind spots. Some are trivial, some profound. One of the most profound biases we share is the bias of belief preservation. When we succumb to this bias, we often make objective evidence subservient to our beliefs. This bias is seen nearly every time an old and proud organization doesn't face the facts of a changing reality. Sears ignored Wal-Mart for years because Wal-Mart was not a "department store." GM ignored foreign manufacturers in the early 1980s because they "only made subcompacts." In Chapter Six, we asked, "What am I seeing that I'm denying?" The natural extension is to ask, "Why?"

2. ARE MY SELF-IMPOSED BOUNDARIES PREVENTING ME FROM SEEING THE BIGGER PICTURE?

When we make sense of the world around us, we always do so within self-imposed boundaries, and, unfortunately, the tighter the boundaries are, the easier it is to find a solution. The scandal of prisoner maltreatment in Iraqi prisons was at first the work of a "few bad apples," which made it an easy problem to resolve. Only over time did we see the full scope of a system that had run amok. Remember that the answer to "Why?" is generally found in the bigger system environment.

FIGURE 10.1. THE SENSE-RESPONSE CYCLE OF REFLECTING

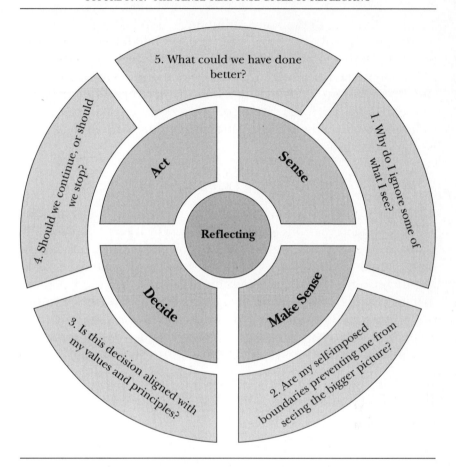

3. IS THIS DECISION ALIGNED WITH MY VALUES AND PRINCIPLES?

People and organizations are notorious for saying the right words to describe values and principles but acting without regard to them. As individuals, we may profess to have a strong sense of "family," and yet we travel and take assignments and regularly miss our kids' games and birthdays. At the turn of this century, the Ford Motor Company talked of its dedication to the environment yet it produces some of the least fuel-efficient vehicles on the market. Do you walk the talk in your dealings with others?

4. Should We Continue, or Should We Stop?

The question of stopping or continuing a course of action is rarely dealt with in an objective fashion: egos, pride, and fear get in the way. Economists talk about the sunk cost of a decision and tell us that these past costs should not be considered as we move forward. But all you have to do is look at a handful of over-budget projects to see that this advice is rarely considered in the real world. The willingness to exercise self-regulation while caught up in the action is all too often missing.

5. What Could We Have Done Better?

All projects and programs *should* have a close-out phase during which we uncover lessons learned that *should* be used to improve our performance on the next program or project. However, our experience is anything but that. We see successful project managers rushing to get onto their next assignment, and we see poor project managers simply relieved that "it's over." In both cases, they miss the opportunity for improvement. We would be surprised if more than 15 percent of large projects lead to real learning for their organization. We are too busy to take the time to improve. What a shame.

Benefits, Risks, and Challenges of Reflecting

All of the Prepared Mind skills have benefits, risks, and challenges associated with their development and use. Here is our starting list for the skill of Reflecting. Add to, subtract from, and modify them to fit your reality.

Benefits of Improving Your Skill of Reflecting

Improving a skill takes time and energy, and before expending either, we need to be assured that the benefits are worth the effort. Consider the following points.

Self-Revelation
Socrates, who laid the foundation for Western philosophical thought, said, "The unexamined life is not worth living." The

biggest benefit for improving our skill of reflecting is that we get a better sense of who we really are.

Wisdom

In a world that is overloaded with data, we are starved for wisdom: the ability to discern what is true and right. Taking the time to reflect on our actions is one of the best paths to building wisdom in ourselves.

Anchoring

Deep learning, which is enabled by reflection, allows us to see patterns and anchor ourselves in long-term ideas, principles, and values and helps us not be blown about by the winds of reaction. Reflective people decide and respond more than they react.

Perspective

Those who are reflective often become the person the group turns to for counsel and perspective. Why? Because reflective people keep the big picture in their minds and are able to see and articulate connections between a particular action or piece of information and the big picture.

RISKS OF REFLECTING

An overemphasis on a newly developed skill can result in experiencing downside risks. Consider the following points.

Not Liking What We See

If one of the benefits of reflecting is finding out who we are, a potential downside is that we may not like the person we find. We may be better than we think, but we have to face the risk that our self-image will not live up to the truth we see in the mirror. Taking on a disposition of humility and learning keeps us open to changing ourselves and consequently keeps us from claiming to be perfect.

Time

Reflecting, like so many of the other Prepared Mind skills, takes time to develop and use. In times of crisis, we may sacrifice precious time as we reflect on the situation. Many of the exercises offered in this chapter, like the Daily Examen, call for a short amount of time to be taken each day for this skill. We take time to work out physically, so why wouldn't we want to take time to work out mentally and perhaps spiritually?

Emotional Distress

Even if we are reflective and begin to see things in new ways, there is no guarantee that others will reflect and get it too. This may lead to feelings of frustration, isolation, or depression. It seems that one of the keys here is not to expect change from reflection without practicing the skills of learning and enabling. Help people observe patterns, and ask them reflective questions repeatedly. Sooner or later, they will start to reflect as well.

Dissonance

Reflection can cause dissonance in ourselves and or in others when our image of our world does not map to our world. What do we do about it? We can and should look at it as an opportunity to exercise the skill of challenging and learning so we do something constructive with the dissonance and are willing to sit with it for awhile.

CHALLENGES TO REFLECTING

Here are four challenges you might face as you try to improve your skill of reflecting:

- Pressure to act
- No process
- Unarticulated principles and values
- Fear of discovery

Pressure to Act

Pressure to act fast and act continuously work together to create a vicious circle of nonthoughtful work. The adage of the 1990s of "fire, ready, aim" gave us speed but usually not sustainable business. It takes courage to say "stop," but we all know that leadership requires courage. Typically, if we do not stop, reflect, and regulate ourselves, down the road some entity outside ourselves will regulate us and define our opportunity space for us. We need to make thought and action a both-and requirement for business, not an either-or choice.

No Process

School and work are very good at teaching us how to analyze, how to do, how to decide and act, and sometimes how to defend our decisions. However, we have not had as many opportunities to learn how to reflect. Maybe it has been considered a luxury or a nice-to-have but not a need-to-have. Maybe it has been considered too soft and inactionable. However, as we see the demand for leadership and more thoughtful work at all levels rising, we realize that reflection is a necessity for leadership.

Unarticulated Principles and Values

There is a great moment in the movie *The Natural* when Glenn Close says, "I believe we all have two lives: the one we learn with and the one we live with after that." While those of us who profess to believe in the principles of the Prepared Mind feel that learning is continuous, there is something to that quote that rings true. The early part of life is often about figuring out our principles and values that we will then use in the rest of our lives. The skill of reflection helps both aspects of life. However, in order to articulate and rearticulate our principles and values, whether as individuals or as an organization, we have to use metacognition to examine what we think and how we think and generalize them to more guiding overall principles and values. Experience will test and challenge these principles, but you have to know what they are in the first place in order to have an anchor for your behavior and a mirror for your reflection.

Fear of Discovery

"Don't go there" is a current catchphrase when talking with someone (even yourself) about a sensitive subject. Some people do not want to reflect because they fear they might find out something about themselves or their actions that they do not recognize, cannot explain, or do not like. Reflection does not have to be judgmental. Also, the ups and downs in life usually force most of us, at one time or another, to "go there" whether we want to or not. It is important to know how to go there and not feel threatened by it before the harsh hand that reality sometimes deals us forces us to.

Applied Reflecting: The Talent Problem

Consider these examples of questions and activities Prepared Mind leaders might engage in as they confront the talent problem from the reflecting point of view:

- An executive might reflect on actions that saved the company in the short term (downsizing or outsourcing, for example) but made it so lean that it's anorexic. Has she cut the training budget and simultaneously weakened the "bench strength" of the organization? What could she have done differently? Or, more important, what did she do or neglect to do that got the company into the dilemma that triggered the downsizing. She is not a victim. What was her role?
- A middle manager might look at peers and ask if he had helped them or simply complained about them. We talk of teamwork, and yet we operate under the tacit belief that knowledge is power, as if it were something to be hoarded rather than shared. What is your contribution to the success of your peers? What are you afraid of?
- An individual contributor might question her role in maintaining her state-of-the-art knowledge of needed technology. The trigger to lifelong learning is found in the value we place on our skill set. How valuable is yours?

BUILDING YOUR SKILLS

Here are a few more ideas to use in building your skill of reflecting.

REFLECTING AND DOING

One way to slow the train and be smart about business is to combine metacognition with making what is tacit or implicit explicit. We are asked by one company after another to help them help their employees become more thoughtful and consultative and serve less as order takers. We advise them to encourage their employees to ask questions like, "Why?" and "Tell me what you are try-ing to achieve so I can give you the best resource." This is asking them to make explicit what is tacit and implicit to them. The more you practice this technique with an attitude of service, the more re-flection and thoughtful action becomes baked into interactions.

When you see yourself or others reacting or just jumping to the first answer, stop to ask yourself (or them) how thinking about the situation is using your (or their) capacity for metacogni-tion. The best consultants are excellent at helping clients think about their own thinking and giving them alternatives to think about their issues and requests in new ways. There is always a spirit of doing and delivering service, but inserting these core concepts and prac-tices of reflection helps us do the best thing given the standards and circumstances.

LEARN A PROCESS FOR REFLECTION

Making a short list of good questions explicit and using them every day may sound simplistic, but little things can often make a big dif-ference. An executive from one of the world's largest oil compa-nies once shared a story about his father that he had incorporated into his daily practice. While he was growing up, he observed that every morning after breakfast, his dad went into his study for five minutes, closed the door, and then came out and carried on his day. The oil executive waited over fifty years to finally ask his dad what he did in his study each morning. His father's reply was that every morning, he asked himself two questions: "What is my pur-pose in life? How am I going to carry it out today?"

The father told the son that his purpose did not change, so the answer to the first question was always "to teach and learn." (The man was a businessman, by the way.) However, the answer to the second question varied every day, depending on what was on his calendar. He said this exercise always grounded him and gave him a compass for the day. What the son did not see was that at night, when everyone else had gone to bed, his dad spent a few minutes going back over the day and asking himself, "How did I do?"

Ask people of integrity and inner peace and strength how they do it, for these qualities usually result in part from reflection.

ARTICULATE YOUR PRINCIPLES AND VALUES

One of the most systematic ways for thinking about your thinking and making what you believe explicit is to write it down. Do not worry about "good writing." Just scribble notes in a journal, or write a letter to a friend talking about what you believe and why. Give examples of when you have seen these beliefs come to life through your decisions and actions. Give examples of when you have felt off because your decisions and actions violated some previously unarticulated value or principle. You can start with ten minutes of reflection three times a week by doing this exercise. Explore beliefs with others in a nonconfrontational way.

EASE INTO DISCOVERY

Begin small with just one aspect of your life or work. Make up even just one metacognitive question for yourself like, "What was I thinking when I chose that option?" and practice reflection. If you need a little help getting started, ask a trusted mentor to ask you questions and call out inconsistencies until you become more aware of your own habits and regulating mechanisms. Mentors are not just for young professionals. Some of the wisest and most continuously successful executives we know ask others they trust to help them continue to discover the best that is within them and when their actions do not mirror what they have determined as their own "best practice."

MORE QUESTIONS TO CONSIDER

- **Beginner's Mind.** The Zen concept of Beginner's Mind deals with maintaining many possibilities.

  Take a current problem, and list the possible answers you can think of. Now think like a beginner, a naive newcomer, and double the list by asking "dumb" or "obvious" questions. Write them down. What do you see?

- **René Descartes.** Consider the following quote from Descartes: "If you would be a real seeker after truth, it is necessary that at least once in your life you doubt, as far as possible, all things."

What happens if you doubt some of your business or personal truths? Make a list of all those things you assume to be true. What do you see when you allow yourself to doubt some of them?

- **The Red Hat.** Edward de Bono's *Six Thinking Hats* is a comprehensive outline of thinking modes.[6] The Red Hat deals with feelings and intuition.

  What does your situation feel like? Ignore your head for a while; what does your gut tell you to do? Write the reasons your situation makes you mad, happy, jealous, worried, and so on.

GO FORTH AND REFLECT

Make a commitment to leave this chapter prepared to apply the skills of reflecting, even if you have just one strategy in mind. Review and reflect on all the exercises and tips in this chapter for developing your reflection skills, and choose one to start with today.

Chess is like life in that you need to see three moves ahead.
                                    —Unknown Grand Master

The Prepared Mind reflects on the causes of events to uncover the basic principles that drive them. Understanding basics gives the power to predict and control outcomes at a higher-than-chance level. Basic principles are masked and operate three causes beneath the surface of events. Practice seeing three causes deeply by reflecting on (in order) the environment, mental states, and the universals that drive a given event.[7]

CHAPTER ELEVEN

CONCLUSION
Preparing for Tomorrow

*The Bay of Pigs debacle occurred in part because
President John F. Kennedy and his key advisors could
never give it sustained attention for more than forty-five
minutes at a time.*
RICHARD E. NEUSTADT AND ERNEST R. MAY

We opened this book with the observation from Louis Pasteur that "chance favors the prepared mind," and in the subsequent chapters we explained the eight skills of the Prepared Mind and how their use can make you a more effective leader. We close the book with a question and some suggestions on how you can answer that question by using the Sense-Response Cycle and the eight skills of the Prepared Mind.

The question is simple: How will you prepare for your tomorrow? You may be a company executive or a newly hired individual contributor. You may be involved in manufacturing or in services, and it could be for a profit-seeking institution or a nonprofit. The specific circumstances don't matter. What matters is that every one of us has to be prepared for our tomorrow, whatever it may be.

DEALING WITH TOMORROW

Leaders have three choices when it comes to dealing with tomorrow's problems and opportunities:

- Wait for events to happen and react to them as best they can. In this case, the cycle is reduced to "sense, then act."
- Jump on the bandwagon of changes clearly under way and do their best to adapt to the changes. The Sense-Response Cycle is used, but minimal time is spent in making sense.
- Anticipate the changes, and take an active role in shaping their future. The cycle is used in a balanced and meaningful way. The more you can anticipate your future, the more prepared and influential you will be.

To use the metaphor of a radar screen, there are minor events entering the outer ring of our mental radar screen that should be seen as clues to future events (Figure 11.1). This ring is your anticipation zone; if you pay attention to events in this zone you will have enough time to prepare for your future outcomes, both good and bad. There are events with clearer outcomes in the middle ring of our radar screen that show clear intent. As we sense events in the adaptation zone we have the time to adapt our mental maps and the actions of our organization before their inevitable conclusion. Finally, there are here-and-now events to which we can

FIGURE 11.1. CLUES TO FUTURE EVENTS

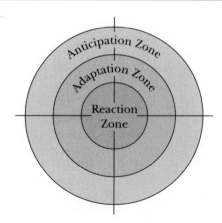

only react. Once events have entered the reaction zone they are generally out of our control; they control us.

Future events, both good and bad, are going to happen. How can you best use the time available to you?

The Sense-Response Challenge

In the grand scheme of things, one of the hallmarks of the past couple of centuries has been the acceleration of the pace of change. We don't know for sure what challenges and opportunities tomorrow will bring us, but we do know that, as in the past, some of us will see them and others won't. The overarching challenge for today's leaders is to learn ever faster ways to prepare for whatever will come our way.

In order to rise to this challenge, we have to look at the Sense-Response Cycle (Figure 11.2) and figure out how to increase its speed. We suggest you use the eight skills of the Prepared Mind to prepare yourselves to:

- Sense sooner.
- Make sense faster.

FIGURE 11.2. SENSE-RESPONSE CYCLE DEMANDS

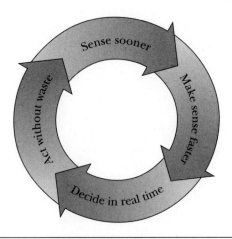

- Decide in real time.
- Act without waste.

Some of us will anticipate our future, others will have to react to what we create.

Observing in Support of the Sense Phase

Observing is the skill most aligned with the sense phase of the Sense-Response Cycle. How will we use it to sense those things that will be important to our future? Part of the answer can be found by attending to the anchoring concept of pattern recognition and considering how it helps us prepare for the future by understanding enduring patterns from the past and looking for them as we try to discern our future.

When it comes to systems, certain patterns seem to repeat. And so if we can recognize a pattern as it evolves today, we can predict tomorrow's probable outcome. Exhibit 11.1 lists four of these patterns, often referred to as systems archetypes, along with a brief description and examples.

How can you use the skill of observing to help you prepare for your tomorrow? Consider the following:

- *Watch for the evolution of known archetypes, and address their implications early.* For example, price wars are an example of escalation, and, historically, we know that everyone loses when escalation occurs. The key is to change the game and escape the trap of escalation. Will any of the major airlines win the fare wars? Not until they change the game.
- *Watch for slow change in existing mental maps.* Staying with the airline example, Southwest Airlines is no longer unique, and ever so slowly, its workforce is getting older, more tenured, and therefore more expensive. Southwest has had a great run, but its competitive model and advantages are slowly eroding.
- *Watch for new entrants with new approaches to serving "your" customers.* Are convenience stores a challenge to the fast food industry? They haven't been one in the United States, but they are in Japan. They are not categorized as restaurants, but people do spend money buying breakfasts and lunches there.

EXHIBIT 11.1. FOUR SYSTEMS ARCHETYPES

Archetype	Past Examples	Recent or Emerging Problems	Applicable to Your Future?
Escalation: Both parties see the other's actions as threats, so they do more in defense of their own position. And on it goes.	The buildup of atomic weapons in the Cold War Airline price wars Automobile rebates	Renewed tensions between unions and company management	
Fixes that fail: The fix quickly reduces the symptom of the problem, but the unintended consequences of the fix over time actually make the problem worse or create new problems.	DDT (long-term use was an ecological disaster) Chlorofluorocarbons (contributed to the hole in the ozone layer) Housing projects in major cities Executive stock options	Failure of employee stock options to increase morale or loyalty Outsourcing of noncore processes leading to "corporate anorexia" and other unintended consequences	
Success to the successful: Resources are given to the successful party, ensuring future success.	Declaring young managers as "high potentials" and giving them a disproportionate share of attention Fictitious earnings growth and stock price	Shift of U.S. business alliances to India and Asia ("friendlier" environment) rather than Europe "Clean books" and stock price	
Tragedy of the commons: People destroy a common resource in working for their own best interests.	Water use in the West Fishing grounds Grazing land	Health care system collapse as boomers age and overload the system	

- *Investigate surprises, and watch for new combinations.* For example, computers started as "number crunchers" and then morphed to word processors and then morphed to photo archives and now are morphing again into entertainment storage and retrieval devices. TiVo was a surprise to both the computer and the television industries.

REASONING TO SENSE AND MAKE SENSE

Once we have sensed changes in our environment, we have to figure out what they mean. Reasoning is aligned with the transition from sensing to making sense, and the anchoring concept of mental models is used both consciously and unconsciously. As we try to make sense of what we observe, the question we have to constantly ask ourselves is, "Do we have a valid mental model of the future, and does what we are seeing fit these models?" For example, is your mental model based on "more of the same" or "everything is chaotic"? Do you see a future that is a modification of today or something that has to be invented along the way?

One of the problems with developing a valid mental model of the future is that our expertise gets in the way. Consider the story of Arthur C. Clarke, one of the most respected writers of science fiction who has been writing interesting stories about the future since the early 1950s. As we conducted our research for this book, we read one of Clarke's earliest stories, "The Sands of Mars," to see how well he had been able to look into the future.[1] The story, written in 1951, was about a reporter's trip to the "red planet." His description of the atomic engines that powered the spacecraft made sense inasmuch as atomic power was then a reality and people were speculating as to how it might be used. His descriptions of weightless space travel and dealing with the vacuum of space were well imagined. He clearly understood the need for minimizing weight in the rocket in order to conserve fuel. And that is where his expertise got in the way.

Clarke described a scene in which the main character was going to document his experiences of space flight. In preparation for writing his report, our fictional reporter pulled out his lightweight typewriter and the pack of ultralight carbon paper that he would use. Clarke was a writer and he just "knew" that a good typewriter was an essential tool and that a good portable was certainly state-of-the-art. Although calculating machines (computers) had been used during World War II to calculate artillery and naval gun trajectories, these were numbers, not words, and he missed a clue about the future.

Our explanation of his inability to "invent" a new means of preparing a report was that he could not, so would not, see beyond something he knew so well. A typewriter was permanently etched in his mental model.

In much the same way, one of us was involved with a major automotive supplier a few years ago and had the opportunity to discuss the future of the automotive industry with senior executives in preparation for a training session with a large number of middle managers. The topic of fuel cells was raised, but most of the senior executives saw this technology as a long-range issue. However, the training session included an exercise where teams of middle managers were to write a disaster scenario for the company. It was amazing to see how many of the teams created a scenario around the impact of fuel cell technology in the short run. What didn't one group observe what the other group was concerned about? Time will tell which group is right, but that's not the issue. The issue was that two groups of managers had different radar screens and therefore different mental models of the future.

As you construct your mental model of your future, the model should include the possibility of surprise, and, going back to the skill of observing, you need to look for possible surprises that would affect your mental model. What could surprise you? Consider Peter Drucker's point of view: there is a set of assumptions that define an organization's theory of business and there are certain steps to be taken to make sure the theory is valid.[2] His explanation of the three categories of assumption can be summarized:

- Assumptions about the environment in which the organization functions. When you think "environment," think of everything that is "out there," from customers to competitors to complementers.
- Assumptions about the mission of the organization. When you think "mission," think of the organization's reason for be-

ing. Sometimes this is hard for profit-seeking businesses but easy for the nonprofit sector. Try these: What is the mission of Ford Motor Company? What is the mission of Habitat for Humanity?

- Assumptions about the needed core competencies of the organization. What does the organization have to do better than anyone else if it is to accomplish their mission?

Think of these three sets of assumptions as answering the following questions: What can we be? What do we want to be? What do we have to be?

Along with his explanation of an organization's theory of business, Drucker posed four questions you can use to test the validity of the theory of your business:

1. Do your assumptions about environment, mission, and core competencies fit reality? What are you observing that should modify any of these?
2. Do your assumptions about environment, mission, and core competencies fit each other? Do you see conflict and how your mental model of the business should change?
3. Does everyone in your organization know and understand your theory of business? Who is in the know, and who is clueless?
4. Do you test your theory of business constantly?

Simple mental model; simple test. What are your answers to the four questions?

Most people can go back and explain the earlier theory of business. Some can explain today's theory of business. But what about tomorrow? Are you and your organization prepared for your organization's future theory of business?

IMAGINING IN SUPPORT OF THE MAKE-SENSE PHASE

Part of the challenge of the make-sense phase of the Sense-Response Cycle is the need to create a picture of the future without all the facts at hand. Try as we might, we cannot prove our future; we can only imagine it. And this is where the anchoring concept of fore-thought comes into play.

How can you apply your skill of imagining to prepare for your future? One way is to recall that the ability to imagine is funda-mental to the whole concept of innovation. Since that's the case, we can look at past innovations (prior knowledge) and what was or could have been imagined and then use that to make sense of our future. Consider the following:

- What do contact lenses, diapers, ballpoint pens, and cameras have in common? They are all disposable. What is it about your business that could be made disposable? What is your insight about your disposal future?
- What do Rogaine, fantasy sports, retirement planning, and Harley Davidson motorcycles have in common? Boomers. What is it about your business that could be "generational"? What will the boomers need next? What about the Xers and the millennials?
- What do D-cell batteries, light bulbs, computer keyboards, and automobiles have in common? They are all standardized or have standard components. What is it about your business that you could standardize to appeal to future customers or clients?
- What do fountain pens, roll-top desks, retro-clothing, and the 2005 Ford Mustang have in common? The past. Can you provide future appeal to customers by taking them back to the past?

CHALLENGING TO IMPROVE THE DECIDE PHASE

Is your view of the competitive landscape, the problem, or the op-portunity the only and correct view? Obviously not. As you prepare for your tomorrow, you may want to engage in the anchoring con-cept of perspective taking, that is, seeing the bigger picture from as many points of view as needed. For an example, refer to Figure 11.3, which portrays a mind map drawing we used in a workshop with a client who wanted to investigate innovation as a means of growth.[3]

In the beginning, the client simply wanted to understand the innovation process to follow. The seven hexagons in the middle of the map provide a basic overview of the process and the requirements for both physical and psychological support. However, the more we talked, the more it became clear that much more had to be taken into consideration—for example:

- Would their culture help them or hold them back?
- Did they all agree as to the need? Was sustaining innovation enough, or did they want (or need) to hit the market with disruptive innovation?
- What skills did they have? More important, what skills would they need?
- What could they change, and what would they have to leave alone?

As we continued to view management's dictate of "become innovative" from many different perspectives, we developed a series of questions that had to be answered and would require the full range of Prepared Mind skills. A short list of the questions raised is shown along the top of Figure 11.3. The most interesting and hard-fought question was, "What business are we in?" Until that question was debated and clarified, the call for innovative behavior was not bringing an aligned response.

How are you going to use the skill of challenging to prepare for your tomorrow? Accept the reality that you, your company, and your industry are part of a large complex adaptive system. Consider a few of the characteristic of complex adaptive systems (CAS) and see what they might tell you about your future:

- *CASs are sensitive to small change.* Note the impact that a couple of degrees of warming have on glaciers, wetlands, and winter snows. To what is your business ecosystem sensitive? Price of oil? Interest rates? Political stability? Find the key leverage points, study their changes, and see your future.
- *CASs adapt.* Environmentalists warn us that we are destroying the earth's ecology, and that may be true. But in the long run (the very long run), the earth will adapt and survive. The human

FIGURE 11.3. INNOVATION MIND MAP

Observe	Reason	Imagine	Challenge
Seeing the world anew	Using structure to come to conclusions	Constructing new mental models	Taking a defensible position
How fast is the marketplace changing?	How could an idea pipeline work here?	What would give us a competitive advantage?	What business are we in?
Who or what is new?	What is the impact on the profit model?	What might "different" look like?	What assumptions are feeding the active inertia here?

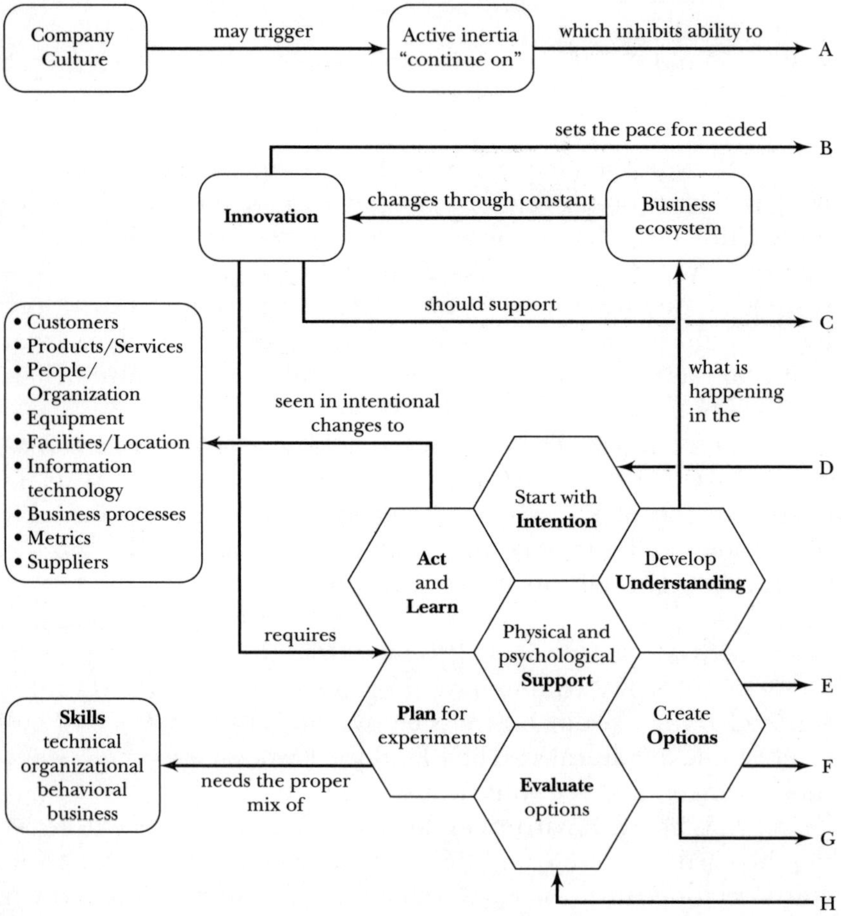

Company Culture — may trigger → Active inertia "continue on" — which inhibits ability to → A

Innovation — sets the pace for needed → B

Innovation ← changes through constant — Business ecosystem

should support → C

- Customers
- Products/Services
- People/ Organization
- Equipment
- Facilities/Location
- Information technology
- Business processes
- Metrics
- Suppliers

seen in intentional changes to

what is happening in the

Start with **Intention**

Develop **Understanding**

Act and **Learn**

Physical and psychological **Support**

→ D

requires

Plan for experiments

Create **Options**

→ E

Skills technical organizational behavioral business

needs the proper mix of

Evaluate options

→ F

→ G

→ H

Decide	Learn	Enable	Reflect
Defining a course of action	Creating and modifying mental maps	Bringing about new understanding and behaviors	Reviewing and adjusting a personal point of view
Who should be our customer?	What don't we know that we should?	How should innovation be perceived at this company?	Why is innovation not a core competency here?
What products and services should we offer?	What rate of change can the customers use?	Who has to get on board?	Why have we failed or succeeded at past innovation?
How can we do it cost-effectively?			

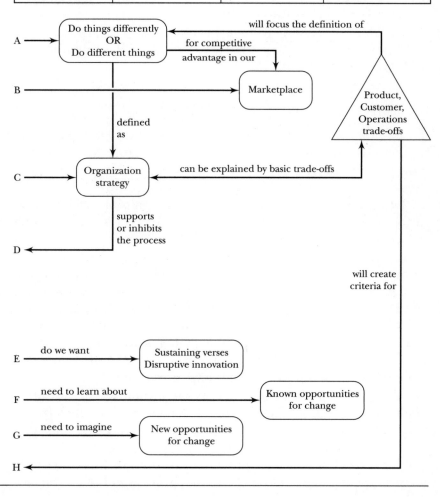

race might not, but the earth will. Think about the changes and pressures that your personal or organizational environment is subject to. This system *will* adapt, and if you can see the large-scale changes, you can see the future. Think about the airline industry for a minute. Cost and competitive pressure are enormous. Can you see a different industry emerging?

- *CASs have both linear and nonlinear feedback mechanisms.* Much of our strategic planning is built on the assumption of linear cause-and-effect relationships. Linear: Fuel prices go up; delivery costs go up. Nonlinear: iPod looks "cool," sales explode. If you can understand some of the nonlinear mechanisms at work you have a chance to see further into the future.

Learn about complex adaptive systems, and apply what you find out to your business

LEARNING TO IMPROVE THE DECIDE PHASE

As we think about the future awaiting us, we may want to pause and think about what we have learned about the future from the past. Using the anchoring concept of transfer, what can we take from the past into the future? We know six things for sure.

First, leaders have always had to deal with tomorrow, and we can learn from historical examples. We are certainly not the first to face an unknown tomorrow. People have done this throughout all of time; some have prospered, and others have not. The challenge we face is how we can learn from their tomorrows—our history. As we examine the successes and failures of those who came before us, we see people who did not imagine a future that others could clearly see. We see people, comfortable in their role as industry leader, who could not challenge themselves and change. We see executives who refused to let their people lead them to a new tomorrow. These things need not happen to you.

The second thing to consider as you ponder tomorrow is that small warning signs abound, helping us to anticipate much of our future if we pay attention. For example, there were warning signs pointing to the destruction of the World Trade towers on September 11, 2001, but an intelligence failure slowed the make-sense phase of the Sense-Response Cycle. We saw them only after the fact.

Third, we do not have to simply wait for tomorrow; today's actions shape our future in intended and unintended ways. When Henry Ford created a moving assembly line, it was no accident, for he intended to build cars for the masses. He was creating a future, and he knew it. However, the inevitable drudgery of assembly line work was an unintended consequence. As we try to plan our future, we also have to be concerned about the unintended consequences of achieving what we expect to achieve.

Fourth, the future holds both losers and winners; we have only to look to the world of technology to see dramatic examples. As we consider the future, we have to consider the consequences of inaction as well as action. Western Union was at the top of the telegraphy game and had the opportunity to own the emerging telephone technology—and chose not to do so. It lost by doing nothing. Honda started manufacturing motorcycles in the United States and continued to expand into anything that needed an engine. It has been winning by seeing other futures for its capabilities. When we act on behalf of our future, we need to consider changes we might invoke as well as the impact of active inertia— that is, doing what we've always been doing.

The fifth consideration is that tomorrow looks different to different people: no one is right; no one is wrong. However, the sum of these different views forms the totality of tomorrow. The future of the automobile industry is not solely in the hands of the automobile companies with the biggest R&D budgets. It can be seen through the eyes of the fuel cell researchers, the oil companies, the legislative bodies, consumers, and others. The answer to "Why?" is always found in the larger system. And so as you consider the future of your organization, you have to consider the future of the business ecosystem in which you operate. The dot-com bubble of the late 1990s was a perfect example of this. The Internet was expected to change everything, but the Internet cognoscenti did not spend enough time listening to themselves. The old brick-and-mortar companies did *not* stand still and wait for the Internet start-ups to change the world. Many, but certainly not all, of the old economy companies acted quite quickly because they also saw the future every bit as clearly as the new economy companies did.

Finally, tomorrow belongs to a younger generation, and we should feel a sense of responsibility to give them a tomorrow that is as unimpaired as possible. We have to be aware of how we will affect the future for those who will follow us. We curse the foolishness of those who came before us and damaged the land and the water and the air. We should not do the same to those who follow us.

DECIDING AND REFLECTING-IN-ACTION AS WE ACT

How will you prepare for your tomorrow? The most straightforward answer we can provide is to say that action and reaction have to take place early and often. We could spend most of our lives in the make-sense phase if we wanted to because it is so comfortable. We could just immerse ourselves in the data and information and not make a move until we were sure of ourselves. However, we all know that that is not practical or even realistic. The world would pass us by, and before long, we would be watching the taillights of the future we intended to see head-on.

An anchoring concept for the skill of deciding is the concept of commitment. Similarly, an anchoring concept for the skill of reflecting is self-regulation. When you combine these concepts and skills, you can quickly come to the realization that failure is an option; it's just that you want to make sure you learn and move forward from each and every (small) failure. The reality of business is that it can be viewed as complex and at times chaotic. We can figure out a complex system, given enough time and money, but we can never figure out a chaotic system. We have to try things and see how the system responds. We have to create purposeful change and see what the system does.

What could you change in your system? Think about the following categories of catalysts to understand your future:

- *Your competitors.* Will you have the same competitors in the future? What have you observed about their behaviors? Can you expect them to continue on into the future? If you attack them in some way (pricing, services, or distribution, for example), will they retaliate in a rational manner? If not, then what happens?
- *Your customers.* Will their buying criteria change? How are new customers changing the basis of competition in your industry? Who is underserved? Who is overserved? What if you focused on smaller but growing customers instead of your best (current) customers?

- *Your products and services.* Where are they in their life cycle? Can you assume that today's products and services will satisfy tomorrow's customers? If they are in the mature stage of their life cycle, what will replace them? What if you dropped a solid but stagnant product line?
- *Your people and how you are organized.* Will today's skill base produce tomorrow's products and services? What if you hired people from another industry? What might they see, and how might they change things?
- *Your physical and knowledge assets.* Can you assume that today's profile will serve the needs of tomorrow's customers? What if you paid your best customers to brief you and your team on what they see changing?
- *Your location.* Are you in the right place for tomorrow? What if you moved your office to a remote site? How would your view of the world change?
- *Your metrics.* Remember that metrics drive behavior. Will you be measuring the right things? What metrics could you use to get a better sense of how your future will be different?

Look for problems and opportunities that will change or make obsolete your mental map of business success. All we know for sure is that tomorrow will look different than today. We may have to change some things in order to remove some of the haze.

ENABLING THE ACT PHASE BY ASKING THE RIGHT QUESTIONS

The work involved with preparing for your tomorrow starts with answering five basic questions. We are posing these questions for an organization, but the questions could and should be considered in a personal sense as well. The questions that all of us need to ponder as we prepare for our future are:

1. Where are we?
2. How is our reality changing?
3. Where are we going?
4. How will we get there?
5. What assumptions are we making?

As you consider your answers to these questions, we will point out the obvious Prepared Mind skill or skills that would be used to answer them, and then we will point out the complementary skills that, if used, will give you a richer answer and help you better prepare for your tomorrow.

Where Are We?

This is the opening question for the sense phase of the Sense-Response Cycle, and it should address the facts of the day. Unfortunately, this question is not raised often enough in organizations; all too often, we assume that we know the current state of the company (usually a financial view) and so does the rest of the organization.

The obvious skill to be used in answering this question is the skill of Observing. We need to open our eyes and ears and see what our customers, competitors, workers, and society think of us. We need to compare ourselves to similar companies and prepare an objective answer to the question.

However, we should dig deeper and get further insight. Think of using other Prepared Mind skills as you answer this question. We could challenge and ask what's good and bad about our current situation. We could reflect and ask if we planned to be where we are today or were forced into this position by external events that we should have seen.

How Is Our Reality Changing?

This question should be used to address the Achilles' heel of most of us: the ability to recognize and deal with slow change. People don't get fat overnight, and companies don't become noncompetitive overnight either. What happens is that the mental map we use to orient ourselves and navigate the problems and opportunities confronting us slowly becomes obsolete, and we don't notice.

As we consider this question, we see the blending of observing and imagining in the question, "I wonder what *this* could mean?" We will see some of the dots, but it will take good imagination to connect them. In addition to using the obvious skills, we might want to learn from the past as we study shifts that we as well as others have missed. Technology changes have always brought on new applications, so we should look for clues of emerging applications (and problems). And each generation of workers brings its own set of assumptions, values, and work/life issues. How prepared are we to attract and manage the diverse workforce that we inevitably face?

Where Are We Going?

This is a two-part question. The first part is to look at your assessment of your current situation and combine it with your insights about a changing reality and project where you would wind up if you do nothing. This part of the question assesses the momentum of your organization today and projects it into the future. Where will our inertia take us, and is that where we want to go? We often see successful companies that seem to miss the curve in the road. It's not what they did that got them in trouble; they kept doing what had made them successful in the past. It's just that their customers or industry changed, and they did not see the changes in time to navigate the curve and not go off the road.

The second part of the question is at the heart of our plans and dreams. It's as large as the "vision stuff" that executives talk about. And it's as practical as the explanation of the goals of a project on the manufacturing floor. In order to answer this question, we often resort to the rational and logical part of our brain and enlist our reasoning skills. We ask rational questions about market share and market growth, and we extrapolate today's performance and express tomorrow's goals.

However, if you applied the skill of learning on a proactive basis, you might add to the question, Where *could* we go? And that question might cause you to learn as much as you can about innovation, for example. Who are your nonconsumers, and how might you capture them? How much improvement can your mainstream customers absorb? What are you offering that both current and future consumers will want or not want?

If you view this question from a challenging point of view, you might ask an additional question: Should we go to where our existing plan takes us, or is there a better destination?

If you view this question from an enabling point of view, you might take the time to see that other people in your organization have a more valid point of view.

If you consider this question while imagining, you might create a business that is entirely new. Consider eBay. Auctions have existed as a means of commerce since humanity lived on a barter economy. But we could never have auctions on a worldwide scale until the creation of the Internet. Look at emerging technologies, and consider the second-order effects of their implementation: What will emerge that is new and innovative, and how can you either lead that innovation or adapt it to your particular situation?

How Will We Get There?

The obvious skills to use here are the skills of reasoning and deciding. However, if you are not careful, you might find yourself in the position of satisficing. You know where you are; you have an idea as to where you want to go; and if you're not careful, you will try to implement the first good plan that is laid on the table. Ideas are not plans, and in order to lead effectively, you need to show everyone your map. That would require that you enable your team and give them the opportunity to help you plan.

Answering the "How?" question requires us to better learn and understand some of the fundamental truths of good project management. For example, moving an organization into the future requires a solid blend of technical, organizational, and business skills, all of which we either have to learn or enable others to participate. Furthermore, trade-offs are inevitable, and the very act of prioritizing means we need to be able to challenge in a meaningful and constructive way.

What Assumptions Are We Making?

Our assumptions usually hide in the background and are taken for granted. Bringing them into the foreground requires both good reasoning and a willingness to challenge. We need to spend the time investigating the "why" of our plans and operations. We need to review the assumed cause-and-effect relationship of the plan and determine what has to be in place for them to work as we hope they will.

Assumptions underlie all of our decisions, past and present, and sometimes the easiest way to expose today's assumptions is to go back in time and think of past assumptions that were patently wrong. The trick here is to see how past (bad) assumptions and the decisions we made show up in failures and problems: they really stand out as we think about them. But you need to distinguish between whether someone made a bad decision or whether the assumptions were bad, which is not always easy to do. Once you've warmed up your brain on the past, dig into today and look for the assumptions that were or are in place to get to the mix of decisions you operate under today. Once you have uncovered the assumptions in use today, it's time to challenge them. How many are necessary? How many are wrong? How many are slowly changing?

Be Constantly on Alert

Today will morph into tomorrow, but it will do so rather slowly for any individual in spite of all of the worry about the speed of change. This is the hard part because none of us is very good at dealing with slow change; for the most part, an organization's responses to changes in its environment is careful and measured.

Regardless of your role, preparing your mind and using the eight skills should improve not only your organization but your satisfaction with it. Of course, there are never any guarantees; some organizations are too hidebound to deal with innovative thinking. But worthwhile organizations almost always have champions. You may have to look hard to find them; you may already know who these champions are. Use your strengths wisely, seek out others with complementary strengths, and work mindfully.

That, in the end, is really what leadership is all about.

Notes

Introduction

1. Gerald L. Gelson, *The Private Science of Louis Pasteur* (Princeton, N.J.: Princeton University Press, 1995).
2. We are indebted to the insights of Ronald A. Heifetz for a description that paints the conditional nature of leadership in a broad context. Heifetz wrote in *Leadership on the Line* (Boston, Mass.: Harvard Business School Press, 2002): "To act outside the narrow confines of your job description when progress requires it lies close to the heart of leadership, and to its dangers" (p. 24). We describe how we build on his concept of leadership in detail in Chapter One.
3. Heifetz, *Leadership on the Line,* p. 24.

Chapter One

1. Andy Grove, *Only the Paranoid Survive* (New York: Currency Doubleday, 1996), p. 3.
2. The issue of speed was at the heart of a study done by Richard Foster and Sarah Kaplan of McKinsey and Company and summarized in their book *Creative Destruction* (New York: Currency, 2001). The issue is the speed of change for an entire industry, and the punch line is that a company needs to change itself at least as fast as the industry is evolving or it risks becoming irrelevant.
3. In Jim Collins's book *Good to Great* (New York: HarperBusiness, 2001), it is telling that those companies considered great did not have change management programs. Instead, change is part of the culture of those companies. Even when companies have to change radically and have not demonstrated a continuous trek to greatness, their leaders think beyond popular wisdom and prepare their companies for a reimagined future that builds in innovation, change, and curve jumping as part of the new way of doing business. Lou Gerstner's first two years at IBM were an example of this. He knew that time was not on his side, and he acted appropriately to the situation. Many of the changes he implemented, including getting employees closer to the customers, were about staying in touch with the outside world so

change could happen more quickly in response to real need that was understood at all levels of the organization. This new mind-set and practice would help keep IBM ahead as a leader, not just a survivor. Louis V. Gerstner, *Who Says Elephants Can't Dance? Inside IBM's Historic Turnaround* (New York: HarperBusiness, 2002).

4. This image of catching us off guard applies not only to threats in our internal and external environments but also to opportunities. It is generally accepted that Xerox's slide in the late 1990s and the discontinuation of its famed research organization, PARC, was due to ongoing failure to make sense of, decide, and act on the many inventions that were discovered within Xerox, costly lost opportunities such as the original Apple. Could the reason that innovation is so difficult in most companies be due to faulty Sense-Response Cycles? Many authors blame such failings on organizational systems and culture, but only Prepared Minds can outsmart systems and turn faulty cycles into progressive ones. Individuals experience faulty Sense-Response Cycles, and so do organizations.

5. Warren Bennis, *On Becoming a Leader* (Reading, Mass.: Addison-Wesley, 1994).

6. James M. Kouzes and Barry Z. Posner, *The Leadership Challenge* (San Francisco: Jossey-Bass, 2003).

7. Bill George, *Authentic Leadership: Rediscovering the Secrets to Creating Lasting Value* (San Francisco: Jossey-Bass, 2003).

8. Charles Handy, *The Age of Unreason* (Cambridge, Mass.: Harvard Business School Press, 1990).

9. Ronald A. Heifetz, *Leadership Without Easy Answers* (Cambridge, Mass.: Belknap Press, 1994). See also Ronald A. Heifetz and Marty Linsky, *Leadership on the Line: Staying Alive Through the Dangers of Leading* (Boston: Harvard Business School Press, 2002).

10. This kind of change is the most difficult because it requires people to be open to changing their minds. Most of us do not like to be told by an outside source that we need to change our minds and actions. We tend to take this as a sign that someone is telling us we are wrong or someone is exercising power over us. We may comply behaviorally but not change our minds. That is why Heifetz advocates learning as the main lever of change, because learning helps people internalize the need to change not just comply with an external agent.

11. Jean Egmon, "The Use of Adaptive Leadership and Adaptive Learning Strategies in Organizations Facing Market Extinction" (unpublished doctoral dissertation, University of Illinois at Urbana-Champaign, 1999).

12. For example, in the 1970s, a young professor from Harvard, Michael Porter, presented a concept of strategy that was elegant in its sim-

plicity. He described company strategy as the pursuit of either being the low-cost provider or being different in a way that would appeal to customers. He also defined the executive nightmare of being "stuck in the middle." Porter's books, *Competitive Advantage: Creating and Sustaining Superior Performance* (New York: Free Press, 1985) and *Competitive Strategy: Techniques for Analyzing Industries and Competitors* (New York: Free Press, 1980), continue in print after more than twenty years. Following this simple (but not easy) model, any number of companies embarked on cost-reduction or differentiation-focused strategies.

As time went on, executives, consultants, and academics built on or amplified Porter's thinking. In the early 1990s, inspired by Porter's model, Michael Treacy and Fred Wiersema analyzed market leaders and developed their concept of Operation Excellence as an expansion of Porter's thinking about low-cost providers. They also defined Product Leadership and Customer Intimacy as ways companies can differentiate themselves from their competition. Their book, *The Discipline of Market Leaders* (Cambridge, Mass.: Perseus Books, 1995), became the blueprint for strategy workshops across the country.

13. One of these is our Known Future: those things based on demographics that are so powerful that we know they will happen. An example is the impact the baby boom generation has on business. This generation is so big that it actually shapes the needs of some organizations. Another future we have to consider is our Hazy Future: those things that will happen but have an unknown magnitude. An example is the relative acceptance of new products and services. Finally, every organization has to face a Bolt-from-the-Blue Future: those low-probability, high-impact events that can force a fundamental change in strategy; 9/11 was a perfect example of this.

Chapter Two

1. Heifetz
2. Theodore Levitt, "Marketing Myopia," *Harvard Business Review,* July–Aug. 1960, pp. 45–56.
3. As we wrote this book, we tried to blend the rigor of academic research with the language used in businesses throughout the world. From a cognitive psychology point of view, we should be discussing *schema* at this point, but that is not common language for the intended audience of this book. However, the common term of *mental model* is too vague. So we have decided to follow the intent of the metaphor used in the beginning of this section and stay with the map metaphor. Just like the human mind, maps depict real things, like cities and towns and rivers that are connected (by roads). Our term *mental maps* is used

to consider the knowledge that we have and how these entities are connected. We introduce schema as an anchoring concept in Chapter Seven.

4. The concept of the iceberg comes from Northwestern University's Center for Learning and Organizational Change.

5. For more on double-loop learning, see Chris Argyris, *On Organizational Learning* (Oxford: Blackwell Publishing, 1999). For more on systems thinking, see Peter Senge, *The Fifth Discipline: The Art and Practice of the Learning Organization* (New York: Doubleday/Currency, 1990).

6. Steven Covey, *The Seven Habits of Highly Successful People* (New York: Simon & Schuster, 1990).

Chapter Three

1. The story of Silver Blaze is found in a collection of Arthur Conan Doyle's books, *The Complete Sherlock Holmes* (New York: Doubleday, 1930).

2. See John Naisbitt, *Megatrends: Ten New Directions Transforming Our Lives* (New York: Warner Books, 1988); Faith Popcorn, *The Popcorn Report: Faith Popcorn on the Future of Your Company, Your World, Your Life* (New York: Doubleday, 1991); and Clayton Christensen, *The Innovator's Dilemma* (Boston: Harvard Business School Press, 1997).

3. Thomas S. Kuhn, *The Structure of Scientific Revolutions* (Chicago: University of Chicago Press, 1962), p. 11.

4. Kuhn, *Structure of Scientific Revolutions*, p. 111.

5. Ellen Langer, *Mindfulness: Choice and Control in Everyday Life* (Reading, Mass.: Addison-Wesley, 1989).

6. Chris Argyris and Donald Schön, *Organizational Learning II* (Reading, Mass.: Addison-Wesley, 1996).

7. Thomas H. Davenport and John C. Beck, *The Attention Economy: Understanding the New Currency of Business* (Accenture, 2001).

8. William James, *Principles of Psychology* (New York: Holt, 1890), p. 403.

9. I. Roth, "An Introduction to Object Perception," in I. Roth and J. P. Frisby, *Perception and Representation* (Philadelphia: Open University Press, 1986).

10. This was pointed out years ago in Kuhn's *Structure of Scientific Revolutions* and was popularized in the 1980s by Joel Barker's books and videotapes about the power of paradigms. For a summary of his material, see Barker, *Paradigms: the Business of Discovering the Future* (New York: HarperCollins, 1992).

11. Gary Hamel and C. K. Prahalad, *Competing for the Future* (Boston: Harvard Business School Press, 1994).

12. Adapted from Mark Clare and Jean Egmon, "Knowledge Cards" (2005). See Third-Angle.com. Clare and Egmon usually give people entire

decks of the cards to practice the "soft skills" that are really the most difficult and vital in leadership. For more information, e-mail egmon@northwestern.edu.

Chapter Four

1. Peter Senge, *The Fifth Discipline: The Art and Practice of the Learning Organization* (New York: Doubleday/Currency, 1990).
2. P. N. Johnson-Laird, "Freedom and Constraint in Creativity," in R. J. Sternberg (ed.), *The Nature of Creativity* (Cambridge: Cambridge University Press, 1988).
3. A. Newell and H. A. Simon, *Human Problem Solving* (Upper Saddle River, N.J.: Prentice Hall, 1972).
4. Dietrich Dörner, *The Logic of Failure* (Reading, Mass.: Addison-Wesley, 1996).
5. Rachel Carson, *Silent Spring* (Boston: Houghton Mifflin, 1962).
6. Peter Drucker, *Management: Tasks, Responsibilities, Practices* (New York: HarperCollins, 1973), p. 543.
7. Adapted from Mark Clare and Jean Egmon, "Knowledge Cards" (2005). See Third-Angle.com.

Chapter Five

1. Michael Porter, "What Is Strategy?" *Harvard Business Review,* Nov.–Dec. 1996, pp. 61–78.
2. The phrase "city on a hill" is an image taken from the Gospel of Matthew and used in John Winthrop's 1630 writing, "A Model of Christian Charity."
3. Howard Gardner, *Frames of Mind* (New York: Basic Books, 1983). See also Howard Gardner, *Intelligence Reframed* (New York: Basic Books, 1999).
4. Stephen R. Covey, *The Seven Habits of Highly Effective People* (New York: Simon & Schuster, 1989).
5. Roger von Oech, *A Whack on the Side of the Head* (New York: Warner Books, 1983). Michael Michalko, *Thinkertoys* (Berkeley, Calif.: Ten Speed Press, 1991).

Chapter Six

1. Donald A. Sull, *Revival of the Fittest: Why Good Companies Go Bad and How Great Managers Remake Them* (Boston: Harvard Business School Press, 2003).
2. Joseph Schumpeter, the Czechoslovakian-born American economist known for his theories of the development of capitalism, coined the phrase "creative destruction" in his 1942 work, *Capitalism, Socialism and Democracy* (New York: HarperCollins, 1962).

3. The story is told in Jack Stack's book, *The Great Game of Business* (New York: Currency Doubleday, 1992).

4. Michael Treacy and Fred Wiersema, *The Discipline of Market Leaders: Choose Your Customers, Narrow Your Focus, Dominate Your Market* (New York: Perseus Books, 1997).

5. Many executives have taken them to task for a simple view of strategy. These executives miss the power in this simple model: to consider the constant trade-offs that take place in all three vertices of the triangle formed by the three disciples. You have to excel in one of the disciplines, but you can never fall behind in either of the other two. The model is a great discussion tool and should not be used as a formula.

6. Leon Festinger, *A Theory of Cognitive Dissonance* (Evanston, Ill.: Row, Peterson, 1957).

7. Karl E. Weick, *Sensemaking in Organizations* (Thousand Oaks, Calif.: Sage, 1995).

8. Ronald Heifetz claims that this use of challenging in getting others to learn and do adaptive work is one of the key responsibilities of adaptive leaders—those who lead change. Ronald Heifetz, *Leadership Without Easy Answers* (Cambridge, Mass.: Belknap Press, 1994).

9. In Chris Argyris's terms, the "espoused theory" does not match the "theories in use" of the culture. See Chris Argyris and Donald Schön, *Organizational Learning II* (Reading, Mass.: Addison-Wesley, 1996).

10. More recent work around cognitive dissonance theory has focused on the emotional response to feeling responsible for unwanted consequences of an action. Sometimes in order to reduce that tension, people find a way, psychologically, to disown responsibility. In these cases, challenging the person about his responsibility, challenging a group, or challenging oneself becomes critical to prevent the game of passing the buck.

11. John Steinbeck, *The Short Reign of Pippin IV* (New York: Viking Press, 1957).

12. Mark Tennant and Philip Pogson, *Learning and Change in the Adult Years* (San Francisco: Jossey-Bass, 1995).

13. Adapted from Mark Clare and Jean Egmon, "Knowledge Cards," (2005). See Third-Angle.com.

Chapter Seven

1. Louis V. Gerstner, *Who Says Elephants Can't Dance?* (New York: Harper-Business, 2002).

2. L. L. Thompson (ed.), *The Social Psychology of Organizational Behavior* (New York: Psychology Press, 2003).

3. Gary Klein, *Sources of Power: How People Make Decisions* (Cambridge, Mass.: MIT Press, 1998).

4. Daniel Goleman, *Emotional Intelligence: Why It Matters More Than IQ* (New York: Bantam Books, 1995).

5. Jean Egmon, "Meta Macrocognition: A New Way of Seeing the Big Picture" (working paper, Complexity in Action Network, Northwestern University, 2005).

6. D. Kahneman, P. Slovic, and A. Tversky (eds.), *Judgment Under Uncertainty: Heuristics and Biases* (Cambridge: Cambridge University Press, 1982).

7. A. Brown, "Knowing When, Where, and How to Remember: A Problem in Metacognition," in R. Glaser (ed.), *Advances in Instructional Psychology* (Mahwah, N.J.: Erlbaum, 1978).

8. J. R. Anderson, *Cognitive Psychology and Its Implications* (New York: Freeman, 1985).

9. Edward Tenner, *Why Things Bite Back: Technology and the Revenge of Unintended Consequences* (New York: Vintage, 1997).

10. Paul Nutt, *Why Decisions Fail: Avoiding the Blunders and Traps That Lead to Debacles* (San Francisco: Berrett-Koehler, 2002).

11. Researchers on decision making and risk generally classify decisions into three domains: (1) riskless (decision making under certainty), (2) decision making under uncertainty, and (3) decision making under risk (see, for example, Thompson, *Social Psychology of Organizational Behavior*). In scenario 1, riskless decision making or decision making under certainty focuses on how people make choices among sure courses of action, like ordering from a menu at a fine restaurant where any choice is good. Few business decisions are like this anymore. If leaders are spending their time on these kinds of decisions, it probably means they are not aiming high enough. At the same time, we don't want to discount the importance of seemingly small or risk-free decisions. Using a decision matrix to determine the location of a conference or the selection of one candidate among a pool of highly qualified can help the confidence in the selection and support the decision for those stakeholders who are affected by the outcomes.
    In scenario 2, decision making under uncertainty is when you do not know what the future will bring and cannot assign meaningful probabilities to it. These are decisions that are difficult to quantify but may have a huge impact. As leaders, we try to do everything to predict or limit results. We conduct pilot studies. We do needs assessments. We test-market a product. However, like planning an outdoor barbecue for next Saturday, you really have no idea as to whether it will rain,

so it is likely that you will develop alternative decisions to enact at the last minute if Plan A does not work.

In scenario 3, decision making under risk (or risky choice), the decision maker knows the probabilities and knows that decisions are by nature risky. Like a hedge fund, they can lead to big gains or big losses. The key here is to spend the time to identify the risks before making a decision.

In times of crisis, it is often the qualitative criteria that provide the answer. At the same time, the habit of thinking quantitatively can protect the integrity of our decisions in accordance with our finances. Many thought leaders in the field of decision making encourage leaders to learn to think quantitatively, even if real numbers are elusive. See, for example, J. Baron, *Thinking and Deciding*, 3rd ed. (Cambridge: Cambridge University Press, 2000).

For instance, tennis players think quantitatively when they quickly consider the trade-offs of where to hit a shot based on the probabilities that it will go out versus winning a point if it does not go out. These players do not have any real statistics in their minds. However, their thought processes take them down the path of reasoning quantitatively, often with implicit memory of where their shots usually land when they hit them under similar conditions. It is great when we have statistically proven models to aid our decisions. Even when we don't, it is good to use the skill of reasoning and thinking the problem through as being quantifiable.

12. Dorothy Leonard-Barton refers to this trap as core rigidities in "Core Capabilities and Core Rigidities: A Paradox in Managing New Product Development," *Strategic Management Journal*, 1992, *13*, 111–125.

13. Jean Egmon, "The Use of Adaptive Leadership and Adaptive Learning Strategies in Companies Facing Market Extinction" (unpublished doctoral dissertation, University of Illinois at Urbana-Champaign, 1999).

14. Kathleen Eisenhardt has looked at the differences between fast decision makers and slow decision makers in "Speed and Strategic Choice: How Managers Accelerate Decision Making," *California Management Review*, 1990, *32*(3), 39–54. It is also informative for developing strategies for overcoming common pitfalls of decision makers.

15. Ellen J. Langer, *Mindfulness* (Reading, Mass.: Addison-Wesley, 1989).

16. Nancy R. Tague, *The Quality Toolbox* (Milwaukee: American Society for Quality, 1995).

17. Adapted from Mark Clare and Jean Egmon, "Knowledge Cards" (2005). See Third-Angle.com.

Chapter Eight

1. Peter Drucker, *Managing in a Time of Great Change* (New York: Dutton, 1995).
2. Malcolm Gladwell, *The Tipping Point: How Little Things Can Make a Big Difference* (Boston: Little, Brown, 2000).
3. D. E. Rumelhart and D. A. Norman, "Accretion, Tuning, and Restructuring: Three Modes of Learning," in J. W. Cotton and R. Klatzky (eds.), *Semantic Factors in Cognition* (Mahwah, N.J.: Erlbaum, 1995).
4. Peter B. Vaill, *Learning as a Way of Being: Strategies for Survival in a World of Permanent White Water* (San Francisco: Jossey-Bass, 1996).
5. Henry Petroski, *To Engineer Is Human* (New York: Vintage Books, 1982).
6. Adapted from Mark Clare and Jean Egmon, "Knowledge Cards" (2005). See Third-Angle.com.

Chapter Nine

1. Jim Collins, *Good to Great* (New York: HarperBusiness, 2001).
2. Abraham Maslow, *Motivation and Personality* (New York: HarperCollins, 1954).
3. David McClelland, "Toward a Theory of Motive Acquisition," *American Psychologist,* May 1965, pp. 321–333.
4. Victor Vroom, *Work and Motivation* (New York: Wiley, 1964).
5. B. F. Skinner, *Science and Human Behavior* (Old Tappan, N.J.: Macmillan, 1953).
6. Frederick Herzberg, "One More Time, How Do You Motivate Employees?" *Harvard Business Review,* Jan.–Feb. 1968, pp. 53–62.
7. Richard Boland and Fred Collopy from the Weatherhead School of Management at Case Western Reserve University have been arguing Nobel laureate Herbert Simon's case that design, intelligence, and choice are the three fundamental pillars of business problem solving. At the Center for Learning and Organizational Change, we take what we know about designing learning environments and designing organizations and apply it to the way we think about everything from strategy to marketing to technological tools to community space.
8. Don Norman, *Emotional Design: Why We Love (or Hate) Everyday Things* (New York: Basic Books, 2004).
9. A. Collins, J. S. Brown, and S. E. Newman, "Cognitive Apprenticeship: Teaching the Crafts of Reading, Writing and Mathematics," in Lauren B. Resnick (ed.), *Knowing, Learning and Instruction: Essays in Honor of Robert Glaser* (Mahwah, N.J.: Erlbaum, 1989).
10. Cognitive apprenticeship was invented by A. Collins, J. S. Brown, and S. E. Newman, "Cognitive Apprenticeship."

11. See garlikov.com. S. B. Merriam and R. S. Caffarella, *Learning in Adulthood: A Comprehensive Guide,* 2nd ed. (San Francisco: Jossey-Bass, 1999).

12. P. Hersey and K. K. Blanchard, *Leadership and the One Minute Manager* (New York: Morrow, 1999).

13. Adapted from Mark Clare and Jean Egmon, "Knowledge Cards" (2005). See Third-Angle.com.

14. Adapted from Clare and Egmon, "Knowledge Cards."

Chapter Ten

1. Albert Bandura, *Social Foundations of Thought and Action* (Upper Saddle River, N.J.: Prentice Hall, 1986).

2. Henry Petroski, *To Engineer Is Human: The Role of Failure in Successful Design* (New York, St. Martin's Press, 1985).

3. Petroski, *To Engineer Is Human,* p. 62.

4. Jack Mezirow, *Fostering Critical Reflection in Adulthood: A Guide to Tranformative and Emancipatory Learning* (San Francisco: Jossey-Bass, 1990).

5. Peter F. Drucker, "The Theory of Business," in *Managing in a Time of Great Change* (New York: Truman Talley Books/Dutton, 1995).

6. Edward de Bono, *Six Thinking Hats: An Essential Approach to Business Management,* rev. ed. (Boston: Back Bay Books, 1999).

7. Adapted from Mark Clare and Jean Egmon, "Knowledge Cards" (2005). See Third-Angle.com.

Chapter Eleven

1. Arthur C. Clarke, *Prelude to Mars: An Omnibus Containing Two Complete Novels, Prelude to Space and Sands of Mars, and Sixteen Short Stories* (New York: Harcourt, 1965).

2. Peter F. Drucker, "The Theory of Business," in *Managing in a Time of Great Change* (New York: Truman Talley Books/Dutton, 1995).

3. Mind-mapping techniques have been popularized by Tony Buzan and others over the past twenty years or so. For an explanation of mind mapping and how to create mind maps, you may want to read any of Buzan's books. For example, try *The Mind Map Book* (New York: Plume Books, 1996) or *How to Mind Map* (New York: HarperCollins, 2002).

ACKNOWLEDGMENTS

As with so many others things in life, the writing of our book is the result of the insight, questions, and guidance that we had from many fronts. Interviews with dozens of executives across many industries gave us insight into the mental skills they saw present or absent in business successes and failures. We came to them with a conceptual model, and they gave generously of their time in teasing out the needed nuances. The master's degree students in Northwestern University's Learning and Organizational Change program's summer '04 class (LOC 455) gave us a sense of what skills could and could not be learned in a formal setting and ways the book could weave theory and practice to make it practical and credible for any reader. Leslie Stephen provided editorial coaching and encouragement that revealed wisdom and talent that produced a book and helped us grow. And, as always, family and friends gave us patient support.

Bill wishes to call out three people in particular for their help. Jan Churchurillo read and commented on much of the manuscript. Her frank and honest criticism was both encouraging and invaluable. Jon Atchue gave Bill the opportunity to take some of his ideas and "play with the minds" of managers and executives during workshops at two major corporations. Finally, Don Zimmer's passionate front-porch military history lessons were great in grounding concepts in the harsh reality of real battles won and lost.

Jean wishes to thank Dave Curtin, who reviewed an early version of the book and immediately pulled out ideas that served as springboards for new ways of thinking and working. Dave also employed his wonderful Irish sense of humor and diplomacy to point out areas in need of a new way of writing. Chris Lowney, a published author in the leadership field, kept me honest about what leadership is and challenged us to say something new about leadership in *The Prepared Mind*. Ali Niederkorn, a long-time colleague at Northwestern and in consulting, provided invaluable perspective about content and process.

ABOUT THE AUTHORS

Bill Welter is the managing director of Adaptive Strategies, a firm specializing in business education and consulting. He has over thirty-five years of varied military, engineering, consulting, and teaching experience. These four careers have given him ample opportunity to view, experience, and reflect on the reality of Louis Pasteur's quote that "chance favors the prepared mind." In the Marine Corps, he learned that success depends on people who believe in their mission and know what to do. As an engineer, he learned that strategy without good execution is a waste of time and energy. During his years of consulting, he learned that organizational and behavioral skills are the foundation of all successful projects. And as an educator, he learned that understanding context is needed for deep insight.

Jean Egmon is a faculty member in managerial economics and decision sciences at the Kellogg School of Management at Northwestern University and the director of the Complexity in Action Network at Northwestern, the corporate and government outreach and application arm of the Northwestern Institute for Complex Systems. She is also president of Third Angle, an advisory and development firm that improves innovative capacity by using interdisciplinary research and techniques from management, engineering, complexity science, and cognition and by providing networking and knowledge brokering between researchers and organizational leaders committed to breakthrough thinking and action at multiple levels of business.

INDEX